DT   Wright, Richard,
510.2 1908-1960.
.W74
1974 Black power

DATE			
DEC 17 '81			
JAN 7 '82			
AUG 9 '82			
DEC 05 1989			

BLACK POWER

KWAME NKRUMAH,
Prime Minister of the Gold Coast

BLACK POWER

A Record of Reactions
in a Land of Pathos

by

RICHARD WRIGHT

GREENWOOD PRESS, PUBLISHERS
WESTPORT, CONNECTICUT

Library of Congress Cataloging in Publication Data

Wright, Richard, 1908-1960.
    Black power.

    Reprint of the ed. published by Harper, New York.
    1. Ghana--Description and travel. 2. Ghana--
Social conditions. I. Title.
[DT510.2.W74 1973]   916.67'03'3   73-13457
ISBN 0-8371-7136-9

Grateful acknowledgment is made to:

Dodd, Mead & Company for permission to reprint 8 lines from
"When Malindy Sings" from THE COMPLETE WORKS OF PAUL
LAURENCE DUNBAR;

Harper & Brothers for permission to reprint the first verse of
"Heritage" from COLOR by Countee Cullen. Copyright, 1925,
by Harper & Brothers, Copyright, 1953, by Ida M. Cullen.

This edition originally published in 1954 by Harper & Brothers,
New York

Reprinted with the permission of Ellen Wright

Reprinted in 1974 by Greenwood Press, Inc.,
51 Riverside Avenue, Westport, Conn. 06880

Library of Congress catalog card number 73-13457
ISBN 0-8371-7136-9

Printed in the United States of America

10 9 8 7 6 5 4 3

TO WHOM IT MAY CONCERN:

      This is to certify that I have known Mr. Richard Wright for many years, having met him in the United States.

      Mr. Wright would like to come to the Gold Coast to do some research into the social and historical aspects of the country, and would be my guest during the time he is engaged in this work.

      To the best of my knowledge and belief, I consider Mr. Wright a fit and proper person to be allowed to visit the Gold Coast for the reasons stated above.

                        Kwame Nkrumah,
                        Prime Minister.

Accra,
4th May, 1953.

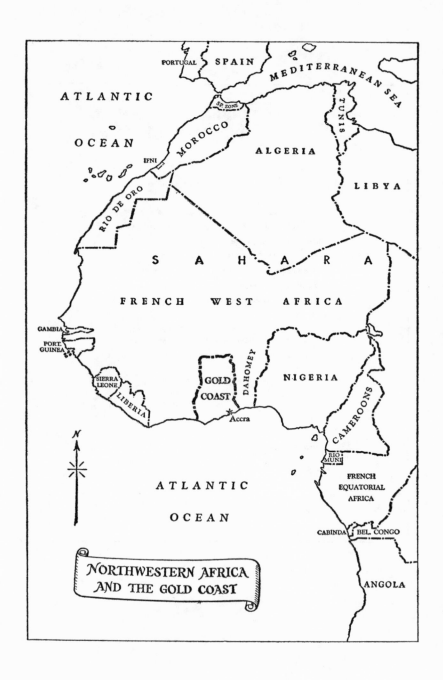

NORTHWESTERN AFRICA
AND THE GOLD COAST

TO THE UNKNOWN AFRICAN

who, because of his primal and poetic humanity,
was regarded by white men as a "thing" to be
bought, sold, and used as an instrument of production; and who, alone in the forests of West Africa,
created a vision of life so simple as to be terrifying,
yet a vision that was irreducibly human . . .

What is Africa to me:
Copper sun or scarlet sea,
Jungle star or jungle track,
Strong bronzed men, or regal black
Women from whose loins I sprang
When the birds of Eden sang?
  One three centuries removed
  From the scenes his fathers loved,
  Spicy grove, cinnamon tree,
  What is Africa to me?

— COUNTEE CULLEN

Not till the sun excludes you do I exclude you . . .

— WALT WHITMAN

The entire course of development of the human race, from whatever point of view it may be regarded, whether intellectual, economic, industrial, social, or ethical, is as a whole and in detail coincident with the course of transmitted social heredity.

— ROBERT BRIFFAULT

APROPOS PREPOSSESSIONS

In today's intellectual climate—a climate charged with ideological currents in the service, paid or voluntary, of some nation, party, movement, or interest—it behooves a writer reporting in nonfictional terms on vital material to lay before the reader his working frame of reference, his assumptions and preoccupations. If the present writer were less serious or responsible, he would not be concerned about this, but since he knows that he is dealing with material out of which our destiny will partly be shaped, he is anxious to place himself in a position where the reader will have no doubts as to what he is up to.

During my lifetime I've witnessed a radical change engulf more than half of human society; some nations have disappeared and new ones have risen to take their places; some social classes have vanished and others have come into being. . . . These changes were not unexpected on my part; indeed, I labored to help bring them about. My belonging to a minority group whose gross deprivations pitched my existence on a plane of all but sheer criminality made these changes welcome to me. From 1932 to 1944 I was a member of the Communist Party of the United States of America and, as such, I held consciously in my hands Marxist Communism as an instrumentality to effect such political and social changes.

Today I am no longer a member of that party or a subscriber to its aims. Let it be said that my relinquishing of membership in that party was not dictated by outside pressure or interests; it was caused by my conviction that Marxist Communism, though it was changing the world, was changing that world in a manner that granted me even less freedom than I had possessed before. Perhaps, in time, I could have brought myself to accept this Communist suppression of freedom on a temporary basis, but when historic events disclosed that international Communism was mainly an instrument of Russian foreign policy, I publicly and responsibly dropped its instrumentality and disassociated myself from it.

Yet, as an American Negro whose life is governed by racial codes written into law, I state clearly that my abandonment of Communism does not automatically place me in a position of endorsing and supporting all the policies, political and economic, of the non-Communist world. Indeed, it was the inhuman nature of many of those policies, racial and otherwise, that led me to take up the instrumentality of Communism in the first place. . . .

Hence, the problem of freedom is still with me. The Communist instrumentality which I once held in my hands has built up a slave empire of 800,000,000 people; and the Western world, of which I am an uneasy member, has not materially altered many of its attitudes toward the aspirations of hundreds of millions of minority peoples caught by chance, time, and culture within its wide sway of power.

In this dilemma of a divided world one elementary fact stands out undeniably: the victories of the Communist instrumentalities were largely won by skilled Communist appeals to the Western sense of justice, by Communist exploitation of the thwarted traditional hopes of Western man. In fact, it can be definitely stated that Communist strength is predicated upon Western stupidity, moral obtuseness, foolish racial jealousies—of the abandonment by the West of its own ideals and pretensions. . . . ("Capitalistic contradictions," the Communists call it.)

If Western man has irrevocably decided that his record of dealing with the colored part of mankind is just and beyond criticism, that his way of life is perfect, that he has a godlike right to determine and time the development of mankind according to his own convenience, that his mere presence in this world is a blessing to the less fortunate, that he will make no meaningful concessions to the sense of justice and freedom which he himself helped to instill in men's hearts—if this is the stance of Western man, then the last and strongest weapon of the West has been voluntarily surrendered to the Communists, the most solid moral ground of the last two thousand years has been gratuitously vacated, and the chances of a Communist global victory thereby immeasurably enhanced.

The aim of this book is to pose this problem anew in an area of the world where the issue has not yet been decided, an area that is proving a decisive example for an entire continent. The Western world has one last opportunity in Africa to determine if its ideals can be generously shared, if it dares to act upon its deepest convictions. China has gone the desperate way of totalitarianism; India teeters on the brink; and now has come Africa's turn to test the ideals that the West has preached but failed to practice. . . .

Let me be honest; I'm not too hopeful. The Western world does not even yet quite know how hard and inhuman its face looks to those who live outside of its confines. One of the aims of this book is to show you that face in its characteristic historical expression, to show you that face in terms that maybe you can understand and recognize. I don't know. It may well already be too late. If you can feel that the person who presents these perhaps unwelcome facts to you does so with the desire of making you aware of your moral stance, of making you realize how others see and judge you, then you might read these lines with care.

In presenting this picture of a part of Africa, I openly use, to a limited degree, Marxist analysis of historic events to explain what has happened in this world for the past five hundred years or more. If anyone should object to my employment of Marxist methods to make meaningful the ebb and flow of commodities, human and otherwise, in the modern state, to make comprehensible the alignment of social classes in modern society, I have but to say that I'll willingly accept any other method of interpreting the facts; but I insist that any other method *must not exclude the facts!*

But my utilization of Marxist instrumentalities of thought does not necessarily commit me to programs or policies popularly associated with Marxist philosophy. The measures which I recommend at the end of this book do not derive from any programmatic theories of any political party. They are derived from my concern about human freedom, from what I know of the world, from what I saw and felt in Africa, and the concrete situation of the Convention People's Party of the Gold Coast.

This book seeks to provide Western readers with some insight into what is going to happen in Africa, so that, when it does happen, they will be able to understand it, so that they will not entertain the kind of illusions that held forth about China; my point is that if Africa today is in turmoil, it is not merely the omniscient hand of Moscow that is fomenting all the trouble; but that, given the harsh background of Africa and the numbing impact of the West that it has suffered, what is happening was bound to happen. Frankly, this current mania of ascribing *all* the world's unrest to Russian Communists simply credits the Russians with more intelligence than they actually possess.

The issue of who is to blame in a colonial nation that is determinedly actuated by Western ideals to throw off the yoke of foreign rule is a tricky one. The popular assumption is that colonial people are happy and that only evil foreign agents are stirring up strife, but the facts of life in the Gold Coast do not bear out such tortured contentions. Indeed, the greatest incentive to the growth of Communism in Africa today would be the attempt on the part of the West to throttle the rise of African nations; such an attempt at crushing African aspirations would drive the Africans straight down the road that China is so bloodily traveling. . . . That road began with Mau Mau.

The historical material in this book is drawn exclusively from bourgeois sources, if that is of any comfort to anybody. The interpretations of facts, their coloring and presentation, are my own, and, for whatever it is worth, I take full responsibility for them. And I think that time will bear me out.

This volume is a first-person, subjective narrative on the life and conditions of the Colony and Ashanti areas of the Gold Coast, an area comprising perhaps the most highly socially evolved native life of present-day Africa. The choice of selecting the Gold Coast for such an intensive study was my own and the judgments rendered are not comparative. I felt that it was time for someone to subject a slice of African life to close scrutiny in terms of concepts that one would use in observing life anywhere. Thus, some conclusions arrived at in these pages might well startle or dismay those who like to dote on "primitive" people. . . .

Africa challenges the West in a way that the West has not been challenged before. The West can meanly lose Africa, or the West can nobly save Africa; but whatever happens, make no mistake: THE WEST IS BEING JUDGED BY THE EVENTS THAT TRANSPIRE IN AFRICA!

RICHARD WRIGHT—Paris: May, 1954

PART ONE

APPROACHING AFRICA

Only in one particular did the freedom accorded in the slave trade differ from the freedom accorded in other trades—the commodity involved was man.

ERIC WILLIAMS' *Capitalism and Slavery*

I . . .

The table had been cleared and the coffee was being poured. The Easter Sunday luncheon was almost over and we were stirring the sugar in our cups. It was so quiet that the footfalls from the tranquil Paris street below echoed upward. It was one of those moments when, for no reason, a spell of silence hangs in the air. I sipped my coffee and stared at the gray walls of the University of Paris that loomed beyond the window.

One of my guests, Dorothy, the wife of George Padmore, the West Indian author and journalist, turned to me and asked:

"Now that your desk is clear, why don't you go to Africa?"

The idea was so remote to my mind and mood that I gaped at her a moment before answering.

"*Africa?*" I echoed.

"Yes. The Gold Coast," she said stoutly.

"But that's four thousand miles away!" I protested.

"There are planes and ships," she said.

My eyes ranged unseeingly about the room. I felt cornered, uneasy. I glanced at my wife.

"Why not?" she said.

A moment ago I had been collected, composed; now I was on the defensive, feeling poised on the verge of the unknown.

"Africa!" I repeated the word to myself, then paused as something strange and disturbing stirred slowly in the depths of me. I am African! I'm of African descent. . . . Yet I'd never seen Africa; I'd never really known any Africans; I'd hardly ever thought of Africa. . . .

"Kwame Nkrumah, the Prime Minister, is going to table his motion for self-government in July," Dorothy said.

"It would be a great experience for you," my wife said.

I heard them, but my mind and feelings were racing along another and hidden track. *Africa!* Being of African descent, would

3

I be able to feel and know something about Africa on the basis of a common "racial" heritage? Africa was a vast continent full of "my people.". . . Or had three hundred years imposed a psychological distance between me and the "racial stock" from which I had sprung? Perhaps some Englishman, Scotsman, Frenchman, Swede, or Dutchman had chained my great-great-great-great-grandfather in the hold of a slave ship; and perhaps that remote grandfather had been sold on an auction block in New Orleans, Richmond, or Atlanta. . . . My emotions seemed to be touching a dark and dank wall. . . . *But, am I African?* Had some of my ancestors sold their relatives to white men? What would my feelings be when I looked into the black face of an African, feeling that maybe his great-great-great-grandfather had sold my great-great-great-grandfather into slavery? Was there something in Africa that my feelings could latch onto to make all of this dark past clear and meaningful? Would the Africans regard me as a lost brother who had returned?

"Do you think that the Gold Coast will be self-governing soon?" I asked. I genuinely wanted to know about the political situation in the Gold Coast, yet another and far more important question was trying to shape itself in me. According to popular notions of "race," there ought to be something of "me" down there in Africa. Some vestige, some heritage, some vague but definite ancestral reality that would serve as a key to unlock the hearts and feelings of the Africans whom I'd meet. . . . But I could not feel anything African about myself, and I wondered, "What does being *African* mean . . .?"

". . . and they are fighting for self-government," Dorothy was explaining. "It would be wonderful if you could be there when the first black Prime Minister in history asks the British for the freedom of his people."

"Yes," I said. "How long does it take to get there?"

"One day by plane and twelve days by ship," Dorothy said.

Was Africa "primitive"? But what did being "primitive" mean? I'd read books on "primitive" people, but, while reading them, their contents had always seemed somehow remote. Now a strange reality, in some way akin to me, was pressing close, and I was dismayed to discover that I didn't know how to reac' to it.

"Just what level of development have the people there reached?" I asked Dorothy.

"You must ask George about that," she said. "He's been there. . . . But you'll find their development mixed. You'll find Christians and pagans . . ."

"I want to see the pagans," I said impulsively.

"Why?" my wife asked.

"I know what a Christian African would have to say, but I don't know what paganism is—"

"It's *all* there," Dorothy said emphatically. "And if you're going to attend the session of the Legislative Assembly in which the Prime Minister will make his bid for freedom, you'd better see about passage."

"I'll go by ship, if I go," I said. "That would give me time enough to read up on the history of the country."

"You *must* go," my wife said.

The fortuity of birth had cast me in the "racial" role of being of African descent, and that fact now resounded in my mind with associations of hatred, violence, and death. Phrases from my childhood rang in my memory: one-half Negro, one-quarter Negro, one-eighth Negro, one-sixteenth Negro, one thirty-second Negro. . . . In thirty-eight out of the forty-eight states of the American Federal Union, marriage between a white person and a person of African descent was a criminal offense. To be of "black" blood meant being consigned to a lower plane in the social scheme of American life, and if one violated that scheme, one risked danger, even death sometimes. And all of this was predicated upon the presence of *African* blood in one's veins. How much of me was *African?* Many of my defensive-minded Negro friends had often told me with passion:

"We have a *special* gift for music, dancing, rhythm and movement. . . . We have a genius of our own. We were civilized in Africa when white men were still living in caves in Europe. . . ."

To me talk of that sort had always seemed beside the point; I had always taken for granted the humanity of Africans as well as that of other people. And being either uninterested or unable to accept such arguments, I'd always remained silent in such conversations. My kind of thinking was impotent when it came to explaining life in "racial" terms. On countless occasions I'd heard white men say to me:

"Now, you take the racial expression of the Negro . . ."

And I'd looked off uneasily, wondering what they meant. I was accounted as being of African, that is, Negro, descent, but what were these "racial" qualities that I was supposed to possess? While in the presence of those who talked confidently of "racial" qualities, I would listen and mull over their phrases, but no sooner had they gone than my mind would revert to my habitual kind of thinking that had no "race" in it, a kind of thinking that was conditioned by the reaction of human beings to a concrete social environment. And I'd ask myself:

"What are they talking about?"

Over the Easter Sunday luncheon table, I mapped out my voyage. I wanted to see this Africa that was posing such acute questions for me and was conjuring up in my mind notions of the fabulous and remote: heat, jungle, rain, strange place names like Cape Coast, Elmina, Accra, Kumasi. . . . I wanted to see the crumbling slave castles where my ancestors had lain panting in hot despair. The more I thought of it, the more excited I became, and yet I could not rid myself of a vague sense of disquiet.

I excused myself from the table and consulted the Encyclopaedia Britannica and the description of the Gold Coast it gave was vivid, replete with dangerous reptiles, gold, and diamonds. There were only three short paragraphs about the people who were described as being of the "Negro race." The Gold Coast was about four degrees from the Equator and teemed with mineral and agricultural wealth. I returned to the table.

"Do you think I'll have any trouble getting in?"

"You'd better apply for your visa at once," Dorothy advised. "If you have any trouble, get in touch with the Prime Minister. Meanwhile, George'll tell Nkrumah that you want to come. . . ."

"Just what's the setup in the Gold Coast? Are foreign affairs in the hands of the British?"

"Yes; and finance and the police too," she said.

"And the rest of the cabinet ministers are African?"
"Yes."
"I'm going," I said. It was decided.

II ...

On the platform of Euston Station in London I saw swarms of Africans, Western in manner and dress, for the first time. The boat-train compartment in which I sat was cold and I huddled in my macintosh, longing for my heavy coat which was packed in my trunk. Outside the train window the landscape was as bleak as any described by D. H. Lawrence or Arnold Bennett or George Moore. . . . I drifted to sleep, then I was awakened by the train jolting, slowing. I looked out of the window and saw Liverpool. . . .

This was the city that had been the center and focal point of the slave trade; it was here that most of the slavers had been organized, fitted out, financed, and dispatched with high hopes on their infamous but lucrative voyages. Suffice it to · say that the British did not originate this trading in human flesh whose enormous profits laid the foundations upon which had been reared modern industrial England. The honor for the launching of that crusade against Africa rested upon the pious shoulders of the Portuguese who had had the right, under a papal bull of 1455, to subject to servitude all infidel peoples. Later it fell to the daring of the English to rear that trade into a system whose functionings would in some manner touch more than half of the human race with its bloody but profitable agitations—the consequences of which would endure for more than four hundred years.

In dredging through books for material on the background of the Gold Coast, I purposefully confined my reading to the historical facts presented by the British themselves, many of whom, like Sir Alan Burns, Eric Williams, W. E. Ward, and K. A. Busia, etc., are still living and active. I found that though the British might at times be guilty of a kind of intriguing understatement, they never hid facts, even when those facts contradicted their own moral notions. The sketchy backdrop which follows came not from Socialist or Marxian, but from conservative British sources.

The search for short sea routes, the thirst for gold and spices, and Columbus' discovery of the New World set in motion international economic rivalries that have not subsided even to this day. I've often wondered why the assault upon Africa was called "imperialism" even by ardent revolutionaries, why such a mild word as "exploitation" was ever used to describe it. The simple truth is that it consisted of a many-centuries-long war waged by the peninsula of Europe, with the sanction of Catholicism, against the continent of Africa. In that campaign the odds were on the side of the superior organization and technical development of white Europe which, when pitted in war against the fragility of an essentially agricultural and tribal people, smashed those people, dealt them a blow from which they have never recovered. Indeed, so unimportant were Africa's millions deemed that no real account of that long campaign was ever fully or properly recorded.

True, forms of rigorous servitude existed even among European whites when the slave trade was launched, and, in those days, Liverpool had had but a modest share of it. Yet, there existed in England the conditions, the attitudes, and the impulses which would easily lend themselves with passion to the slave trade. The first slaves to toil for Europeans in the New World were not Negroes, but the indigenous Indians who, alas, were found to be temperamentally unsuited for arduous labor under tropic suns, and new sources of human instruments had to be sought. The next experiment in harnessing human beings to the plantations of the New World involved poor white indentured servants and convicts, and, during the sixteenth and seventeenth centuries, the word "convict" had a meaning that conveniently covered a wide area of people.

There existed a widespread system of kidnaping men, women, and children and spiriting them aboard ships bound for the colonies of the New World. England's feudal laws recognized three hundred capital crimes, and an Englishman could be hanged for picking a pocket of more than three shillings. Guided more by a sharp eye for the needs of the colonies than by humanitarian motives, many

Englishmen, from 1664 to 1667, prayed for transportation to the colonies instead of death for those who stole more than four shillings' worth of goods, a silver spoon, or a gold watch. So vast and steady was the spawn that Newgate and Bridewell dumped upon the shores of the New World, especially in New York, Pennsylvania, Virginia, Georgia, etc., that even Benjamin Franklin protested.

But whence the ascendancy of Liverpool in this trade? With Spain and Portugal advancing conflicting claims to the newly discovered territories, the Pope stepped in, in 1493, and issued a series of papal bulls which gave the East to Portugal and the West to Spain. But the always protesting Anglo-Saxons were in no mood to recognize the right of even a Pope to divide up the world as he wished, and the English, the Dutch, the Swedes, the Germans, and finally even the French would accept no such papal edicts as binding. Every son of Adam felt he had a God-given right to share in the human loot—and share he did.

Slavery was not put into practice because of racial theories; racial theories sprang up in the wake of slavery, to justify it. It was impossible to milk the limited population of Europe of enough convicts and indentured white servants to cultivate, on a large and paying scale, colonial sugar, cotton, and tobacco plantations. Either they had to find a labor force or abandon the colonies, and Europe's eyes turned to Africa where the supply of human beings seemed inexhaustible. So the process of stealing or buying Africans to work the lands bought or stolen from the Indians got under way. . . .

If the Europeans were cruel to the infidel Africans, they were not much less cruel to their own Christian brothers. The African simply inherited a position already occupied by indentured white servants and criminals, and the nightmare called the Middle Passage—the voyage from Africa to the West Indies or America—had long been made by declassed Anglo-Saxons from England to America, and they'd been packed like herring in the holds of ships. . . . The tenure of the indentured servant was limited; for the African, this limitation was waived and he was bound for life. But, when the indentured white servant was eventually freed and settled on his own land, he

found his lot doomed by the ever-increasing hordes of African slaves
whose output reduced the conditions of his life to that of a debased
class whose aims were feared by the slave-owning aristocracy. The
plantation owners and the moneyed men of the mother country
regarded these newly freed whites as constituting a threat in two
directions: they didn't want those poor whites to advance claims
for democratic rights which no colonial society could possibly
tolerate; and the budding manufacturing interests of England feared
that the rootless whites would turn to manufacturing and become
their competitors. Thanks to slavery, the poor whites of the New
World were retarded for more than two centuries in their efforts to
gain political and social recognition, and it was not until the Civil
War in America abolished slavery, thereby enthroning industrial
production as the new way of life, that it could be said that the
New World had had any real need of poor white people at all. . . .

The kidnaping of poor whites, developed in England, had but
to be extended to the African shoreline and the experience gained
in subjugating the poor whites served admirably for the taming of
the tribal blacks. A hungry cry for sugar rose from all Europe, and
blacks were siphoned from Africa to grow the cane. The colonial
plantation became an economic and political institution that aug-
mented wealth and power for a few aristocrats, spread misery for
countless blacks, and imperiled the democratic hopes of millions
of whites.

Eric Williams reports in his *Capitalism and Slavery* that the Stuart
monarchy entrusted the slave trade to the Company of Royal Ad-
venturers Trading to Africa, and these gentlemen, in 1663, in-
corporated themselves for a period of one thousand years! Hitler's
clumsy dreams were picayune when compared with the sanguine
vision of these early English Christian gentlemen. . . . The African
trading companies were regarded not only as commercial enter-
prises, but as training schools for all those who wished to deal in
slaves and African matters. The scheme, bold in scope and daring
in design, enabled the English to establish a monopoly to steal or
buy slaves from the Straits of Gibraltar to the Cape of Good Hope,
unload British-manufactured goods in Africa, sell the slaves to the

planters in the West Indies or America; they then would load their
empty ships with plantation produce to keep the growing mills of
England busy. It was foolproof; you couldn't lose. . . . The human
bodies involved in this circular trade were incidental; it was just
trade. . . . Of course, the colonial planters complained of the
quality of the goods and the prices exacted by the English, just as
the Africans complain today, but what could they do?

In 1698, however, this monopoly was broken and the right of
free trade in slaves was equated to the natural rights of all Englishmen, and the English not only stocked their own colonial plantations with slaves but managed to supply black human beings to
their imperialist rivals as well.

But Liverpool. . .? Though London and Bristol exceeded Liverpool
in importance as a slave port in 1755, Liverpool quickly forged
ahead and, between 1783 and 1793, 878 Liverpool ships carried
303,737 slaves whose sterling value has been estimated as being over
fifteen million pounds. This trade was a sky-dropped bonanza to the
English, for it was conducted in terms of exchanging English
manufactured goods for slaves whose sale in the West Indies and
America supplied England with raw materials. English bullion had
not to be touched to keep this vast circular movement going. Until
1783 the whole of English society, the monarchy, church, state, and
press backed and defended this trade in slaves.

Out of the welter of this activity English mercantile ideas and
practices grew up; a classic concept of a colony emerged and has
endured more or less until this day: colonies are areas to be kept
economically disciplined and dependent upon the mother country.
Colonists were obliged to ship their produce to England in English
bottoms, and they could buy no goods but English goods unless
those goods had first been shipped to England. A colony, therefore,
became a vast geographical prison whose inmates were presumably
sentenced for all time to suffer the exploitation of their human,
agricultural, and mineral resources. Then, as well as now, no native
industry was tolerated; everything from sugar to shoes was shipped
from the mother country, taxed by colony customs; and, after it

had passed through many hands, it was sold to the native to enable
him to enjoy the blessings of Christendom.

Once slavery had become a vested interest in Liverpool, its
importance stretched far beyond the mere buying and selling of
slaves. Britain's merchant navy was nursed and reared in the slave
trade; her seamen were trained in it; shipbuilding in England was
stimulated by this trade in flesh. . . . And Liverpool itself flourished.
Eric Williams' *Capitalism and Slavery* relates that: "In 1565 Liverpool had 138 householders, seven streets only were inhabited, the
port's merchant marine amounted to twelve ships of 223 tons. Until
the end of the 17th Century the only local event of importance was
the sieging of the town during the English Civil War. In collecting
ship money Strafford assessed Liverpool at fifteen pounds; Bristol
paid two thousand. The shipping entering Liverpool increased four
and one half times between 1709 and 1771; the outward tonnage
six and a half times. The number of ships owned by the port
multiplied four times during the same period, the tonnage and
sailors over six times. Customs receipts soared from an average of
£51,000 for the years 1757 to £648,000 in 1785 . . ."

In 1790 the abolition of the slave trade would have ruined Liverpool; her estimated loss from abolition was then computed at over
seven and a half million pounds. Profits from the slave trade built
Liverpool docks; the foundations of the city were built of human
flesh and blood. . . .

Yet, how calm, innocent, how staid Liverpool looked in the
June sunshine! What massive and solidly built buildings! From my
train window I could catch glimpses of a few church spires punctuat-
ing the horizon. Along the sidewalks men and women moved unhurriedly. Did they ever think of their city's history? I recalled once
having asked a lower-class Englishwoman what she thought of the
colonies, and she had sucked in her breath and had told me:

"I'm sorry, but they'll have to go it on their own. We've bled
ourselves white to feed them, to lift them up; now they've got to
stand on their own feet. We've had enough of carrying them on our
shoulders."

I went through immigration, customs; I was the only American on board. Despite the sunny sky, it was cold. I stood on deck and stared at the city. What a drably respectable face on this city that had had such a past. . . .

At five o'clock I heard a long, dull blast and felt the ship easing out to sea, heading, as thousands of English ships before her, toward African waters. . . . In those days those ships had carried cotton and linen goods, silks, coarse blue and red woolen cloths for togas, guns, powder, shot, sabers, iron and lead bars, hardware of all kinds, copper kettles, glittering beads, masses of cheap ornaments, whiskey, and tobacco. The cargo in the hold was not terribly different even today. Only this time there were no handcuffs, chains, fetters, whips. . . .

The dogged English had lost thousands of men, as seamen and soldiers, seeking gold and slaves in the hot climate of West Africa, and yet they'd kept sending their boys. Was it imagination or lack of it? Now that mercantilism was dead and industrialization was the cock of the walk, what would the English do with their colonies? What would they do with a surplus of 20,000,000 too many Englishmen reared on the easy profits of selling manufactured goods to backward peoples? Even Argentina today was industrializing herself and had but little need for English goods. The art of manufacture was no longer a secret, and machines had a nigger-loving way of letting even black hands operate them. Africans were talking boldly of hydroelectric plants and the making of aluminum. . . . True, the British could help technically in all of this, but British aid was timed by the capacity of Africans to absorb techniques which the world today knew could be mastered by anybody. . . .

III...

Next morning a steward seated me at a table at which sat a tall, slightly bald African. We exchanged greetings and he introduced himself as Justice Thomas of the Nigerian Supreme Court.

"You're American?" he asked.

"Yes."

"First trip to Africa?"

"Yes."

"You know, my grandfather was a slave in the West Indies," he told me. "He'd been stolen from Africa and sold. He managed to make his way back to Africa and he settled in Freetown. He was a Christian and gave his children an education."

"That's interesting," I said.

"My ideas are Left," he told me and waited.

That sounded strange to me. If you are a Leftist, you act it, you don't talk it. And I knew that I'd been farther Left than he'd ever dream of going. I nodded and waited.

"I believe in doing things for the masses, but it must be done with dignity," he told me. "I'm pro-British and pro-African. I'm for the United States."

"Uh hunh," I said and waited.

"You're going to the Gold Coast?"

"Yes."

"What do you think of Nkrumah?" he asked me.

"I don't know. I'm going down to find out," I said.

He launched into a description of one of his most recent cases; it seemed that he had presided at a trial of nineteen men and that he had sentenced them to long prison terms.

"Who were these men and what had they done?" I asked.

"They were Africans and they'd engaged in violent actions against the government," he told me. "By the way, what do you do?"

"I write," I said.

"What do you know about Communism?" he asked me.

"I was a member of the Communist Party of the United States for twelve years," I told him.

He blinked, sighed, and shook his head.

"Are you a Communist now?"

"No."

"Why did you leave?"

"I embraced Communism because I felt it was an instrumentality to help free the Negroes in America," I explained to him. "But, in time, I found that instrumentality degrading. I dropped it of my own accord. I was not driven out; I was not frightened out of Communism by American government agents. I left under my own steam. I was prompted to leave by my love of freedom. My attitude toward Communism is a matter of public record."

As breakfast ended, he hauled from his pockets several bottles of garlic tablets, yeast pills, and vitamin capsules; he was an ardent follower of Gayelord Hauser, blackstrap molasses and all. He continued to talk ramblingly, leaping from subject to subject. I listened.

"That Nkrumah's done a great job," he told me. "I know his secret. He embraced the masses. One neglects the masses at one's peril. . . . What do you think?"

"Embracing the masses seems to be a habit with politicians today," I said.

"You wouldn't mind if I asked that you be assigned to my table, would you?" he asked me.

"Not at all," I said. "It'd be a pleasure."

After breakfast I sat on the cold deck, mulling over Justice Thomas as the ship rolled gently through a wind-swept, leaden sea. I'd been told that we'd not find any warm weather for three days. The deck was quiet; the ship seemed to be settling down for a long run. The passengers were restrained, English, and so was the food.

At lunch, after we had greeted each other, Justice Thomas proclaimed:

"You see, we Freetowners have been in contact with Europe for a long time. We are called Creoles. It's from us that the English draw their best African leaders, teachers, doctors, lawyers. If we didn't have the help of the English, we'd be swamped by the natives in Sierra Leone. We in the Colony are but a handful, about 100,000, and the tribal people number almost 2,000,000. Against such numbers, we few literates rule by prescriptive right. It's not democratic; we don't pretend it is. What happened in the Gold Coast will never happen in Sierra Leone. No, sir! No tribal rabble will sweep us out of our positions!"

"Look, just what do you think of the tribal Africans?" I asked him.

"I like to live well," he said, grinning and looking at me frankly. "I love good food, good whiskey. . . . These natives running naked

in the bush—" His nostrils wrinkled in disgust. "You don't know
Africa." He lifted his right hand and cupped it to my ear and
whispered: "There are men in Nigeria who still enjoy human flesh—"
"Cannibals?" I asked.

"God, yes," he assured me solemnly. "They are not ready for
freedom yet. This business of having five and six wives . . . It's
barbarous. I chose one wife and I stick to her. I can support more
than one, but I want only one. I could have followed my people's
customs, but I wanted to rise out of the mire. The British did *not*
make me a Justice of the Supreme Court of Nigeria because they
liked my black skin. They did it because of what I've got up
here. . . ." He tapped his balding skull. "When Thomas sits on a case,
the British know that it's useless to appeal against it. When a man
appeals against a decision of mine, the British ask: 'Who tried that
case?' If the answer is: 'Thomas,' the British will say: 'The decision
is sound, for Thomas is a sound man.'" He laughed with self-
satisfaction. "I know my English law. The British are hard but
fair, and they trust me."

"Do you ever think of developing your country?" I asked him.

"No; my talent doesn't run in that direction," he said.

"What professions will your children follow?"

"Law and medicine," he said promptly.

"Suppose your son wanted to be a mining engineer. . . ."

"That would be difficult," he admitted.

"That's why we drove the English out of America," I told him.
"Mr. Justice, it all depends upon how free you want to be. I'm
neither anti- nor pro-British, but if I lived under British rule and
wanted to develop and exercise my natural and acquired powers
and the British said no, I'd be anti-British. Tell me, do you believe
that the American colonies were right in taking their independence?"

He grinned at me.

"It's not the same thing," he said. "*We* are different. These boys in
Africa want to go *too* fast. You and I have been in touch with the
Western world for two, three hundred years—"

"Say, you know, if you were not black, I'd say that you were an

Englishman. In fact, you are more English than many English I've met," I told him.

Reactions flickered across his face; then he decided to laugh.

"I *am* English," he said.

"But you cannot live like the English," I reminded him.

"What do you mean?"

"Do you have the British constitution in Sierra Leone?"

"No; but—"

"Why not?"

"They are not *ready!*"

"What do you call *ready*? Are people civilized and ready to govern themselves when they become so desperate that they put a knife at the throat of their rulers? Must the native rulers of all of Britain's colonies be graduates from prisons?"

He rubbed his chin and grinned at me. "But it mustn't go *too* fast," he mumbled stubbornly.

"Who's to time this development?" I asked.

We had reached an impasse. As we ate I looked past his shoulder and he looked past mine. We were still friendly, but we knew that we could not agree. It was not ideology that separated us, but fundamental attitudes toward life.

"I like Americans," he said as he left the table; there was something wistful in his eyes.

IV...

We were in the Bay of Biscay and the ship pitched and rolled; I liked that, for it made me feel that I was really on the ocean. Heaving seas and tossing ships never made me ill. I always pictured in my mind the ship lurching forward and I could see the prow dipping, churning the sea, throwing up spray and foam as it lunged forward; and then I knew that the stern had to lift and, at the same moment, I knew that the huge ship had to roll to the right and I could feel it tilting—seeing it in my mind's eye—and then feeling the weight of the water of the ocean resisting and forcing it back into an upright position which it would hold for a moment, perilously balancing itself in the sliding waters; and I would wait for the ship to roll in the opposite direction, to the left; and I'd know that this same motion would have to be repeated endlessly, and I agreed with it, identifying myself with the ship and visualizing all of its motions as being necessary and natural, even when the pitching and rolling accompanied each other. . . .

That afternoon the sun came out for the first time and the sea turned from slaty gray to green; we were getting into deep waters.

It was 'my first voyage on a ship so purely English. With the exception of a Syrian or two, a German, some Africans, and a few vague Mediterranean nationalities, the ship's passengers were mostly men and women going to Africa to assume civil service jobs or returning from a few months' leave in England. Dull, repressed, stolidly English, they spent most of their days playing cards, ping-pong, or drinking. They were a mediocre lot to administer the destinies of millions of blacks. . . .

Each morning on deck, each Englishman had a cheery "Good morning," but evidently such a greeting exhausted him, for he'd remain taciturn for the rest of the day. It was just as well, for it was the Africans that I really wanted to talk to.

When I went up on deck Sunday morning for a stroll, I passed the forward foyer and heard that Anglo-Saxon, nasalized singing of psalms that had been so long familiar to my ears. A Church of England service was being conducted and, discreetly peering through the half-transparent curtains, I could see rows of white and black faces, heads lifted, mouths opened, giving praises to God. Several times I traversed the deck in order to observe without offending; I was curious as to how Africans and Englishmen served the same God.

I saw black faces well mixed with the white, which meant that, in confronting God, they drew no color line. I'd always accepted a Jim Crow Holy Ghost as being rather natural, indeed, inevitable; for, if God had entrusted the running of this earth to the white man, then He did so to prepare us all for the Jim Crow social stratification of life beyond the grave. Heaven had a color line and that was why white men, staunch Christians, reflected so much racial bias in their daily dealing with their fellow blacks. . . .

But why had the British drawn no color line in matters mystical and metaphysical? Upon reflection, however, I discovered that the British could not, in a black continent, draw a color line in religious matters and prove that God was a common Father. Jim Crow religious services would surely defeat the aims, economic, cultural, and political of *Pax Britannica*. So, on Sundays, the redeemed infidels stood shoulder to shoulder with their white masters to sing praises to "Him from whom all blessings flow . . ."

Upon the ship as a whole there was no color line, and yet it was strange how the English and Africans, after having closed ranks to acknowledge God on Sundays, kept more or less to themselves on weekdays. I didn't detect any desire on the part of the British to avoid the Africans; indeed, it was the other way around. The Africans, mostly returning students, were distant, reserved with the British. I learned later in Africa that they not only didn't yearn for the company of the British, but wanted them as far away from Africa as possible; they spoke their white tutors' language with an accent, entertained British values with self-consciousness, and seemed definitely to prefer the company of their own tribal folk to that of their alien overseers.

At lunch the judge remarked casually:

"I didn't see you at service this morning."

"That's right."

"Everyone is welcome, you know."

"I don't profess any religion," I said.

He stared at me. I don't think that he quite knew how to accept that; I doubted if he'd ever heard anybody say anything like that before in his life.

"You are an atheist then?"

"I couldn't even qualify for that. I'm nothing in matters religious."

"What reasons do you give for rejecting God?"

"I don't reject or accept Him."

"Who do you think made the world?"

"I don't know. *Must* I know that?"

"But how do you account for all of this—" He waved his hand to include the ship and the vast ocean beyond it.

"Look, Mr. Justice, please don't tell me that this universe is a kind of watch and that somebody just *had* to make it," I chided him, laughing.

"No; I wasn't going to say that," he smiled.

"I'm not proud, scornful, or anything like that. I just don't know and I don't feel compelled to say that I know about God," I told him.

"You have attended church services?"

"How could I have ever escaped such in my youth?"

"I don't know what I'd do if I didn't pray to God sometimes," he said.

"What do you tell God in your prayers?" I asked him.

"About myself, my worries—"

"Did you ever discuss the white man with God?"

He laughed.

"You are funny!" he said.

"You're funny too," I said. "If I prayed to God, that would be the first thing I'd take up with Him. Especially if I were an African. You see, I'm practical—"

"But don't you think that the African has been improved by accepting Christianity?"

"He's certainly more docile," I said.

That shook him, but he managed to confess:

"I don't doubt it."

V . . .

As we sailed from Freetown I saw my first real tropical sunset. From the blue-gray waters of the sea and the hills of Sierra Leone there rose a purplish mist that melted into the yellow and red and gold of the clouds that spread themselves for miles along the horizon. The dropping sun proclaimed itself in a majestic display of color that possessed an unearthly and imperious nobility, inducing the feeling that one had just finished hearing the dying, rolling peal of a mighty

organ whose haunting chords still somehow lingered on in the form
of those charged and spangled lances of somber fire. The ship sliced
its way through a sea that was like still, thick oil, a sea that stretched
limitless, smooth, and without a break toward a murky horizon. The
ocean seemed to possess a quiet but persistent threat of terror lurking just beneath the surface, and I'd not have been surprised if a
vast tidal wave had thrust the ship skyward in a sudden titanic
upheaval of destruction.

As I watched the sea and the sky I knew that it was from feelings
such as these floating in me now that man had got his sense of God,
for, when such feelings stated themselves in him, he felt that some
powerful but invisible spirit was speaking to him; and he fell on his
face, asking to be saved from the emotion that claimed him, afraid,
not so much of the sea or the sky, but of the fantastic commotion that
bubbled in his heart. But I stood still, detached, watching the sea
and the sky and at the same time hearing the echoing declarations
that they roused in me. . . .

These feelings I do not deny, and I've not been the first to feel
them. I do not know why they are such as they are, what they really
mean, but I stand before them with the same attention that I stand
before this sea and this sky. I refuse to make a religion out of that
which I do not know. I too can feel the limit of my reactions, can
feel where my puny self ends, can savor the terror of it; but it does
not make me want to impose that sense of my terror on others, or
rear it into a compulsive system. Detached, I contain my terror,
look at it and wonder about it in the same way that I marvel about
this sea and sky.

The sunset dies and is gone; I can no longer see it; I can only feel
the feeling of wonder that still lives in me.

I admit the reality of the feeling; but I would not rig up devious
forms of sacrifice to rid myself of it, for that would be the surest way
of stifling it, killing it for all time.

At last, tropic weather. A blue horizon. Balmy breezes. A hot sun.
The rustle of water filled the air as the ship glided forward through
southern seas.

Night fell swiftly and overhead the stars, huge and chaste, glimmered faintly. One could now smell the sea.

I awakened one morning and looked out of my porthole and saw, looming through a warm mist, the Canary Islands. I shaved, showered, dressed, and went up on deck. Mr. Justice sauntered smilingly toward me, attired in tropic finery.

"Good morning!" he boomed. "Let's go ashore. . . ."

"Do you know Las Palmas?" I asked.

"Like the palm of my hand."

"All right," I said.

After breakfast the ship docked and the judge and I descended the gangplank.

"Once, when I was passing through Las Palmas," the judge rambled, "somebody offered to take me to a house of prostitution."

"Did you go?"

"I refused," Mr. Justice said with moral indignation. "I never let anybody take me to places like that. Things like that are to be found by yourself. I pity the man who can't find a woman."

I blinked, trying to keep abreast of his strange moral notions. Another African passenger joined us; he lived in the Gold Coast, but he'd been born in Togoland. I noticed that he was intimidated in the august presence of Mr. Justice, but he didn't seem to mind me. I was an American and he knew that I drew no class lines. This chap—I'll call him Mr. Togoland—was careful at all times to walk just a few steps behind Mr. Justice, not to interrupt him as he handed down his lofty opinions, and to pay deference to his every move. We hired a taxi.

"Where're we going?" Mr. Togoland asked.

"I don't know," I said.

The driver turned and jabbered in Spanish, then grinned and drew with his palms the imaginary outlines of a plump woman-shape.

"Gurrls?" he asked in a thick accent.

"What do you say, Mr. Justice?" I asked.

Mr. Justice turned to Mr. Togoland and asked:

"You want to meet some girls?"

"Where?" Mr. Togoland asked.

"In a house," the judge said.

Mr. Togoland was a YMCA official and he looked at me and grinned.

"I'd like to *see* some," he ventured timidly. "Just to look at."

"I'll accompany you gentlemen," I said. "But I'm *only* looking. I didn't come thousands of miles to pick up diseases from Spanish women in the Canary Islands."

"Let's go then!" the judge shouted.

He was uneasy; he had changed his role and he was not certain as to how I was taking it. He placed his hand in a fatherly manner on my shoulder as the taxi bumped along in the bright sunshine.

"You know," the judge floated on, "my father used to make many trips here for business. In those days it was usual for a man to leave his calling card with the madam in a house of prostitution."

"Leave his calling card? Why?" I asked.

"That was to show other customers that only men of distinction went there," Mr. Justice explained.

"But I don't have any calling cards," I told him.

"You don't understand. Let me tell you a personal story," Mr. Justice said, relaxing, smiling. "Years ago, when I was a young man, I went into one of those houses. When I presented my card, the madam said: 'Why, your name is familiar to me. Wait a moment; I'll find a card with a name on it like yours. . . .' The madam pulled out from a closet a big glass bowl in which calling cards were kept. She fished around in it and a few minutes later she pulled out my father's calling card, all yellow and dusty—"

"No kidding," I protested.

"On my honor, she did," Mr. Justice swore. "Boy, oh, boy, was I proud!"

"A kind of following in your father's footsteps," I suggested.

"Yes! That's it exactly," he said and went into guffaws of laughter.

The taxi pulled up in front of a pale green cement house; the driver got out and rapped twice on a door panel—that, no doubt, was a signal. Well, I told myself, I'm a stranger, but I feel pretty safe in the presence of a judge of the Nigerian Supreme Court.

No one will dare to pick my pocket in there; if they do, they'll find themselves tangling with the majesty of British jurisprudence. . . .

We were admitted by a squat, ugly woman. Nobody in our group spoke Spanish and I tried French.

"We want to drink some beer and talk to the girls," I told her.

She was more than agreeable; she let us in and ran down a dim hallway, knocking on doors and calling out girls' names. Mr. Justice, Mr. Togoland, and I sat down. In fifteen minutes twenty girls of all ages and sizes and personalities filed in sleepily, ranged themselves obligingly along the walls and looked at us with detached and casual eyes. I saw white matter at the edges of their eyelids and their faces appeared as though in dire need of a good wash. They yawned, but when our eyes caught theirs, they smiled shyly. The linoleum floor was littered with cigarette butts and a stale odor hung in the air. Some of the girls squatted on the floor; they wore thin pajamas but had no brassières. They asked for cigarettes and we passed some around. We drank, talked, joked, the madam doing the translating.

I watched Mr. Justice's eyes roving greedily among the girls.

"Don't let me cramp your style, Mr. Justice," I whispered to him.

"Oh, I'm happy," he said, laughing.

"Do what you want to do," I told him.

In comparison with the self-conscious stodginess of the British ship, this whorehouse was a citadel of simplicity, honesty, and straightforwardness. How relaxed everyone was! Even the haunting specter of Communism was absent. Since there was no need here of pretense or lying, one could afford to allow one's human impulses to come to the fore. It occurred to me that this shabby whorehouse was perhaps the only calm and human spot in this strongly entrenched Catholic city of Las Palmas where Franco's Fascism was in blatant evidence on so many billboards. . . . And perhaps these lost and sinful girls, pretty and always receptive, were the only free people in the entire islands. . . . Without doubt they were the only real democrats within reach. They were genial and they accepted everybody regardless of race, creed, or color; that is, for a price. . . . While we were talking and drinking, a black sailor came in and one of the girls rose promptly to serve him, taking him down the hall to a room.

Mr. Justice was nervous; he crossed and uncrossed his long legs. He drummed his tense fingers on the arm of the sofa. Too many wheat germs, I thought. At times he gazed thoughtfully at the ceiling, as though pondering some tricky point of law. Mr. Togoland's eyes shone as he looked from girl's face to girl's face, then glanced at their breasts which were like dim shadows under their sheer pajama tops. We ordered another round of beer and, as Mr. Justice tilted back his head to drink, I glanced shyly at him. When my eye caught his, he bent suddenly forward and laughed so loud and long that he spluttered beer spray across the room.

The girls were excited at his odd behavior and wanted to know what he was laughing at. I shook my head, knowing that moral subtleties of that genre were much too abstruse for prostitutes, no matter how generous they were.

"You are a knockout," Mr. Justice said to me, simpering.

"You are a killerdiller," I told him.

"It's wonderful being with you," he said.

"The pleasure is all mine," I said.

I knew that he was hotly longing to make a serious approach to one of the girls, but, out of deference to me—or was it the moral attitudes with which he had hemmed himself in during the past few days that was inhibiting him?—he was afraid to act and be himself. I could have easily put him at his ease, could have spoken a sentence and released him from the high-flown sentiments of honor and Christianity and he could have done what he wanted to do, but I was perverse enough to make him sit there on top of his platitudes and grin nervously. After all, I thought, it would certainly boost his chances in the other world if he could find enough self-control to forgo his impulse toward animal pleasure. And, if he persisted in building up his façade of pretense, if he must continuously fling Christianity and imperialism in my face, then let him squirm and wriggle a bit on the hook of his own hypocrisy—and that's exactly what he did. Every time he worked up enough spunk to start pawing one of the dusty-skinned Spanish girls, I'd look at him intently,

reminding him with a reproving glance of his august position as a
defender of British and Christian values, and he'd throw himself
back on the sofa, slap his thighs, and let out a storm of embarrassed
laughter. And I joined in his laughter, laughing at his predicament.
Mr. Togoland looked from one to the other of us, wondering what
was happening.

"What a life," Mr. Justice said, sheepishly wiping his mouth with
the back of his hand.

"You can say that again," I assured him.

The girls chatted among themselves and threw out a few English
words, urging us to drink. The squat madam hustled in with bottles
of cold beer, anxious to drum up trade of a more solid nature. I
drank and kept my eye on Mr. Justice, grimly determined not to
give him a break. If he wanted a girl badly enough, he'd have to
show me what a staunch individualist he was, how morally independent the British had taught him to be. But it was he who finally
sighed and said:

"I guess we'd better go."

We paid for our drinks and climbed back into the taxi. Mr. Togoland was wistful and grateful, but somehow disappointed.

"Was that the first time you've ever been in such a place?" I
asked him.

"Yes," he sighed. He glanced shyly at Mr. Justice. "And in such
company," he murmured, deeply impressed.

Mr. Justice was silent, serious, reflective. The white Spanish-
styled villas flew past the taxi window. We came in sight of the
ocean where the sun splashed and glittered on the seascape. Ships
idled at anchor. Gulls wheeled in the dazzling blue, crying hungrily.

"Listen," Mr. Justice began soberly, "those houses are safe, well
run, clean. They're all right. I know that all of the leading British
administrators, merchants, and soldiers in West Africa go to such
houses when they visit Las Palmas. . . ."

"Then it *must* be all right, if *they* go there," I said tersely.

Mr. Justice looked at me searchingly, surprised.

"Of course, it is," he said. "Did you *doubt* that?"

"I've *never* doubted the wisdom of the British," I said.

"Oh, come now," he chided me uneasily. "Be fair."
"I'm not a fair man, Mr. Justice," I informed him.
"I don't understand you," he said slowly.
"I understand *you*," I said.

V I . . .

As we entered West African waters, the sea was choppy, with
whitecaps showing. A blue mist hung on the horizon and, I was
told, the humidity in the air was a foretaste of what I'd encounter
in the Gold Coast.

At dinner I watched Mr. Justice take his wheat germ, his yeast
tablets, his vitamins, and his laxative sticks. I struggled against an
oblique sympathy that was dawning in me for the man. How England had mangled his soul! The truth was that the judge was living
in the wrong century. His enslaved grandfather had desperately
pulled himself out of servitude, had lifted himself above the
tribal level, and, in doing so, he had been akin to the millions of
Europeans and Americans of the nineteenth century who had so
valiantly overthrown the remnants of feudalism. Mr. Justice represented the victory of enlightenment: he could read, he could vote,
he was free; but he was adamant against the hungers of the new
generation.

Mr. Justice's grandfather had been a hero to him, but I doubted
if Mr. Justice's children would regard him in a heroic light. He
wanted his children to be black Englishmen. But would his children
want to be that? Were there not much bigger and more exciting
battles for them to fight? Mr. Justice had succeeded at the moment
when history was about to nullify his triumphs, and he was already confused and bewildered at the new social and political
currents swirling about him.

We were now in tropic waters, almost opposite Dakar. The
horizon was continually shrouded in mist. The sea was smooth, with
a tiny whitecap here and there. Hourly the heat and humidity

mounted and I imagined that the temperature on shore must have been very high.

That afternoon I wandered down into third class and found a group of young African students. I insinuated myself into their conversation and steered it toward politics. One undeniable fact informed their basic attitudes: Russia had made a most tremendous impression upon the minds of these world's outsiders. From where these colonial boys stood, Russia's analysis of events made sense. The first inescapable fact was that it was *only* from Russia—not from the churches or the universities of the Western world—that a moral condemnation of colonial exploitation had come. On this moral ground abandoned in embarrassment by the West, the Russians had driven home telling ideological blows.

The foremost conviction I found in them—or maybe you'd call it mood—was that nobody should strive for a unique or individual destiny. This was, of course, in essence, anti-Christian, even if the befuddled boys holding such notions did not know it. The historic events of the past forty years had made them feel that the only road into the future lay in collective action, that organized masses constituted the only true instrument of freedom.

This was not Communism; it was its impact; it was not the ideology of Marxism; it was its influence. The methods of imperialists have made it easy for these boys to embrace the idea of "masses," and the masses they have in mind are black masses. . . . Of Communism *per se* they wanted none, but they keenly appreciated the moral panic into which Russia had thrown the Western world. And they were aware of the huge mass of empiric material available about the techniques of making uprisings, general strikes, all kinds and degrees of actions that could paralyze the economic activities of imperialist powers. . . .

One rather heady young man expressed himself about Russia as follows:

"Russia's a gadfly! I'm not for her, but I'm not against her! Let her stay where she is and harass the West! Why are the British treating us a little better? They're scared of our going over to the Russians, that's all. If Russia were defeated tomorrow, a tide of reaction would set in in all the colonies. But, with the Cold War raging, even an Englishman, when he passes you on deck, is willing to say 'Good morning'!"

Their resentment against the British went far beyond economic issues. They swear that they'll rename many of their towns, rivers, villages and they'll christen them with names that their fathers gave them. They despise names like Gold Coast, Mumford, and Queen Anne's Point; and they are determined to rename their country Ghana. . . . I'm afraid that white Westerners will look on in dismay when they leave the Gold Coast and wonder what all their labors were for; they may go so far as to accuse the Africans of ingratitude. . . .

That night the ship washed through a steamy, tropic sea. A lighthouse whirled a powerful beam every few seconds through the velvet dark. The air smelled of rain. The winking red and green lights of a plane floated through the sky with a sound so faint that it emphasized the silence of the sea. Overhead the blackness was studded with points of star fire floating in a haze of silver; the sky seemed heavy, rich, about to swoop with a ripened load toward the heaving surface of the water.

Next day the sea was a flat, gray disc whose surface stretched toward a vague horizon. During the night it had rained and now drops of water clung to my porthole. The ship plowed through slaty seas that looked like viscous oil. The heat was so enervating that I felt sleepy, heavy, filled with unrest. The slightest exertion brought sweat to my face, yet the sky was never really bright; the sun's rays could not penetrate the overhanging mist. The day wore on and a kind of grayness pervaded the world and there was no line between the sea and the sky.

PART TWO

THE NERVOUS COLONY

Detribalization breaks down traditional ideas and introduces some of the Western; exploitation sharpens the ensuing restlessness into discontent; missionary education provides leaders and unwittingly furnishes much of the ideology and patterns of expression, for African revolts are frequently a mixture of religious fanaticism and anti-European sentiment.

The Marginal Man, by EVERETT V. STONEQUIST

VII...

When I awakened on the morning of the 16th of June, I was at once conscious of a strange, dead quiet. The ship's diesel engines had ceased to throb; stillness gripped my narrow cabin. We had docked! I leaped out of my bunk-bed and peered through the porthole and saw Africa. . . .

I dressed hurriedly and went on deck; an African city, under a blanket of blue mist, lay spread out before me. The heat was heavy, close, wet; and the city—Takoradi—seethed with activity at even this early hour. On the wharf was a forest of derricks, cranes, sheds, machines and, as I looked closer, I could see that they were being operated by black men—a fact that must have produced pain in the heart of Dr. Malan of South Africa, for he had sworn that black men were incapable of doing these things.

I studied the swirling crowd on the docks and found it hard to distinguish men from women, for practically everyone had a richly colored cloth draped about him, and almost everyone was barefooted except the policemen who, to my horror, were dressed in dark blue wool! I wondered how they could stand it. . . .

At the breakfast table I took my farewell of Mr. Justice who was continuing the voyage to Lagos, Nigeria.

"I wonder what you're going to make out of Africa," the judge said reflectively, chewing.

"I don't expect to find too much there that's completely new," I drawled.

"Africa's strange, *strange*," he assured me.

"My background's rather strange too," I informed him.

He laughed and shook his head.

"If you get to Nigeria, you must look me up," he said. "Don't forget me."

"I shan't forget you," I told him.

I descended to the customs shed where it was twice as hot as it had been on board. A young man approached me.

"Mr. Wright?"

"Yes."

"I'm meeting you for the Prime Minister."

He was Mr. Ansah, short, black, alert, a personal friend of Nkrumah. He guided me through customs and informed me that a government transport bus would take me to Accra, the capital. Emerging from the customs shed, I saw Africa for the first time with frontal vision: black life was everywhere. My eyes were riveted upon a woman wearing a brightly colored length of cloth which held a baby strapped to her back; the infant's legs were sprawled about the woman's hips and thighs, and the tiny head of the baby lolled in sleep with sweat beading on its forehead. The cloth held the weight of the baby's body and was anchored straight across the woman's breasts, cutting deeply into the flesh. Another woman was washing in a pan set on the ground; she was bent at an angle of forty-five degrees in the broiling sun, her black child also sound asleep upon her back. The babies of other women were awake, their wide, innocent eyes avoiding the broad blank expanse of their mothers' backs, looking at the world from side to side. Then I was startled by a European family threading its way through the black crowd.

"They are the minority here, hunh, Mr. Ansah?" I asked.

He roared with laughter.

"It's good *not* to be a minority for once, eh?" he asked.

"I admit it," I said. "Say, how do they behave?"

"All right," he said. "It's the high officials who need watching. Individuals like these are generally polite; they have to be. They're dependent upon us, you see."

We walked past black traffic officers, black policemen, gangs of black workmen; and, in the locomotive of a train, I saw a black fireman and a black engineer. The whole of life that met the eyes was black. I turned my attention to my host.

"You're a businessman, I take it?"

"Yes. I hope you're not opposed to businessmen."

"Not if they're working for the freedom of their country," I told him.

He laughed heartily and grabbed my hand.

"Just what do you do?" I asked him.

"Timber. I cut it, dress it, draw it, and ship it to all parts of the world."

"How many men do you employ?"

"About two hundred. Say, would you mind coming with me to the store? I must do a bit of shopping. . . ."

We entered a huge, modern store that reminded me of a unit in the American Atlantic and Pacific grocery chain; it was managed by the British but staffed with Africans. As Mr. Ansah shopped, I wandered about. I examined an enameled pot that would hold about a quart of liquid; it was priced at £1! Or $2.80! A salesman came up to me.

"You wish to buy something, sar?"

"No; I'm just looking."

"You're American, aren't you, sar?"

"Yes; how did you know?"

"Oh, we know, sar," he said. Another salesman joined him. "What part of Africa did you come from, sar?"

I stared at him and then laughed. I felt uneasy.

"I don't know."

"Didn't your mother or grandmother ever tell you what part of Africa you came from, sar?"

I didn't answer. I stared vaguely about me. I had, in my childhood, asked my parents about it, but they had had no information, or else they hadn't wanted to speak of it. I remembered that many Africans had sold their people into slavery; it had been said that they had had no idea of the kind of slavery into which they had been selling their people, but they had sold them. . . . I suddenly didn't know what to say to the men confronting me.

"Haven't you tried to find out where in Africa you came from, sar?"

"Well," I said softly, "you know, you fellows who sold us and the white men who bought us didn't keep any records."

Silence stood between us. We avoided each other's eyes.

"Are you going to stay with us, sar?"

"I'm visiting."

There was another silence. I was somehow glad when Mr. Ansah returned. We went back to the docks. It was so hot and humid that I felt that my flesh was melting from my bones. I climbed into the government bus and shook hands with my host. The bus rolled slowly through streets clogged with black life. African cities are small and one is in the "bush"—the jungle—before one knows it. Ten minutes out of Takoradi was enough to make Africa flood upon me so quickly that my mind was a blur and could not grasp it all. Villages of thick-walled mud huts heaved into view, tantalizing my eyes for a few seconds, and then fled past, only to be replaced by others as mythical and unbelievable. Naked black children sat or squatted upon the bare earth, playing. Black women, naked to the waist, were washing their multicolored cloths in shallow, muddy rivers. The soil was a rich red like that of Georgia or Mississippi, and, for brief moments, I could almost delude myself into thinking that I was back in the American South. Men, with their cloths tied at their hips, were cutting grass at the roadside with long cutlasses. Then I saw a crowd of naked men, women, and children bathing in a wide, muddy stream; the white lather of soap covered their bodies, and their black, wet skins glistened in the morning sun.

Then, to my right, the Atlantic burst in a wide, blue, blaze of beauty. Along this coastline Africa had been in contact with Europe for more than five hundred years. What kind of relationship had these people had with Europe that left them more or less what they were . . . ? Travelers' accounts in 1700 tell of having seen thousands of tracks of antelope, elephants, and other wild animals in the areas through which my bus was speeding. Wild life has vanished from here now. Those not slain by hunters have been driven deeper into the dense jungles. But the customs of the people remain almost unaltered . . .

In 1441 a Portuguese navigator, one Antonia Gonzales, launched the slave trade on these shores by kidnaping a few Africans; evidently the Christians of Portugal liked the services of those blacks,

for Gonzales returned in 1442 for another shipload. Thus were inaugurated those acts of banditry which, as the decades passed, were
erected into an institution that bled Africa and fattened Europe. In
the beginning of the sixteenth century the slave trade took on a
definite historic pattern and soon became the dominant passion of
the Western world.

It had not, however, been for slaves that the Europeans had first
sailed down the coast of West Africa; they'd been trying to prove
that the world was round, that they could find a route to India,
seeking to determine if Africa was a peninsula. They had become
distracted by the incredibly rich gold dust to be found on the
Guinea Coast and, in 1455, there had sprung up what was known
as the "silent trade," a kind of coy and furtive bargaining between
the predatory Europeans and the frightened but gullible natives. . . .
Europeans would leave heaps of cheap trinkets upon the ground and
then retire a half day's march away; the Africans would steal out,
examine the shoddy merchandise, and place tiny piles of gold
dust upon each heap. The Europeans would then return and try
to determine if the gold dust left was an adequate payment for the
goods; if they felt that it was not, they'd retire again and the Africans
would sneak up. If the Africans wanted the goods badly enough,
they'd increase the tiny piles of gold dust. . . . Confidence being
somewhat established in this manner, the Portuguese, according to
historical records, had once traded extensively for gold in the very
neighborhood through which my bus now sped.

The kaleidoscope of sea, jungle, nudity, mud huts, and crowded
market places induced in me a conflict deeper than I was aware of;
a protest against what I saw seized me. As the bus rolled swiftly
forward I waited irrationally for these fantastic scenes to fade; I
had the foolish feeling that I had but to turn my head and I'd see
the ordered, clothed streets of Paris. . . . But the string of mud villages stretched out without end. My protest was not against Africa
or its people; it was directed against the unsettled feeling en-
gendered by the strangeness of a completely different order of life.
I was gazing upon a world whose laws I did not know, upon faces
whose reactions were riddles to me. There was nothing here that I

could predict, anticipate, or rely upon and, in spite of myself, a mild
sense of anxiety began to fill me.

The bus stopped and I stared down at a bare-breasted young girl
who held a huge pan of oranges perched atop her head. She saw
me studying her and she smiled shyly, obviously accepting her
semi-nudity as being normal. My eyes went over the crowd and I
noticed that most of the older women had breasts that were flat
and remarkably elongated, some reaching twelve or eighteen inches
(length, I was told later, was regarded as a symbol of fertility!),
hanging loosely and flapping as the women moved about—and
intuitively I knew that this deformation had been caused by the
constant weight and pressure of babies sagging upon their backs
and pulling the cloth that went across their bosoms. . . .

Some of the roofs of the huts were made of thatched straw and
others were constructed of rusty corrugated tin. Many of the mud
huts—commonly known as swish huts—had been fairly recently
erected and were of a reddish-brown color; others were old, showing cracked walls half washed away by the torrential tropic rains,
and their color tended toward a tannish yellow. I learned later that
these swish huts had been known to withstand tropical weather
for more than seventy years, so strongly were they built, and that
they were cool and comfortable to sleep in. What fascinated me was
the manner in which the swish hut structures ordered the manner of
living; or was it that the African manner of living had preordained
the odd structure of the huts . . . ? They were so constructed that
they formed a vast rectangle, three sides of which were solid walls
of clay rooms whose doors fronted a wide courtyard; the fourth wall
of rooms had a narrow opening serving both as exit and entrance.
A dwelling unit of this sort was referred to as a compound, and,
in its enclosure, washing, cooking, mending, carpentry, and a
score of other activities took place. A compound of this nature was
a variant of a stockade and it was believed that the Africans resorted to this mode of building when they wanted to protect themselves from slave snatching.

Bit by bit my eyes became accustomed to the naked bodies and
I turned my attention to the massive and green landscape, above

which drifted that inevitable blue haze. I sped past plantations of banana trees, palm trees, coconut trees, orange trees, and rubber trees; then there loomed wawa trees and mahogany trees; cottonwood trees, white and tall and straight, stood like monuments amidst the green forest. Cocoa trees crowded the countryside with their red, brown, and yellow pods, then came patches of cocoa yam, cassava, and pineapple. But these plantations were like no plantations I'd ever seen before; there was no order, no fences, no vast sweeps of plowed earth such as one sees in the American Midwest—there was just a profuse welling of plants in a tangled confusion stretching everywhere, seemingly with no beginning and no end.

The bus rocked on through thick jungle; then, half an hour later, roared into another batch of mud villages. As we slowed for a crossroads, I stared again at the half-nude black people and they returned my gaze calmly and confidently. What innocence of instincts! What unabashed pride! Such uninhibitedness of living seemed to me to partake of the reality of a dream, for, in the Western world where my instincts had been conditioned, nude bodies were seen only under special and determined conditions: in the intimacies of marriage, in expensive nightclubs, in the clandestine rendezvous of lovers, in art galleries, or in the bordels of the kind that Mr. Justice liked to haunt . . . ; and only men of undoubtedly professional stamp—doctors, artists, undertakers—were permitted, by the tolerance of the state or the indulgence of society, to deal with nudity, and then only behind closed doors. Yet, as I stared out of the bus window, I was amazed at the utter asexuality of the mood and the bearing of the people! Sex *per se* was absent in what I saw; sex was so blatantly prevalent that it drove all sexuality out; that is, it eliminated all of that evidence of sublimated and projected sexual symbolization with which Western men are habitually prone to decorate their environment in depicting to themselves the reality of the hidden bodies of their women. The hair of the women was plainly done, wrapped tightly in black strings and tied in plaited rows close to the skull; no rouge or powder showed on any woman's cheeks; no fingernails were painted; and, save for a few tiny earrings of gold, they were bare of ornamentation of every kind.

Undoubtedly these people had, through experiences that had constituted a kind of trial and error, and in response to needs that were alien and obscure to me, chosen some aspect of their lives other than sex upon which to concentrate their passions, and what that other aspect was and the manner in which they concentrated their passions upon it was something that I did not know, nor could I guess at its nature. Was it hunger? Was it war? Was it climate? Or was sex being *deliberately* brought into the open . . . ? Had it been from some taboo originating in their religion? Or had it risen out of the vicissitudes of natural catastrophes? And, again, faced with the absolute otherness and inaccessibility of this new world, I was prey to a vague sense of mild panic, an oppressive burden of alertness which I could not shake off. . . .

Fishing villages, quaint and bleak in the blinding sun, flashed by, then came Elmina, Cape Coast, Anomabu, historic Gold Coast place names that stirred me to a memory of dark and bloody events of long ago. The road twisted through plantation and forest and jungle and again, to my right, the green waves of the Atlantic leaped wild and free, rolling and breaking upon the yellow sands and the grayish rocks of the far-flung shore, and I knew that it was across those stretches of barren beach that hundreds of thousands of black men, women, and children had been marched, shackled and chained, down to the waiting ships to be carted across the ocean to be slaves in the New World. . . .

The bus stopped in a tiny village and I clambered down to stretch my legs; three or four Africans followed me, then the Europeans got off. . . . I strode around the market place and finally halted before a young woman who sat cross-legged and who was nude to the waist. Balanced on her head was a huge tray of peeled coconuts.

"I want to buy a coconut," I told her.

The flesh of her cheeks had been slashed by double marks in two places: tribal marks. . . . Though scarring the cheeks was being done less and less, it still occurred among the more backward elements of the population. In the old days all babies were thus

marked at birth for purposes of identification, and some of the
tribal marks were truly intricate; indeed, there were times when I
had the impression that some delicate cobweb was covering a person's face, so many crossing lines traversed the jaws and cheeks,
reaching from the temple to the chin, from the nostrils to the ears.

The young woman to whom I had spoken burst into embarrassed
laughter, turned and beckoned to a girl friend, mumbled something
to her in her tribal tongue, and pointed to me. Her friend sauntered
over slowly, lifting her cloth and covering her breasts; she evidently
knew something of Western ways. . . .

"You wanna buy?" she asked me, smiling.

"A coconut," I said.

She translated for her friend who, taking a coconut from her tray,
whacked a hole in it with one deft stroke of her cutlass, and handed
it to me, still giggling. I paid her and she tossed my coin upon the
tray and, without looking, her fingers fished around on the tray
and found my change. I stood to one side and drank the coconut
milk, studying her. Her eyes were sloe-shaped; her feet were large
and splayed, the soles coarsened by earth and rain and rocks. The
skin of her arms held a slightly ashened hue. When she became
aware of my gaze, she burst again into laughter, hiding her face.
The Europeans standing nearby turned to look at me and the
girl, and I wondered what they were thinking. . . .

En route again, we sped through several thriving commercial
centers. Now and then, looming up from the beach, and fronting
both the sea and the jungle, were huge white castles and forts, their
lofty ramparts holding decaying gun emplacements that still
pointed commandingly toward both the misty expanse of the Atlantic and the tropically green countryside. These forts and castles
had been built centuries ago by the Portuguese, the Dutch, the
Danes, and the Swedes and they had been designed not only to
ward off attacks and raids of the hostile and desperate natives, but
also those of other European imperialist rivals whose jealous hunger
for gold and slaves made them a prey to be feared. For centuries
these dominating structures had served as storage depots, barracks,
military command headquarters, arsenals, and they also contained

deep dungeons in which kidnaped, bought, or stolen slaves had
been kept for overseas shipment. The iron rings and chains which
had fastened their black bodies to the masonry were still intact.

How had the Europeans gotten a toehold upon this shore? Had
they sneaked in? Had the naïve natives invited them in? Or had
they fought their way forward in bloody battles? It was none of
these; it had been through guile . . . ; a guile which enthroned distrust as a cardinal element in the African attitude toward Europe,
a distrust that lives on in the African heart until this day.

The Portuguese set the pattern in 1481. John II, upon ascending
the throne, organized a huge fleet for the purpose of establishing
a European settlement upon the coast where it had been said that
gold was an article of household use among the infidel natives. Historical records relate that the expedition carried "500 soldiers and
officers and 100 masons and other workers"; they carried enough
stones, cut, prepared, and ready to be fitted into place for the hurried building of a fort; also on board was ammunition, food, and a
priest. . . . The idea had been, by ruse or force, to erect a fort
strong enough to repel rival imperialist attacks and, at the same
time, to compel the respect and obedience of the natives. The
Portuguese strategy was to ask the natives to grant them the right
to build a church in order that they might confer upon them the
blessings of Jesus Christ; the force was to be held in reserve in case
the natives refused to accept such blessings. . . .

Anchoring off Elmina in 1482, the expedition's commander, one
Don Diego d'Azambuja, sought an audience with the native chief,
using a Portuguese who had learned the tribal language as his interpreter. Concealing their arms beneath their imposing and gaudy
clothing, they presented the chief with a sugared demand to establish a Christian church on the coast, extolling the benefits of heart
and spirit that would ensue from such an institution.

The natives and the chief had but a hazy conception of Europe,
but they were practical enough to doubt the word of men who came
thousands of miles in ships to erect domiciles in their land; being
naïve, they guessed erroneously that the white men had been driven
forcibly out of their country, had been reduced to living in their

ships, and now wanted to take their tribal lands for themselves. The Africans, mystical and fanatical lovers of their ancestral soil, could not conceive of people voluntarily leaving their homes and families and traveling vast distances merely for the sake of trade. A tragic misconception! Four hundred and thirty-one years ago, the first African to leave a record of protest, diplomatic yet charged with anxiety, spoke as follows:

"I'm not insensible to the high honor which your great master, the chief of Portugal, has this day conferred upon me. His friendship I have long endeavored to merit by the strictness of my dealing with the Portuguese, and by my constant exertions to procure an immediate lading for their vessels. But never until this day did I observe such a difference in the appearance of his subjects; they have hitherto been only meanly attired, were easily contented with the commodities they received; and so far from wishing to continue in this country, were never happy until they could complete their lading, and return. Now I remark a strange difference. A great number richly dressed are anxious to be allowed to build houses, and to continue among us. Men of such eminence, conducted by a commander who from his own account seems to have descended from the God who made day and night, can never bring themselves to endure the hardships of this climate; nor would they here be able to procure any of the luxuries that abound in their own country. The passions that are common to us all will therefore inevitably bring on disputes; and it is far preferable that both nations should continue on the same footing they have hitherto done, allowing your ships to come and go as usual; the desire of seeing each other occasionally will preserve peace between us . . ." (*A History of the Gold Coast*, by W. Walton Claridge, vol. 1).

But the Portuguese had long before made up their minds that it was well worth their while to risk the terrible climate, and, pretending to be spokesmen of the Gentle Jesus, they hankered not for peace, but for victory. Rebuffed, they soon resorted to threats, which caused the African chief to give an uneasy consent. But, next morning, as the Portuguese workmen were frantically hoisting the prepared stones into place, the natives of Elmina attacked them, wounding

many of their men. D'Azambuja altered his tactics and rained presents and bribes upon the natives, offering profuse apologies. Despite
this, the construction of the fort was pushed night and day and,
in less than a month, a tower had been built against which the
natives were helpless. The Portuguese flag was hoisted and a mass
was said. . . .

The European campaign against the mainland of Africa, but-
tressed by a mixture of religious ideology and a lust for gold, had
begun in earnest; there had been no declaration of war; there had
been no publicly declared aims save those of soul-saving, which
even the Portuguese didn't believe, and, as time passed, European
governments *per se* were not even involved in these calculated as-
saults, for it was the right, endorsed by no less than the Pope, of
any individual merchant, criminal, or adventurer to buy a ship, rig
it out, muster a crew, and set sail for Africa and try his luck.

Fortified with the authority of a papal bull, publicly minimizing
the loot to be had, and extolling the opportunities for Christian
service, John II proceeded at once to safeguard his new possession
by spreading the word that the natives of the coast of West Africa
were cannibals and would eat Europeans; he caused rumors to be
circulated that terrible storms rose four times a year and made the
seas impassable; and he assured the world that no one ought to be
foolhardy enough to venture into West African waters in any other
than a ship of Portuguese construction, for others were definitely
unseaworthy. . . . There followed a partial "blackout" of all information relating to Portuguese activities on the coast of West Africa
until 1500 when other European nations, overcoming the psychological intimidations of Catholicism, disregarded the papal bull and
pushed their way past bloody Portuguese resistance and into the
trade in black slaves and yellow gold.

For 150 years there followed a period of free-for-all warfare
among the Portuguese, the Dutch, the French, the English, the
Swedes, the Germans and the African natives. . . . Relying mainly
upon the authority of their firepower, the Portuguese forbade the
Africans to trade with any other European power, an injunction
which the Africans, of course, resented. The Portuguese penalty for

violating their wishes was to raze and burn African villages, and in time even worse reprisals were meted out. The French, being less strong at sea, were also dodging in and out of the coastal native settlements, trading and keeping a wary eye out for the Portuguese. The English made direct representations to the Africans, trying to dissuade them from trading with the Portuguese, and when the Africans failed to comply, they too burned and destroyed native villages and looted the countryside of goats, sheep, and fowl. Sometimes the English and the French formed uneasy alliances against the Portuguese, hoping that, with such a common front, they could drive them out of West Africa, but such alliances could last only so long as the two respective home countries were at peace with each other. Hence, on many occasions the English and the French, hearing that their respective home countries were at war with each other in Europe, would turn suddenly and attack each other in Africa, even though both of them were under attack by the hated Portuguese.

Toward the end of the sixteenth century the Dutch made a bid to share in the rich spoils by making an alliance with native tribes and arming them with guns (much to the fury of the Portuguese who loved the advantage of gunpowder over spears!) and urging them to fight against the Portuguese whom they had grown to hate. Meanwhile, Portugal became diverted by her rich colonies in the New World and allowed her forts to fall into disrepair and to become undermanned. In 1637 the Dutch made a determined assault upon the Portuguese fort at Elmina and captured it, and five years later they had driven the Portuguese, after 160 years of occupation, out of West Africa altogether.

The Dutch victory on the Guinea Coast went unchallenged for but a short time, for, in 1657, the Swedes built a fort at Cape Coast, which fell to the Danes soon afterward; after changing hands several times, the fort at Cape Coast fell to the English for keeps in 1664. The war between the English and the Dutch changed but little the *status quo* regarding the forts, and when peace came in 1667, the situation was about what it had been before the shooting started.

Then, in 1655, the Germans horned in, building two forts at Sekondi and Axim.

In 1693 the natives around Accra attacked the Danes in their strongly fortified Castle Christianborg and defeated them through trickery and captured the castle, but, a year later, they sold it back to the Danes! From 1694 onwards the Dutch power began to decline slowly under the constant attack of native tribesmen, and, since most of the European interlopers were fighting each other in other parts of the world, forts changed hands only to be given back to their original owners when peace came about at spots far from Africa. When England, therefore, lost her American colonies, she was too weak, in 1785, to contest the Dutch ownership of forts in West Africa.

VIII...

Though the distance from Takoradi to Accra was but 170 miles, it took us all of eight hours to make the journey; it was nearing six o'clock when Accra loomed through the sunset on the horizon.

A smiling but somewhat reserved mulatto woman who spoke clipped and careful English—she was the Prime Minister's secretary —was on hand at the bus station to meet me. The Prime Minister, she told me, was in the Northern Territories on an urgent political mission.

"What *is* the political situation?" I asked her.

"You'll see," she said cryptically, lifting her brows.

She drove me in her English car across Accra, and I could hear the faint sounds of drums beating in the distance, the vibrations coming to my ears like the valved growl of a crouching beast.

"What are those drums?"

"You'll find out," she said, laughing.

"I feel strange; I see and hear so much that I don't understand."

"It'll take you a few days to get into it," she said.

In the sun's dying light we came to a group of modernistic bungalows situated atop a chain of low-lying hills where the heat and humidity were more bearable. These beautiful bungalows, I was told, had been built expressly by the British authorities for the creature comforts of the new African ministers, many of whom had only recently been released from prison where they had been serving terms for sedition. But the wily black ministers, full of an old-fashioned distrust of Europeans, had had the unheard-of temerity to refuse to live in the bungalows, had stifled their natural yen for a modern domicile, and had remained, much to British astonishment, in the neighborhoods of their constituents. Their refusal to accept this British graciousness indicated that they suspected that the bungalows were bait to separate them from the common people and to keep them, as the British had always preferred to remain (as a matter of state policy), aloof and remote. But the African politicians had sensed that the most dangerous thing that they could do was to draw a class line between themselves and the masses of tribal voters who had endowed them with power. . . .

I thanked the young lady, bade her good night, and went to my room which had a screened-in balcony from which I could see the swarming, far-off, faint yellow lights of Accra twinkling in the valley below.

"Massa!"

I turned and saw a steward, dressed in white, black of face, barefooted, his lips hanging open expectantly.

"What is it?"

"Massa want chop?"

"What?"

"Chop? Hot chop? Cold chop?"

I hadn't understood anything; it was my first experience with pidgin English and I shook my head and confessed:

"I don't understand."

"Chop, Massa." He went through the motions of eating, carrying his hand to his mouth and chewing vigorously.

"Dinner?"

"Yasa, Massa. When you want."

When I entered the huge dining room I saw three black boys dressed in white standing at attention. I learned later that one was the cook, one was the steward, and the other was the steward's assistant; in addition there were a gardener, a laundryman, a night watchman (commonly known as "t'ief" man), a man who did the shopping, and an Englishwoman who acted as overseer.

As I sat at the table, my three men disappeared, their coarse-soled feet swishing over the highly polished wooden floor. I sighed. This was Africa too. These servants seemed to know their business; they had, no doubt, been trained in their duties by a tradition left here for a hundred years by English housewives. But that pidgin English! I shuddered. I resented it and I vowed that I'd never speak it. . . . I started; the steward was at my elbow, holding a platter of fried fish; he'd come so silently upon me that I was nonplused.

Early next morning I found a taxi at the roadside and went into the city. I got out at the post office. There were no sidewalks; one walked at the edge of a drainage ditch made of concrete in which urine ran. A stench pervaded the sunlit air. Barefooted men dressed in cloths whose colors were a mixture of red, green, yellow, blue, brown, and purple stood idling about. Most of the women not only carried the inevitable baby strapped to their backs, but also a burden on top of their heads and a bundle in each hand. I reached a street corner and paused; coming toward me was a woman nursing a baby that was still strapped to her back; the baby's head was thrust under the woman's arm and the woman had given the child the long, fleshy, tubelike teat and it was suckling. (There are women with breasts so long that they do not bother to give the baby the teat in front of them, but simply toss it over the shoulder to the child on their back. . . .)

The women's carriage was remarkably graceful; they walked as straight as ramrods, with a slow, slinging motion, moving their legs from their hips, their feet just managing to skim over the earth. When they glanced about they never jarred or jolted the huge burdens they had on their heads, and their eyes held a calm, proud look. In the physical behavior of both men and women there were no wasted motions; they seem to move in a manner that conserved their energies in the awful heat.

In front of the Indian, Syrian, and European stores African women sat before wooden boxes heaped high with red peppers, oranges, plantains, cigarettes, cakes of soap cut into tiny bits, okra, tomatoes, peeled coconuts, small heaps of matches, cans of tinned milk, etc. Men from the Northern Territories, dressed in long smocks, sold from carts piled with cheap mirrors, shoestrings, flashlights, combs, nail files, talcum powder, locks, and cheaply framed photos of Holly- wood movie stars. . . . I was astonished to find that even the children were engaged in this street trade, carrying their wares on their heads either in calabashes or brass pans that had been polished until they glittered. Was it a lack of capital that made the Africans sell like this on the streets? One could buy bread from a little girl who carried a big box, screened-in, upon her cranium; one could buy a concoction called *kenke*—a kind of crushed corn that had been cooked and steamed and seasoned with pepper—from a woman who balanced an enormous, steaming calabash upon her head; one could buy baby bonnets from a woman who had layers of them stored in a brass pan that was borne aloft; yet another woman sold soap from a stack which held at least forty cakes perched atop her skull; one could buy lengths of colored cloth from a woman the top of whose head was a small dry-goods store; one could buy fish, eggs, chickens, meat, yams, bananas, salt, sugar, plantains, cigarettes, ink, pens, pencils, paper—and all of this was but "one flight up," that is, above the heads of the street women who were popularly known as "mammies."

The sun was killing. I sought shade at another street intersection where, around an outdoor water hydrant, a knot of men, women, and children were gathered. They had small tubs, gasoline tins, buckets, pans, anything that could hold water. Boys and girls of eight or nine years of age were balancing tins holding ten or more gallons of water upon their tiny heads and walking off toward their homes with careful strides. A girl, a cloth fastened about her middle, was bent over a basin assiduously doing the family wash. Still another girl, twelve or thirteen, was nude and standing in a small tub and bathing herself in full view. A tiny girl squatted over a drainage ditch, urinating. A man went to the hydrant, took a sip of water from the stream, rinsed his mouth, spat, then damned up the stream in his cupped palms and drank. The girl who had been bathing got out of the tub, dumped the water into the drainage ditch, went to the hydrant, took her place in line and, when her turn came, filled her tub, went a few feet away and dashed the entire contents of the tub over her head, rinsing the soapsuds from her body. She looked down at her gleaming, wet skin, her face holding a concentrated and critical expression. Taking her place in line once more, she filled the tub, lifted it to her head and went mincing off, presumably toward home. . . . A woman came leading a boy and girl by their hands; she carried a big galvanized bucket on her head. When she'd filled it with water, she proceeded to bathe the children with a bar of laundry soap and a sponge made of rough excelsior. She handled them rudely, jerking them this way and that, while she plied the sponge over their eyes, mouths, ears. . . . The girl wore a string of white and blue beads about her hips and a red cloth was pulled tight between her tiny thighs, each end fastened to the beads, front and back. The boy wore nothing.

(Over and above supplying needed water, these outdoor hydrants are really social clubs; it is here that the gossip of the quarter is spread and exchanged, where tall tales get embellished, where marriages, deaths, and births are announced. Sometimes fights take place, or romances are started. Sundry bargains and swappings are struck over petty merchandise. The intimacy of the African communal life can be witnessed in all of its innocence as it clusters about an outdoor hydrant.

(The crowds about the hydrants swell or diminish according to the time of day: there is an early morning crowd of men, women, and children; then a lull comes; toward noon the hydrant is patronized mostly by women who cook or wash; then the afternoon is slow; there are moments when the hydrant is completely deserted. Toward four o'clock the crowds collect again and they last until well into the night. Sometimes at four o'clock in the morning one can see a sleepy-eyed child filling a huge pail with water and walking slowly homeward. . . .)

Beggars were in thick evidence, their black, gnarled hands outstretched and their high-pitched voices singing out:

"Penny, Massa! Penny, Massa!"

So deformed were some that it was painful to look at them. Monstrously swollen legs, running sores, limbs broken so that jagged ends of the healed bones jutted out like blackened sticks, blind men whose empty eye-sockets yawned wetly, palsied palms extended and waiting, a mammoth wen suspended from a skinny neck and gleaming blackly in the hot sun—all of them were men and they sat nude to the waist with cloths draped modestly over their loins. I wondered if they were professional beggars, if they had deliberately deformed themselves to make these heart-wracking appeals? If they had, they had surely overdone it in terms of Western sensibilities, for I was moved not to compassion, but to revulsion. Perhaps for an African temperament conditioned to a belief that a beggar might be some distant relative in reincarnated disguise, such sights might impel donations, might induce a state of pity based upon dread. I don't know. . . .

I wanted to push on and look more, but the sun was too much. I spent the afternoon fretting; I was impatient to see more of this Africa. My bungalow was clean, quiet, mosquito-proof, but it had not been for that I'd come to Africa. Already my mind was casting about for other accommodations. I stood on my balcony and saw clouds of black buzzards circling slowly in the hazy blue sky. In the distance I caught a glimpse of the cloudy, grayish Atlantic.

Night fell and suddenly out of the blue velvet dark came the sound of African crickets that was like an air-raid siren. Frog belches exploded. A soft, feathery thud, like that of a bird, struck the window screen. Reluctantly, I climbed into bed. . . .

Next morning a phone call came from the Prime Minister's office; I was told that at four o'clock I'd be picked up by the Prime Minister's car and that I'd see "something."

And at four o'clock a sleek car entered the driveway. A uniformed chauffeur stepped out and saluted me; I climbed into the back seat. As we went through the city black faces jerked around, recognizing the car. We came to the Prime Minister's residence and pulled into a driveway. I got out and young black faces smiled at me. A few policemen hovered in the background. I was led forward

into a red, two-story brick dwelling that looked remarkably like
a colonial mansion in Georgia or Mississippi. I followed my guide
upstairs, down a hallway, and into a living room.

The Prime Minister, dressed in a smock, was standing in the
middle of the floor.

"Welcome!" he said.

"I'm glad to see you and your people," I told him.

"How are you?"

"Fine, but panting to see your party and your comrades."

He laughed. He presented me to a series of his friends whose
strange names I did not recall, then we sat down.

"I want to take you on a quick tour of the city," he told me.

"I'm truly honored."

"Nothing has been prepared. I want you to see how these people
respond to our appeals—"

"What's going to happen in July?" I asked, referring to the coming
meeting of the Legislative Assembly.

The Prime Minister threw back his head and laughed. I got used,
in time, to that African laughter. It was not caused by mirth; it was
a way of indicating that, though they were not going to take you
into their confidence, their attitude was not based upon anything
hostile.

"You are direct," he said.

"Why not?" I asked.

"You'll have to wait and see," he told me.

I studied Nkrumah; he was fairly slightly built, a smooth jet
black in color; he had a longish face, a pair of brooding, almost
frightened eyes, a set of full, soft lips. His head held a thick growth
of crinkly hair and his hands moved with slow restlessness, betraying
a contained tension. His bodily motions were almost deliberate and
at times his face seemed like a blank mask. One could almost feel
the force of his preoccupations as he would jerk his head when his
attention darted. His questions and answers were simple and to the
point; I felt that he had much more on his mind than he permitted
to pass his lips; he was the full-blown politician whose consciousness

was anchored in concrete, practical concerns pointing toward a fondly sought goal. . . .

His colleagues drew him into a discussion that was conducted in tribal language; when it was over, he announced:

"Let's go!"

His personal bodyguard stood at attention; it was composed of hand-picked militants and faithfuls of the Convention People's Party. He led the way and I followed down into the street where his motorcycle escort, dressed in scarlet, stood lined up near their machines. The Prime Minister waved his hand to signal that all was ready. The motorcyclists raced their engines to a deafening roar; then they pulled slowly into the street, leading the way. The Prime Minister's car, with the Prime Minister seated on my right, followed.

The sun was still shining as we moved slowly forward. The drone of the motorcycles attracted the attention of people on both sides of the street and, spontaneously, men, women, and children abandoned what they were doing and fronted the car. Others rushed pellmell out of shacks, their faces breaking into wide, glad smiles and, lifting their hands upward with their elbows at the level of their hips, palms fronting forward—a kind of half-Nazi salute— they shouted a greeting to the Prime Minister in a tone of voice compounded of passion, exhortation, and contained joy:

"Free—doom! Free—dooooom!"

Ahead of the car the sides of the streets turned black with faces. We reached a wide roadway and the crowds swirled, shouting:

"Free—dooom! Free—dooom!"

"Kwame! Kwame!" They shouted his name.

"Fight! Fight!"

"Akwaba! Akwaba!" ("Welcome! Welcome!")

The road turned into a black river of eager, hopeful, glad faces whose trust tugged at the heart. The crowds grew thicker. The shouting sounded like a cataract. The Prime Minister, smiling, laughing, lifted his right hand as he returned their salute.

The road led into a slum area, and the Prime Minister turned to me and said:

"This is James Town. I want you to see this too. . . . I want you to see all we have, the good and the bad."

The narrow streets filled quickly and the car plowed slowly through nostalgic crowds of men, women, and children who chanted:

"Free—dooooom!"

Many of the women waved their hands in that strange, quivering gesture of welcome which seemed to be common to the entire Gold Coast; it consisted of lifting the hand, but, instead of waving the hand as one did in the West, one held the arm still and shook the palm of the hand nervously and tremblingly from side to side, making the fingers vibrate.

"Free—dooooom!"

My mind flew back to the many conversations that I'd had in Chicago, New York, London, Paris, Rome, Buenos Aires about freedom, and I could picture again in my mind the white faces of friends screwed up in disgust and distaste when the word "freedom" was mentioned, and I could hear again in my memory the tersely deprecating question shot at me across a dinner table:

"*Freedom?* What do you mean, *freedom?*"

But here in Africa "freedom" was more than a word; an African had no doubts about the meaning of the word "freedom." It meant the right to public assembly, the right to physical movement, the right to make known his views, the right to elect men of his choice to public office, and the right to recall them if they failed in their promises. At a time when the Western world grew embarrassed at the sound of the word "freedom," these people knew that it meant the right to shape their own destiny as they wished. Of that they had no doubt, and no threats could intimidate them about it; they might be cowed by guns and planes, but they'd not change their minds about the concrete nature of the freedom that they wanted and were willing to die for. . . .

The crowds, milling in and out of the space between the motorcycles and the Prime Minister's car, chanted:

"Free—dooooom!"

The passionate loyalty of this shouting crowd had put this man in power, had given him the right to speak for them, to execute the mandate of national liberation that they had placed in his hands; and, because he'd said he'd try, they'd galvanized into a whole that was 4,000,000 strong, demanding an end to their centuries-old thralldom. Though still mainly tribal, though 90 per cent illiterate, they wanted to be free of an alien flag, wanted the sovereignty of their own will in their own land. And they had melted their tribal differences into an instrument to form a bridge between tribalism and twentieth-century forms of political mass organization. The women who danced and shouted were washerwomen, cooks, housewives, etc.

"Free—dooom! Free—dooom!" rang deafeningly in my ears.

"They believe in you," I said to the Prime Minister.

"Would you believe that four years ago a demonstration like this was impossible?" he told me. "These were a cowed and frightened people. Under the British it would have been unheard of for people to sing and shout and dance like this. . . . We changed all that. When I came from London in 1948, the mood of these people was terrible. They trusted nothing and nobody. They'd been browbeaten so long by both the black leaders and the British that they were afraid to act."

"Who were the first in the Gold Coast to offer opposition to your efforts to organize your people?" I asked Nkrumah.

"The missionaries," he said without hesitation.

My mind raced back to my reading of the history of the early days of the Gold Coast and I recalled that, from 1553 to 1592, the merchants of England, all staunch Christians, had sent ships to the Gold Coast to engage in trading British trinkets for gold dust and slaves, and some of those ships had been named *John Evangelist, Trinity, Bartholomew, John Baptist,* and *Jesus.* . . .

That the missionaries should have been the first to manifest opposition was, in my opinion, as it should have been. If they had to, the industrial and mercantile interests could come to terms with a rising nationalism. Indeed, during the past five hundred years history has shown that nationalism is one of the necessary but transitional forms of an expanding industrial system, and there was no reason why industrialization and nationalism could not, for a time, coexist, mutually enriching each other.

Religious interests, however, were jealous by their very nature and felt an understandable panic at the emergence of a sweeping nationalism that was bent not only upon creating new institutions for the people, but also new emotional attitudes, values, and definitions. And what could have frightened the men of God more than this wild and liquid emotion that Nkrumah had channeled into a new political party? Religion needed all the emotion of a community allied to its own ends, and when a rival appeal was made for the loyalty of that emotion, religious people must needs be opposed, even if the counterappeal of religion meant a decrease in the basic welfare of the people. Mass nationalist movements were, indeed, a new kind of religion. They were politics *plus!*

"I want to see your party and how it works," I said to the Prime Minister.

He nodded but did not answer.

"Free—dooom! Free—doooom!"

The roar came from all sides. Gratitude showed in the eyes of those black faces for the man who had taken their hand and told them that they had no need to fear the British, that they could laugh, sing, work, hope, and fight again.

I was astonished to see women, stripped to the waist, their elongated breasts flopping wildly, do a sort of weaving, circular motion with their bodies, a kind of queer shuffling dance which expressed their joy in a quiet, physical manner. It was as if they were talking with the movements of their legs, arms, necks, and torsos; as if words were no longer adequate as a means of communication; as if sounds could no longer approximate their feelings; as if only the total movement of their entire bodies could indicate in some measure their acquiescence, their surrender, their approval.

And then I remembered: I'd seen these same snakelike, veering dances before. . . . Where? Oh, God, yes; in America, in storefront churches, in Holy Roller Tabernacles, in God's Temples, in unpainted wooden prayer-meeting houses on the plantations of the Deep South. . . . And here I was seeing it all again against a background of a surging nationalistic political movement! How could that be?

When I'd come to Africa, I didn't know what I'd find, what I'd see; the only prepossession I'd had was that I'd doubted that I'd be able to walk into the African's cultural house and feel at home and know my way around. Yet, what I was now looking at in this powerfully improvised dance of these women, I'd seen before in America! How was that possible? And, what was more, this African dance today was as astonishing and dumfounding to me as it had been when I'd seen it in America.

Never in my life had I been able to dance more than a few elementary steps, and the carrying of even the simplest tune had always been beyond me. So, what had bewildered me about Negro dance expression in the United States now bewildered me in the same way in Africa.

I'd long contended that the American Negro, because of what he had undergone in the United States, had been basically altered, that his consciousness had been filled with a new content, that "racial" qualities were but myths of prejudiced minds. Then, if that were true, how could I account for what I now saw? And what I now saw was an exact duplicate of what I'd seen for so many long years in the United States.

I did not find an answer to that question that afternoon as I stared out of the window of the Prime Minister's car. But the question was lodged firmly in my mind, enthroned there so strongly that it would never leave until I had, at least to my satisfaction, solved the riddle of why black people were able to retain, despite vast distances, centuries of time, and the imposition of alien cultures, such basic and fundamental patterns of behavior and response.

We rode on through the cheering throngs. Whenever the car slowed, the black faces, laughing and excited, with heads thrown back, with white teeth showing, would press close to the windows of the car and give vent to:

"Free—doooom!"

But my emotions were preoccupied with another problem. How much am I a part of this? How much was I part of it when I saw it in America? Why could I not feel this? Why that peculiar, awkward restraint when *I* tried to dance or sing? The answers to those questions did not come until after I penetrated deep into the African jungle. . . . On we rode. The crowds surged, danced, sang, and shouted, but I was thinking of my mother, of my father, of my brother. . . . I was frankly stunned at what I saw; there was no rejection or condemnation; there was no joy or sorrow; I was just stupefied. Was it possible that I was looking at myself laughing, dancing, singing, gliding with my hips to express my joy . . . ? Had I denied all this in me? If so, then why was it that when I'd tried to sing, as a child, I'd not been able to? Why had my hands and feet, all my life, failed to keep time? It was useless to say that I'd inhibited myself, for my inability to do these simple things predated any desire, conscious or unconscious, on my part. I had wanted to, because it had always been a part of my environment, *but I had never been able to!*

"What do you think?" the Prime Minister asked.

"It's most impressive," I said.

"They're an unspoiled, a spiritually virgin people," he said.

We came at last to a block of cement houses; from windows and doorways black faces shouted and called:

"Kwame! Kwame!"

"Free—doooom! Free—dooooom!"

The car stopped and the Prime Minister got out; I followed him.

"What is this?" I asked him.

"This is a meeting of the Women's Division of the party," he told me.

We entered a concrete compound and sat as the meeting, dedicated to reorganization and installment of new officers, got under way. A tall black woman led a chant:

"Forward ever, backward never . . ."

There was a relaxed, genial atmosphere; now and then an easy laugh floated over the crowd. The men, clad in their native togas, sat in the rear, rising occasionally to aid in making seating arrangements. In front sat about two hundred women also clad in their native cloths and, for this ceremony, they wore an enormous amount of gold in their ears, around their necks, on their arms and fingers. The yellow sheen of the gold against the background of black skin made a startling combination in the red rays of the dying sun. There was one fat, black woman who, I'd have said, had at least three or four thousand dollars' worth of gold on her arms and around her neck, and it was pure native gold, mixed with no alloy. . . .

A psalm was sung in English. Next, an African of the Christian persuasion stepped forward and, in English, led the group in prayer. Then came a pagan chief with his umbrella, his staff, his "linguist" and proceeded to pour a libation of corn wine to the dead ancestors. The two religions nestled smugly, cheek by jowl, and the setting sun shone as calmly as usual; there was not a tremor in the universe. . . . After he emptied the bowl by dribbling the corn wine upon the ground, the chief had the bowl filled again and he passed it around to each person nearby and they took three sips. (Three is the lucky number among many Africans of the Gold Coast.)

A series of speakers rose, both men and women, and, in a mixture of English and tribal tongues, exhorted the women to give all their support to the Leader, to the Convention People's Party, and to the struggle for national liberation. To this already turgid brew was added still another ingredient; a woman rose and proclaimed:

"I'm Mrs. Nkrumah!"

A howl of laughter rose from the women. Puzzled, I looked at the Prime Minister; he grinned at me, and said:

"It's a joke."

"I *am* Mrs. Nkrumah!" the woman said in a voice that sought to still all doubts.

The Prime Minister rose and, sweeping his arms to include all the women, said:

"You are *all* my brides!"

The women laughed and clapped. Nkrumah, of course, was a bachelor.

"I have to say that to them," he whispered to me as he sat again. "Now, tell me, do you understand what you are looking at?"

"You have fused tribalism with modern politics," I said.

"That's exactly it," he said. "Nobody wanted to touch these

people. The missionaries would go just so far, and no farther toward them. One can only organize them by going where they are, living with them, eating with them, sharing their lives. We are making a special drive to enlist women in the party; they have been left out of our national life long enough. In the words of Lenin, I've asked the cooks to come out of their kitchens and learn how to rule."

The new women officials to be installed were called to come forward and stand fronting the Prime Minister. A short statement of aims and duties was read to them and, at the end, each woman was asked to raise her right hand and repeat the following oath (I'm paraphrasing this from memory):

"I pledge with all my life my support to the Convention People's Party, and to my Leader, Kwame Nkrumah; I swear to follow my Leader's guidance, to execute faithfully his commands, to resist with all my power all imperialist attempts to disrupt our ranks, to strive with all of my heart to rebuild our lost nation, Ghana, so help me God!"

I was thunderstruck. Nkrumah had moved in and filled the vacuum which the British and the missionaries had left when they had smashed the tribal culture of the people! It was so simple it was dazzling. . . . Of course, before Nkrumah could do this, he would first have to have the intellectual daring to know that the British had created a vacuum in these people's hearts. It was not until one could think of the imperialist actions of the British as being crimes of the highest order, that they had slain something that they could never rekindle, that one could project a new structure for the lives of these people.

But, an oath to a Leader? In the twentieth century? Then I reflected. Well, why not? This oath was perhaps the most rational pledge that these women had ever given in all of their lives. Before this they had sworn oaths to invisible gods, pagan and Christian, and now, at last, they were swearing an oath that related directly to their daily welfare. And would these illiterate and myth-minded women have understood an abstract oath taken to a flag or a constitution? In the light of their traditions and culture, this oath seemed logical to them, for the swearing of oaths was a common feature of their rituals. And, in a society ruled by chiefs decked out in gold and silk, what symbol other than that of a living man, a man whom they could see, hear, speak to, check upon his actions—what symbol other than a living one could make them feel that their oath was really binding . . . ? Indeed, the taking of this oath was perhaps the only act in their lives that they had performed over whose consequences they would have some measure of control. Nkrumah was tapping the abandoned emotional reservoir that Christian religion had no use for; he, in contrast to the Christians who called upon them to attend church service one day a week, was commanding the whole of their lives from day to day and they stood before him willingly, pledging to give. It was not a morality easier than that of the church that Nkrumah was offering them; it was a much harder one and they accepted it!

The slip of paper upon which the oath had been written was given to the Prime Minister and, at once, impulsively, I leaned forward and said to him:

"May I make a copy of that?"

I regretted asking the moment the words had escaped my lips; but I had spoken and there was no backing out.

"What did you say?" he asked me.

"I'd like to make a copy of that oath," I stated.

He glanced off without answering, still holding the slip of paper in his hand. I knew that he knew what I had asked and he seemed to be debating. Would my rash request make him distrust me? Would he think that I'd use the oath against him and his party, his people, his cause? I gritted my teeth, scolding myself for being too forward in my zeal to account for what I saw. . . . He was looking off into space; he had not answered me. Ought I ask him again? I decided not to. Nkrumah had been educated in the United States and he must have known instinctively how such an oath had struck me. And I knew that he couldn't imagine my being shocked and, at the same time, being in complete agreement! But, if he was reticent about this, what about the other things I'd see in the Gold Coast?

Another song was sung and, as we all stood up, the Prime Minister, looking off, slowly and seemingly absent-mindedly, folded

the slip of paper containing the oath and put it into his pocket.
I knew then that I'd never get a chance to copy it. . . . I was of a
mind to remind him that I had asked for it, but discretion became
the better part of curiosity and I inhibited myself. I'd be content
with what I'd heard. Obviously the Prime Minister did not want me
to attach too much importance, politically or psychologically, to that
oath. How could I make him understand that I understood, and
that in general I agreed to it as being an inevitable part of the
twentieth century?

The meeting ended and we were escorted by the roaring motorcycle cavalcade back toward the Prime Minister's home. During the
ride the Prime Minister was poised, aloof, silent. Intuitively, I
knew that he was thinking of my reaction to that oath-taking. . . .
We reached his house and sat upon the lawn under a starry sky and
listened to an African band playing native tunes. Suddenly the
Prime Minister spoke to me:

"Let's go upstairs and talk."

"A good idea," I said.

In his living room we sat on a divan; a steward served some
drinks.

"Did you like what you saw?" he asked me.

"I'm stunned, amazed, and gratified," I told him truthfully. "Like
is no word for what I felt. You've done what the Western world
has said is impossible."

He threw back his head and laughed. A silence hung in the air
for several moments. I felt called upon to say something, to explain,
to justify myself.

"Look, I think you know something of my background," I began.
"For twelve years I was a member of the Communist Party of the
United States. I'm no longer a Communist, but I'm for black people.
I know from history and from my personal life what has happened
to us—at least, I know some of it. I don't know Africa intimately.
That's why I'm here. I'd like to understand all of this. I think that
my life has prepared me to do that."

"I'm a Marxist Socialist," he told me.

"I know that there are political things that have to be told with discretion," I went on. "But I'd like to see and know how you organized all this."

I wanted to be given the "green light" to look, to know, to be shown everything. I wanted the opportunity to try to weigh a movement like this, to examine its worth as a political instrument; it was the first time in my life that I'd come in contact with a mass movement conducted by Negro leadership and I felt that I could, if given a chance, understand it.

He gave me a mechanical nod, but I could see that his thoughts were far away. Then a crowd of men and women pushed their way into the room and there were more introductions.

"He is a novelist," the Prime Minister said, pointing to me.

"*A novelist?*" a tall black man echoed.

"Yes; a novelist," the Prime Minister repeated.

The tall black man's face was baffled; he stared at me, as though he doubted my existence. The Prime Minister saved the day by bursting into a loud and long laugh which was soon joined by all in the room. I sat silent and soon the crowd was talking among themselves in their tribal tongues. The Prime Minister rose and left; he returned a few moments later and sat next to me.

"The ideological development here is not very high," he said.

"Uh hunh," I grunted.

"There are but two or three of us who know what we are doing," he said.

"George gave me a list of your bright boys to talk to," I told him.

"Is Kofi Baako on that list?" he asked.

"Yes."

"Talk to him," the Prime Minister said. "He's my right-hand man."

"Is he here tonight?"

"No; he's in Cape Coast at the moment."

The Prime Minister disappeared and I struck up a conversation with some of the party militants. I wanted to break down their reserve and hear what they thought.

"Do you think that the English will shoot if you press your demands for self-government?" I asked.

A look of horror came over their faces.

"*They* can shoot, but *we* won't," a boy swore.

"They'll never get us in that sort of position," another told me.

Some of the boys who didn't understand English asked what I had said and they formed a knot debating and arguing my question. I was soon standing to one side. It was a strange household. People came and went. Presently a line of women edged into the room; at that moment a band downstairs began a dance tune and the women at once went into that same snakelike, shuffling dance that they had done on the streets earlier in the afternoon. The band boomed louder and the sound of dancing came from downstairs, upstairs, everywhere. . . . I wandered out upon the balcony and saw the Prime Minister dancing alone on the lawn with about ten women around him. African dancing is not like Western dancing; one dances alone if one wants to.

It was hot. I felt exhausted. It was near three o'clock in the morning when I met the Prime Minister entering the living room.

"I must go. I'm dead tired," I said.

"The car will take you home," he said.

We shook hands. A young man escorted me down to the car and soon I was whizzing through the humid night toward the government bungalow.

IX . . .

Next morning when I awakened my sense of amazement at what I'd seen was, if anything, stronger than it had been the day before. I'd seen something new under the sun. What a bewildering unity Nkrumah had forged: Christianity, tribalism, paganism, sex, nationalism, socialism, housing, health, and industrial schemes . . . ! Could this sweep Africa? I could well understand why the British, when they first saw it, thought it was a joke. They could not believe that a black man could take the political methods that Europe had perfected and apply them to Africa.

And, of course, only a native African could do what Nkrumah had done. Five hundred years of European barbarism had made it impossible for any European alive to claim the kind of frenzied assent from these black millions that Nkrumah claimed. To that degree, the Nkrumahs of Africa had something that the Europeans could never take from them. What had given Nkrumah the chance to do this was that the British concepts of education had misfired; they had thought that any African who earned a string of university degrees would never dare to stick his hands into this muck, would feel too much revulsion to do so. . . . From the point of view of British mentality, an education was a guarantee that the educated young African would side with the British, and, what is more, many of them did, especially the young Christians. And the British had never suppressed nationalist feeling *per se;* they'd merely shunted it into ineffective channels.

But the British had neglected to take fully into account that some of the Gold Coast boys would be beyond the confines of British influence, that some of them would soak up Marxism and would return home feeling a sense of racial and class solidarity derived from the American Negro's proud and defensive nationalism. Above all, the British did not take into consideration that the Gold Coast boys could take Marxism and adapt it to their own peculiar African needs. For three decades the Russian Communists had tried to penetrate Africa, sending agent after agent into the jungle, and Nkrumah had, in five short years, so outstripped them that their ideas had become, by comparison, backward!

The indirect rule of the British had, unwittingly, created the very conditions which Nkrumah had organized. And the British had adopted that indirect method of ruling so that the religion and customs of the masses would remain undisturbed. . . . To operate their mines, their timber concessions, and their mills, the British had regimented African tribal life around new social and economic poles, and the exhortation of the missionaries had slowly destroyed the African's faith in his own religion and customs, thereby creating millions of psychologically detribalized Africans living uneasily and frustratedly in two worlds and really believing in neither of them.

But could this liquid emotion be harnessed to modern techniques?

And from where would come the men to handle the work of administration when self-government came? Would Nkrumah have to impose a dictatorship until he could educate a new generation of young men who could work with him with a willing heart? Or would he have to rely upon the dangerous collaboration of the British until such could come about? I'd seen the basis of power in the streets of Accra, but could it be used? And how?

And that fierce optimism? Where did it come from? What justified it? Of course, the Gold Coast had about 4,000 British in a population of 4,000,000 blacks, and one could actually forget that Europe existed.

Last night I hadn't had time to question myself closely regarding that snakelike, shuffling dance, that strange veering and weaving of the body. . . . That there was some kind of link between the native African and the American Negro was undoubtedly true. But what did it mean? A certain group of American anthropologists had long clamored for a recognition of what they had quaintly chosen to call "African survivals," a phrase which they had coined to account for exactly what I had observed. And now, as I reflected upon last night's experience, even more items of similarity came to me: that laughter that bent the knee and turned the head (as if in embarrassment!); that queer shuffling of the feet when one was satisfied or in agreement; that inexplicable, almost sullen silence that came from disagreement or opposition. . . . All of this was strange but familiar.

I understood why so many American Negroes were eager to disclaim any relationship with Africa; they were being prompted by the same motives that made the Irish or the Jew or the Italian immigrant more militantly American than the native-born American. The American Negro's passionate identification with America stemmed from two considerations: first, it was a natural part of his assimilation of Americanism; second, so long had Africa been described as something shameful, barbaric, a land in which one went about naked, a land in which his ancestors had sold their kith and kin as slaves—so long had he heard all this that he wanted to disassociate himself in his mind from all such realities. . . .

The bafflement evoked in me by this new reality did not spring from any desire to disclaim kinship with Africa, or from any shame of being of African descent. My problem was how to account for this "survival" of Africa in America when I stoutly denied the mystic influence of "race," when I was as certain as I was of being alive that it was only, by and large, in the concrete social frame of reference in which men lived that one could account for men being what they were. I sighed; this was truly a big problem. . . .

Restless, I sought the streets of Accra just to look at Africa. And while strolling along I found, for the first time in my life, a utilitarian function for nappy hair; the clerks and school children stuck their red and yellow pencils in their hair in order not to lose them, and they never did, so close and secure did their kinks cling to those pencils. Some children carried their ink bottles and schoolbooks on their heads, their arms swinging free as they walked. I saw a little girl peel an orange to eat it; she broke the orange in two, put one half of it upon her head and proceeded, as she walked along, to eat the other half; when she had devoured it, she reached up nonchalantly and got the remaining half of the orange and commenced to nibble away at it.

Bracing myself to encounter rebuffs, I strayed off the main thoroughfares and entered a maze of warrens—compounds—enclosed by stone walls. I blinked; before me was a scene crowded with scores of men, women, children, and everything seemed to be happening at once. . . . The over-all impression was that the black human beings had so completely merged with the dirt that one could scarcely tell where humanity ended and the earth began; they lived in and of the dirt, the flesh of bodies seeming to fuse insensibly with the soil.

On a nearby stone wall were scores of lizards, red, green, gray; and, when I moved, they scuttled to safety. Chickens moved slowly and unafraid among the children and pecked at piles of refuse. Here and there a sheep or goat stood sleepily. Mangy dogs lay in the sun. A woman was kneeling upon the ground, frying some kind of meat in a smoking pot of deep fat. A girl was pounding *fufu* with a long wooden pole, plunging the pole into a wooden vat in which was a mixture of boiled plantains, yams, and cassava; now and then she paused and added a little water to the yellow, doughlike mass, then pounded again. . . . Still another girl, just a few feet from the *fufu*-pounder, was squatting and tending a bubbling pot that cooked over a pile of stones enclosing a tiny flickering fire. Two men, standing opposite each other, were washing a huge tub of clothes, running their hands down washboards that rested in the same tub. . . . Another was mending a pair of shoes. A tiny little nude girl was grinding red pepper on a stone. A fat woman sat nursing a baby at her right breast while she idly and unconsciously, staring off into space, toyed with the teat of her left breast with the fingers of her left hand. A tiny boy minded some ears of corn that were roasting over an iron grill. Off to one side a group of little girls was playing a strange game that consisted of jumping up and down and clapping their hands—a game called *ampe* which fascinated me no end as long as I was in Africa. The legs of the girls were skinny, their black shoulder blades stuck out at sharp angles, and yet their supply of physical energy seemed inexhaustible.

I took out my camera to photograph the scene and the children let out a warning yell that made every face jerk toward me. At once the women began covering their breasts and the boys rose and ran toward me, yelling:

"Take me! Take me!"

Chances of a natural photograph were impossible, and, not to disappoint the children, I snapped a picture or two of them. I turned to leave and they followed me. I walked faster and they began to run, yelling:

"Take me! Take me!"

I hastily turned a corner, hoping that they'd fall behind; but they came on and on, their ranks swelling as they ran. It was not until I was some five blocks from the compound that they began to fall out, one by one, and return. Didn't their mothers miss them? Wasn't there anyone to look after them? To let tiny children of four and five years of age have that much freedom filled me with wonder. . . .

I entered a store to buy a black bow tie and I found that I could barely make the African clerk understand me. My American accent must have indeed sounded strange to his ears which were used to British English spoken with a tribal accent. I had to repeat myself several times before he could grasp what I meant.

"Who owns this store?" I asked him.

"A Syrian," he said, pointing to the rear.

"Do Syrians own most of the stores?"

"Naw, sar. The Indians own some too."

"How are they to work for?"

"All right *now*," he mumbled, eying his Syrian boss.

"What do you mean by *now?*"

"I mean since the CPP, sar," he said, referring to the Convention People's Party.

"How was that? Why did they change?"

"They were scared that we'd take power and chase 'em out of the Gold Coast if they didn't behave, sar," he told me.

Before the coming of Nkrumah there had been much racial tension between the Africans and the Syrians, but, with the mounting tide of clamor for self-government, the Syrians had abruptly changed their attitudes toward the masses of the Africans, and the Syrians were now considered the largest and steadiest contributors of cash to the coffers of the Convention People's Party. . . .

When I was back upon the streets again I was impressed by what I felt to be a sense of fragility, of delicacy almost, of the physique of the people. For the most part they were small-boned, of medium height, well-developed muscularly but tending toward slenderness. I had an intuitive impression that these people were old, old, maybe the *oldest* people on earth, and I felt a sense of melancholy knowing that their customs, laboriously created and posited for thousands of years, had been condemned as inferior, and shattered by a strong and predatory nation. The delicate strands of that fragile culture, so organically dependent upon the soil and climate of West Africa, so purely woven out of the naked impulses of naked men, could never be reconstituted. We had to depend upon guesses and folk-lore to determine what that culture had once meant to them. True, they still clung, in secrecy and shame, to the ways of their fathers;

but, surrounded by a new order of life, they didn't and couldn't believe in them as they once had.

I was pleased to see that, with but a few exceptions, they did not deliberately disfigure or deform their bodies, distend their lips, or force huge holes in their ears or nostrils. Once or twice I did see women who had induced strange swellings on their skins in order to beautify themselves, but that was rare. (I divined later that their religious customs made such deformations abhorrent to them, for they felt that one's chances of passing, when one died, into the other world depended somewhat upon the degree to which one's body was intact. Circumcision was taboo among the Ashanti, and, among those close to the royal family, the spilling of a woman's blood was also strictly forbidden. An intelligent African doctor told me that no wife of the King of Ashanti could submit to any operation, no matter how urgently needed.)

Wilted from the heat, I made my way back to the government bungalow and found a strange young African waiting at the door to talk to me.

"What can I do for you?" I asked him.

"Dr. Wright—" he began.

"Please, I'm no doctor of any kind," I told him.

"Well, sar," he said, smiling. "I work for the English family next door. . . ."

"Yes?"

"You're an American, sar? Aren't you?"

"Yes; I am."

"Maybe you can help me, sar? Please," he begged.

"I'll try. But what is it?"

"You see, sar, we don't like the British. I met American soldiers during the war and they were nice, sar," he explained. "Now, sar, I want to educate myself. I want to take a correspondence course from America and I need help, sar."

"Just what sort of help do you need and what kind of a course do you want to take?" I asked.

"I want to be a detective, sar," he said.

"What?" I thought that I hadn't heard him.

"A detective, sar. Like the ones you see in the movies," he made himself explicit.

"And you want to take all of this in the form of a correspondence course from America?"

"That's right, sar," he said, smiling, glad that at last I'd understood him.

"Now, just how can I help you in that?"

"Well, sar, money is controlled here. I went to the post office, sar, to buy dollars and they wouldn't sell them to me. They said that I'd have to go to a bank, sar. Well, I went to the bank and they said no; they wouldn't sell me dollars, sar. They said I'd have to get the government to okay my application for dollars. Then I went to the government, sar, and talked to a young Englishman."

"And what did he say?"

"Sar, he said I couldn't have any dollars. . . . You see, sar, the English are jealous of us. They never want us to do anything, sar. . . ."

"Why wouldn't the Englishman let you have the dollars?"

"He just wouldn't, sar. He said that I could take a course in how to be a detective from London, sar."

"From London?" I echoed.

"Yes, sar; that's exactly what he said, sar."

I looked at him, at his pleading eyes, at those half-parted, waiting lips, at the slight stoop of respect in his bodily posture.

"Come onto the terrace," I told him.

He followed me and stood respectfully as I sat.

"Sit down," I said.

"Thank you, sar," he said, sitting.

"From where did you get this notion of becoming a detective?"

"In a magazine. . . . You know, sar. One of these American magazines. . . . They tell about crimes. I got it right in my room now, sar. Shall I get it for you, sar?"

"No; no; that's not necessary. Now, just why do you want to become a detective?"

"To catch criminals, sar."

"What criminals?"

He stared at me as though he thought that I'd taken leave of my senses.

"The English, sar!" he exclaimed. "Sar, we Africans don't violate the law. This is *our* country, sar. It's the English who came here and fought us, took our land, our gold, and our diamonds, sar. If I could be a good detective, sar, I'd find out how they did it. I'd put them in jail, sar."

It was all clear now. But the pathos of it stilled my tongue for several moments.

"Didn't the British tell you not to spend your money taking courses in detective work from either New York or London?" I asked him.

"Naw, sar. They just wanted me to take the courses from London, sar," he said. "But the English courses wouldn't tell me all the truth about detective work, sar. They know better than to do that, sar. Oh, sar, you don't *know* the English!"

"In other words, the English wouldn't give you the *real* lessons in detective work? Is that it? They'd keep the really important secrets from you . . . ?"

"That's it, sar! You can't trust them, sar!"

"To whom would you give this evidence of the criminality of the English?"

"To all the people, sar. Then they'd know the truth. And I'd send some of it to America, sar."

"Why?"

"So they'd know, too, sar."

"And if they knew, what do you think they'd do?"

"Then maybe they'd help us, sar. Don't you think so, sar?"

"Why don't you try studying law?" I asked him, seeking some way to get his feet upon the earth.

"Law's all right," he said hesitantly. "But, sar, law's for property. Detective work's for catching criminals, sar. That's what the English are, sar."

"Just how did you get hold of this magazine?"

"My Massa brought it home, sar."

"And when he got through with it, you read it?"

"Yes, sar. But he threw it away before I took it, sar. I got it out of the dustbin in back," he told me circumspectly.

"Look, let me tell you how most detectives get to be detectives," I said. "They start out as policemen and work their way up. Or they start out as stool pigeons. . . . Do you know what a stool pigeon is?"

"Yes, sar. I know that from the movies, sar."

"American movies?"

"Yes, sar. I see a lot of them, sar."

"Well, a stool pigeon tells stories on his friends, on anybody and everybody. In that way the police come to trust him. In time, if he's really good, he might become a detective. It's not really a good job for you."

He was baffled; for a moment he hung his head in thought.

"But I *want* to be a detective, sar," he said insistently.

"But how can I help you?" I was dejected.

"Well, sar, you can sell me some dollars," he said. "I need seventy-five dollars to pay for the first course, sar."

Where could I start with the boy? His view of reality was warped; it was composed of fragments of Hollywood movies and American pulp magazines and he had lived his life so far from such manu-factured dreams that he was unable to tell what was plausible or implausible in them. And all of this was fed by an inflamed sense of national oppression; he felt that the least move he made to better his condition would be thwarted by the British who were the focal point of the organization of his hate, a hate that would always be his excuse if he failed, no matter what he tried to do or how badly he did it. As long as the Union Jack flew over his country, he could always blame the British for everything.

"Why don't you ask some of the rich Africans to help you?" I suggested.

"Oh, *them*, sar?" He actually repressed a sarcastic laugh.

"Why not?" I demanded.

"They are *worse* than the British, sar."

I saw now that I had to be careful in talking to him, for he had a ready category in which to put anybody with a black skin who disagreed with him. The black man who opposed him was a British collaborater.

"How are they worse?"

"They keep away from their black brothers, sar."

"Look, I don't have any dollars with me in cash. I've only travelers' checks. And they can't do you any good," I told him.

I studied him. Maybe he had been prompted by the police to ask me for dollars? No; his story sounded too pathetic to be false, too understandably human to have been calculated.

"Can't you do something, sar, please? I'm not begging; I've saved the pounds, sar. I can give them to you."

How could I get at the boy? He was hugging to his heart a delusive dream and he was determined not to surrender it; if he had to let that dream go, he'd hate whoever robbed him of it. But that false dream stood between him and his seeing reality for what it was, colored his vision regarding the value of being a detective. . . .

"I'll have to think about this," I told him with a sigh.

He thanked me and left; I went upstairs and sat in a chair and shook my head. Good God. . . . Did the men who had administered this colony before the coming of Nkrumah know that this sort of rot was simmering in the minds of boys? Maybe they had known it and had not cared? No; I was inclined to feel that they had not known it, for, if they had, I was sure that they would have been frightened. But what stunned me most about the boy was his absolute distrust of the British; it was by far the deepest emotion of his life.

Next morning the Prime Minister's office phoned to tell me that I'd be called for at four o'clock and taken to a huge outdoor political rally to be held at the Westend Arena. The Prime Minister was scheduled to speak upon his forthcoming motion for self-government and he indicated that he wanted me to greet his followers with a short speech.

As I was driven toward the rally that afternoon, I could hear the roar of the vast crowd five blocks before the arena came into the line of my vision. Arriving at the edge of the throng, I heard a speaker addressing the audience in Ga, the language of a tribe close to the Accra region. I was led through packed black bodies to the platform where the Prime Minister sat surrounded by his ministers and aides.

Fanning out in front of the platform were more than ten thousand faces whose brown, reddish, and black skins were lit to a blatant distinctness by the long red rays of the setting sun. There were practically no women present, a circumstance that I was to get accustomed to in all public affairs of the Gold Coast. Many of the men were barefooted and most of them wore their native togas. An impression of earthiness rose up from those tense, lifted faces that stretched so far away that they became dim to the eye—faces that seemed like a reality conjured up by a sorcerer from the early days of mankind; they appeared unsubstantial, like figments of a dream that would vanish upon close inspection. Then, at that moment, a roar welled up from ten thousand throats and the crowd's reality not only became real, but suggestive of a menace, a threat. . . .

The speaker threw a challenging question in English requiring a yes or no answer, for he wanted the audience to participate in the meeting, and the crowd hurled a rolling "NO!" that made my eardrums tingle. The speaker switched to Ga and hammered on and on; then he swung back to English, declaring:

"Nkrumah has led you this far and he will lead you on! If you don't support him, he cannot have the power to act for you! You must believe that he'll never let you down! He went to prison for you; he suffered for you; he'll lay down his life for you! You must have faith and trust him! Do you trust him?"

"YES!" the crowd roared.

"Will you follow him?" the speaker asked.

"YES!" the crowd answered.

"Do you believe that he fights for freedom?"

"YES!" the crowd answered.

"Who organized the CPP?"

"NKRUMAH!"

"Who raised the slogan for self-government NOW?"

"NKRUMAH!"

"WHO?"

"NKRUMAH!"

"I ASKED YOU WHO?"

"NNNKKKKRRRUUUMMMMAAH!"

"Will *he* fight for you?"

"YES!"

"Will *you* fight for him?"

"YES!"

"And what are we fighting for?"

"FREE—DOOOOM! FREE—DOOOOOM!"

At times the dialogue between the speaker and the audience became so intimate, so prolonged, so dramatic that all sense of distance between leaders and followers ceased to exist, and a spirit of fellowship, of common identity prevailed among faces young and old, smooth and bearded, wise and simple. . . . The speaker lifted his voice in song and the mass joined in, and the collective sound seemed to rise as high as the skies:

> *There is victory for us*
> *In the struggle of the CPP,*
> *There is victory for us!*
>
> *Sons of Ghana, rise and fight!*
> *Girls of Ghana, rise and shine!*
> *In the struggle of the CPP*
> *There is victory for us!*
>
> *Forward ever, backward never;*
> *In the struggle of the CPP*
> *There is victory for us!*

My turn came to greet the audience and I rose and spoke somewhat as follows:

"Men of Ghana: Your great and respected Prime Minister has extended to me an invitation to see your country, its people, and the rapid rate of development that you are making. It is with pride that I've come to look upon the labor of a man who attended our American schools and who has dedicated his life to the struggle for the freedom of his country.

"I'm one of the lost sons of Africa who has come back to look upon the land of his forefathers. In a superficial sense it may be said that I'm a stranger to most of you, but, in terms of a common heritage of suffering and hunger for freedom, your heart and my heart beat as one.

"Centuries ago the living bodies of our forefathers were dragged from these shores and sold into slavery; centuries ago the bodies of our forefathers formed the living instruments which the white men of Europe used to build the foundations of the Western world; centuries ago we were reduced to nameless, stateless pawns shuffled by the will of Europeans and Americans across the chessboards of history; centuries ago our tribes were so mauled, mixed, and scattered that we could not even speak to one another in a common tongue.

"This is indeed a turgid, cloudy past, a past not of our making or choosing; yet, despite all this, this heritage has brought us a sense of unity deeper than race, a sense of humanity that has made us sensitive to the sufferings of all mankind, that has made us increasingly human in a world that is rapidly losing its claim to humanity. . . .

"Under the leadership of your Leader, the Convention People's Party has roused immense interest throughout America and the world at large. You men are, of all the teeming millions of Africa, the first to step upon the political stage of the twentieth century. What you do will have consequences that will roll down the years. What you achieve in the coming months will to a large degree define the character of the coming struggle for the redemption of Africa.

"Today, in your struggle for self-government, you are presenting to the men of England a political promissory note which the English have declared to be the real moral currency of mankind, and now the world is watching to see if the English will honor their own currency! They asked you to build political parties, and you did! But you did it so much quicker than they thought you could! You are making your bid for freedom in terms which your teachers in England and America told you were correct. Now, in your struggle for self-government, you are presenting for redemption a promise

made to you by the heart of England. Will she honor it? The world
is waiting to see. . . .

"From the 30,000,000 sons and daughters of African descent in
the New World, both in North and South America, and in the
many islands of the Atlantic, I bring you deep-felt greetings.

"I am an American and therefore cannot participate in your
political affairs. But I wish you victory in your bid for freedom!
Ghana, show us the way! The only advice that I can give you is
two thousand years old and was uttered by a Man Whose name is
frequently used but Whose moral precepts millions choose to ignore.
To a great and despoiled Africa, to an Africa awakening from its
slumber, to an Africa burning with hope, I advise you: TAKE UP
YOUR BED AND WALK!"

The handclapping was weak and scattered. Perhaps they were
not used to hearing speakers who did not raise their voices, or
maybe they had not understood . . . ? I sat. The Prime Minister rose
to speak. The chairman asked the crowd to pledge their personal
loyalty to the Leader and I saw twenty thousand palms shoot willingly upward and their colors—orange, brownish, dark yellow, and
dingy gray—made me feel that I was gazing upon a sweep of newly
turned earth. . . . And from the rapt look on their faces I knew
that these men had never before in their lives made such a pledge
to a secular cause. Here was religion melting into politics; prayers
were becoming pledges; hope was translating itself into organization;
devotion was becoming obedience; trust was turning itself into discipline; and reverence was being converted into vigilance. . . .

In his speech the Prime Minister was quiet, restrained; he informed his followers that it was necessary from time to time to
report to them upon progress. He reminded them that if they were
displeased with him that they could dismiss him. He asked for their
trust for the future.

"It was Clausewitz who said that politics is war by other means,"
he told them. "Because our struggle now has entered a quiet phase,
do not think that we are not fighting. We are fighting the same old
battle for freedom with other weapons. . . ."

I watched the faces closely. Did they understand such concepts? I wondered. . . . Could such sophisticated language be grasped by men so new to party struggles? How would this party behave in complicated situations? Could these pledges of loyalty withstand the many snarling currents ahead in the sea of politics?

The Prime Minister spoke on, and the sun, as it went down in the west, was a huge blue-gray ball showing through folds of straggling clouds. Again the vast crowd was asked to pledge its loyalty to the Leader by raising its hands, and again those clay-colored, orange, red, yellowish, brown, and grayish palms lifted skyward, extending as far back in the fading purple light as my eyes could see. . . . And I realized that sprawling over this vast continent were millions of other black people just as eager, as submissive, as trusting, who wanted to hold up their hands and pledge their loyalty to a leader— eager to die, if need be, for their redemption, their justification in the eyes of the world.

The Prime Minister finished and there was applause, singing, chanting. On the platform there was some milling around and talking. A newspaperman came to me and asked:

"We'd like to run your speech in tomorrow's paper. I'm with the *Graphic*. Can we have it?"

Instinctively I turned to the Prime Minister.

"There's a reporter asking to print what I said."

"Have you got it written down?" he asked.

"Yes," I said.

"Let me see it," he said.

I gave him my notes. He took them, looked off solemnly, then folded them slowly. The reporter waited. I waited. Then the Prime Minister came close to me and pushed the notes into the top breast pocket of my suit; he said no word and I said no word. I looked at the reporter and he looked at me. Then the Prime Minister moved silently away. . . . The reporter took a few steps backward, looking around with embarrassment. I did not understand what was happening and I did not want to ask for any explanation in public. Had I said something wrong in my speech? No one had asked to read what I had proposed to say. If they had, I'd have gladly submitted my ideas to be censored. But why had the Prime Minister taken my

notes and given them back to me with such a meaningful gesture?
I wanted to know, but, in the end, I resolved that I'd do nothing; I'd
wait. . . .

I made my way back to the government bungalow in a deeply
thoughtful mood.

X . . .

Next morning I resolved to move at once into the center of the
city and I made the round of the three available hotels. I finally
settled on the Seaview which stood at the edge of the beach and
fronted James Town, the slum area. The Seaview was grim, with
dingy mosquito nets over the beds; there were flies, greasy food,
spattered walls, wooden floors whose cracks held decades of filth.
The cold-water faucets gave forth water that was almost hot, so
exposed to the tropic sun was the plumbing of the establishment.
It was the kind of hotel that one read about in a Joseph Conrad
novel and, what intrigued me most, I had only to go to the balcony
and look down and there was Africa in all its squalor, vitality and
fantastic disorder. . . .

No breezes blew here to freshen the air. My skin was always oily
and wet and tiny mosquitoes bit deeply into my arms and ankles.
The humidity was so dense that each time I shaved I had to clean
a film of sweat from the mirror. An army of stewards was in attend-
ance, dressed in white, their naked feet swishing to and fro day and
night. No one hurried; voices were never raised; the hotel seemed in
the grip of the heat, mastered by it.

At mealtimes fried food, prepared by a chef whose god seemed
to have been named grease, was served. The mattresses on the bed
were damp and stained by God knows what. The locks, keys, and
latches on the doors were rusty and worked with difficulty, so
damaged had they become by the ever-present moisture. The
lavatory, when it was flushed, set up a groaning, howling noise
that penetrated every room of the hotel at all hours. And almost
always one could hear the continuous and mysterious beating of

drums deep in the maze of the streets of James Town. . . . The hotel's veranda was constantly crowded with Africans and Europeans guzzling beer which was used instead of the uncertain and sometimes dangerous drinking water. It was amazing how quickly I got used to the medley of odors; the early morning stench of homemade soap, the noon-hour cooking smells, and the vapors of excrement drifting into the hotel from the open drainage ditches outside.

The hotel was owned by a Greek; there were three hotels in Accra and all of them were owned by foreigners. Africans seemed to have the notion that there was something immoral about a hotel, and when you explained to them how needful hotels were to travelers, to those who had no relatives, they'd only smile or giggle. Pride would have kept any African, if he had had the capital, from operating a hotel, even though he had a Western education from Oxford or Cambridge. Living in tribal families, boasting "brothers" and "sisters" by the hundreds in far-flung towns and villages, an African had only to seek out his tribe to be housed, fed, and taken care of.

Using the Seaview as a base, I made many long excursions into the alleyways and compounds of James Town, in and out of the narrow paths between crummy shacks, and even down to the seashore where the strangely painted canoes of the fishermen lay upon the hot sand. Those inhabitants of James Town who lived near the water front were fisherfolk, and their drying nets, dark brown or purple, could be seen draped over wooden trestles in the sun. If a good catch of herring had come in the night before, the women, their cloths tied at their hips, would be arranging the fish in the sun to dry, laying them in rows side by side upon the red earth, upon palm leaves, or upon the rusty tin roofs. . . . And the cured fish would be shipped into the interior.

In shady places the men could be seen standing or squatting, mending nets, or talking politics, or arranging the details of their next fishing expedition. Now and then, stepping calmly among the sprawling men and women, would come a chief, togaed, sandaled, surrounded by his "linguist" and his elders, a young boy holding a vast umbrella above his head. . . .

Practically no grass grew in James Town and there were but few trees. Above all, there were no flowers. So denuded of blooming things was the African's environment that one wondered if it was by intent. (Someone told me later that the lack of vegetation was to keep down the invasion of snakes, but I doubt if that can account for the scarcity of green stuff around African homes.) It might well be that the nearness of the jungle and its lush creepers have made the African feel that he could derive all the delight he needs in growing and blooming things without bothering to plant anything in front of his door.

I turned down a narrow path and saw a woman bent over, resting on her knees, washing her hair in a tin pan, lathering the soapsuds over her head, her eyes closed. Evidently she had heard my footsteps on the hard red clay, for she paused, cocked her head, and listened for a second with her eyes still closed; then, as I walked on, she resumed her vigorous massaging of her hair. . . .

I came upon a group of old men sitting upon their wooden stools, their naked backs resting against a stone wall; they were talking and their bony black bodies reminded me of those wooden carvings now so rare in Africa and which can be seen only in the drawing rooms of rich Europeans. As I passed them I caught the low, soft murmurs of the Ga language flowing from their lips. They knew undoubtedly from my dress that I was a stranger, yet they evinced no overt curiosity. After I'd gone about twenty yards I turned my head and found them gazing at me. But the moment they knew that I knew that they were staring at me, they turned their eyes away. A stranger incited Africans to a high pitch of interest, but they were sensitive and always tried to hide that interest.

I barged into a crowded compound, walking slowly, as though I had a right to be there. The women, as they saw me approach, stopped their work, reached down and took hold of their cloths and covered their naked breasts. I walked on for a few yards and glanced back; they felt that I had gone and had let their cloths fall again to the ground, not slackening the performance of their domestic duties. . . . It was not because I was a man that they had covered themselves, for there were many men in evidence everywhere. It was not only because I was a stranger that they had exhibited such modesty; it was because I wore Western clothes, shoes, a sun helmet, that they had shrunk and covered themselves. They had performed a gesture in which, according to their customs, they did not really believe. But they had been long taught by the missionaries that it was considered shameful—that *others* considered it shameful—to be naked, and so when they had caught sight of me, they had hastily sheltered themselves. My approaching presence had been like the shadow of the Cross falling athwart the innocence of their simple lives, and, because of their conditioning, they had paid deference to that Cross; but the moment I had gone, they had reverted quickly and naturally to their traditional behavior. The words of St. Paul, that arch inhibitor of men, came to my mind:

What shall we say then? Is the law sin? God forbid. Nay, I had not known lust, except the law had said, Thou shalt not covet.

But sin, taking occasion by the commandment, wrought in me all manner of concupiscence. For without the law sin is dead.

For I was alive without the law once: but when the commandment came, sin revived, and I died.

As I walked on in the hot sun I could sense vast emotional impactions taking place; I could feel dammed-up physical hungers straining like jungle plants for the heat of the sun; and, in the end, I could see that Africa too some day would exhibit those strange and fantastic patterns of Western neurotic behavior that would necessitate the uncovering of all of that which religion was now covering up, that there would be doctors to coax these people to believe again in that which religion had taught them to repress. I could feel the mental suffering and emotional anguish that had yet to come into those innocent lives. . . .

I paused before a young woman selling tin pans and, by pointing, I indicated that I wanted to buy one. At once a group of women gathered about; it seemed that my buying a pan made them feel that they had the right to examine me at close quarters. The woman to whom I had pointed out the pan seemed baffled; she called hur-

riedly to a friend. Soon a crowd of no less than fifteen women were
ranged about me, chattering excitedly. Finally they called an old
man who spoke a little English and he translated. The pan cost seven
shillings and I paid, sweating, wondering why the women were
evincing such interest. As I started off with the pan under my arm,
the old man called me back.

"What is it?" I asked.

The women chattered even more loudly now.

"What you do with pan, Massa? Women wanna know."

I looked at the women and they hid their faces, laughing.

"I'm going to use the pan to boil water. I'm making a chemical
solution in which to develop films . . ." My voice trailed off, for I
could see that he had not understood me.

"They wanna know if you buy it for wife?" the man asked.

"No."

There was another outburst of laughter.

"They wanna know if Massa cook chop in pan?"

"No. I eat in a hotel restaurant," I said.

The women conferred with the man again and he shook his head.
Finally he turned to me and asked:

"Massa, women wanna know if Massa make peepee in pan?"

I blinked in bewilderment. The women were howling with laughter now.

I pushed away, hearing their black laughter echoing in my ears
as I tried to lose myself in the crowd. I learned afterward that it
was considered a disgrace for a man to purchase pots, pans, or food,
that it was an open confession that he had no woman to do such
things for him, and that no decent, self-respecting African would
ever dare be caught buying such a thing as a pan in the public
market. In the eyes of those women I'd lost caste, for they'd been
conditioned in a hard masculine school of detribalized thought
whose slogans regarding women were: keep 'em ignorant, keep 'em
pregnant, and keep 'em ten paces behind you.

That evening the Prime Minister's office called and informed me
that I'd be picked up and taken to Cape Coast to watch the Convention People's Party campaign in a by-election. It seemed that

Kwesi Plange, one of the youngest and brightest members of the
party, had died and that it was now necessary to fill his post with a
man upon whom Nkrumah could rely in the Legislative Assembly.
The Plange seat was being hotly contested by the opposition parties
led by the English-educated old guard. Cape Coast was the educational center of the nation and most of the best educated families
lived there. A Gold Coast slogan went: as Cape Coast goes, so goes
the country. Hence, the Convention People's Party was most anxious
to win. But, so many wild and hot charges had been made by both
the Convention People's Party and the opposition that the out-
come was a tossup and an opposition victory was being predicted
in some quarters.

Next morning at ten o'clock a string of about twenty automobiles
halted in front of my hotel; the cavalcade consisted of sound trucks,
private cars filled with the party's ablest speakers and organizers.
There was one car filled with women only. . . . This rigorous separa-
tion of the sexes seemed to prevail in almost everything the Africans
did; you never saw their women until the time came for them to
make their appearance, and then they moved ghostily, doing their
chores, and, it seemed, at some prearranged moment, they would
vanish as quickly and silently as they had come.

I sat in the car with the Prime Minister and we roared out into
the countryside. A blue haze hung over the green stretches of
forest. Much of the conversation that went on was in tribal language
and it didn't seem to bother them that I couldn't understand; it may
be that they talked their tribal tongue so that I *wouldn't* understand. . . . I felt that some of them regarded me as an outsider who'd
scorn their habits, their manners, and their attitudes. I found the
African an oblique, a hard-to-know man who seemed to take a kind
of childish pride in trying to create a state of bewilderment in the
minds of strangers. Only a man who himself had felt such bewilderment in the presence of strangers could have placed so high and
false a value upon it. They seemed to feel that that which they did
not reveal to me I could never know, but nothing could have been
more erroneous.

On this journey I had an opportunity to observe the Prime Minis-

ter in action at close range. Among his own people he was a demo-
crat, self-forgetfully identifying himself with the common masses
in deed and word each passing hour. He slept, played, and ate with
them, sharing his life in a manner that no Englishman or missionary
ever could. . . . It was his lapsing into a sudden silence that drew a
line between himself and them. His prescriptive right to leadership
was derived from his demonstrating the correctness of his political
tactics. I'd not witnessed any evidence of the fury of which I'd been
told that he was capable, but there was a hidden core of hardness in
him which I was sure that no one could bring to the surface quicker
than an Englishman. . . .

The cavalcade halted in a coconut grove just outside of Cape
Coast, in sight of the rolling Atlantic which sent white-capped
waves breaking in foam upon the rock-strewn beach. Standing to
one side and flanked by his trusted aides, the Prime Minister organized his entry into the town, indicating which car was to enter
first, who was to ride in each car. The loud-speakers of the sound
trucks were tested; an agenda for the day was drawn up; the route
to be taken was mapped out.

To Nkrumah's orders the party men reacted quickly, keenly; here,
less than five hundred miles from the Equator, amidst an appalling
heat and humidity, these blacks whom the world had branded as
being lazy and indifferent went about their duties with a zeal that
would have put even Communists to shame. While this organizing
was transpiring, a crowd of barefooted black boys clustered around.
The Prime Minister asked me:

"How about a drink of coconut milk?"

"That'd be fine," I said.

At his signal the boys raced toward the trees; they did not climb
them; they walked up, so adroitly did they scale the tall, slick tree
trunks. Soon they were nestling in the tops of the trees and coconuts
rained earthward. A tall boy picked them up and, with a cutlass,
whacked holes in them. I was handed one; the juice tasted sweet,
cool, and delicious.

I noticed that the women's contingent stood discreetly to one
side. Such separateness, I was now convinced, must have a deep

basis, a religious origin. At no time did the women mingle with the men; they kept in one compact group, to themselves. I spoke to one and she replied shyly, edging away. . . . She was a fully mature woman and surely she was not afraid of talking to a man. This exclusiveness of the women was undoubtedly due to some powerful tribal taboo too deep for even the Convention People's Party to overcome. . . .

The cavalcade was ready; we got into the cars; the Prime Minister stood up, lifted his hand in the party salute. I sat behind him in the open convertible car. . . . The loud-speakers of the sound trucks blared:

"FREE—DOOOOOM!"

And the procession was off on its political mission. Already the people of Cape Coast, hearing the roar, were crowding into the streets, rushing from their mud or concrete houses to salute and scream:

"FREE—DOOOOOM!"

The Prime Minister knew where his votes were; he hit the slum section first. The people, many of them half naked, flowed out of the warrens and mazes of compounds into the streets and their reactions were vital. They waved their hands in that queer, trembling vibration of the outstretched palm, giving a rolling, veering motion with their bodies as they sang and yelled:

"FREE—DOOOOOM! FREE—DOOOOM!"

"All for you, Kwame!"

"FREE—DOOOOOM! FREE—DOOOOOM!"

The procession wove in and out of the narrow, dusty streets, up and down hill. We passed Cape Coast Castle, built by the Swedes in 1657; it stood white and awesome in the hot sun. It was here that most of the slaves of the entire Guinea Coast had been assembled to be shipped to the New World. With loud-speakers screeching, we finally entered the Cape Coast residential section which fronted the sea; here lived some of the oldest and most respected families of the nation. They boasted a Sir or two, a few Orders of the British Empire, scornfully dubbed by the nationalists as: Obedient Boys of the Empire. . . . It was here that the African elite attitude held forth with bitter mien; it was here that the colony's most famous schools were located; it was here that Drs. Danquah and Busia, the intellectual leaders of the opposition, had raised the nostalgic but futile cry: "Preserve our traditions!"

There was less shouting for "FREE—DOOOOM!" in these quiet and sedate streets. Indeed, a skinny black man with a *pince-nez* athwart his nostrils, a chuck of graying mustache upon his upper lip, wearing his toga like that of a Roman emperor, stood on the wooden steps of his house and shouted again and again:

"I HATE HIM! I HATE HIM! I HATE HIM!"

The loud-speaker grated:

"VOTE FOR WELBECK! VOTE FOR THE CPP! VOTE FOR SELF-GOVERN-MENT NOW! FOLLOW NKRUMAH TO VICTORY!"

After two hours of emotional blitzkrieg upon the inhabitants of Cape Coast, the tour ended; later in the afternoon would come the ideological assault in the form of words hurled in an open-air rally in the center of the city. As we drove toward a private home for lunch, the Prime Minister told me some of his problems.

"We really don't know the exact mineral resources of this country," he said. "The British were only interested in getting rich quick, exporting those minerals which could be carried away to England or some other place. One of our urgent tasks is to find out just what mineral wealth we have locked in our soil.

"We have a wonderful soil out of which to make bricks. We've also found locations with soil from which we can make cement. But the British ship us cement from England. . . . And nothing is done about the natural advantages of making cement here. We'd like to, say, in housing, evolve a distinctly native style of architecture that would be suitable both to our people and to the climate. . . .

"Until today England has decided what was good for us and shipped it to us at prices that they determined. For example, woolens, which are far too hot for this climate, were shipped here and sold. Even now they make our local police wear woolen uniforms in this awful heat. . . .

"Take another example. . . . Our climate is good to grow almost anything, yet 80 per cent of our staple food is imported. No one

has really ever tried to experiment and determine what foods this
soil will grow best. Why should the English care about things like
that? They don't live here. They came here to make money in
government or business and then they go back. And, of course, they
never dreamed that one day the native would arise and say:
"*No more of this!*"
We sat down to lunch and the Prime Minister warned me:
"Take it easy with that food. You're not used to it."
I ignored him and served myself generously with groundnut
soup, *kenke, fufu,* all of which tasted wonderful except for the
fiery red pepper which pervaded everything.
"It may give you trouble," somebody else cautioned me.
"What harm can this good food do me?" I asked challengingly.
The next morning I knew. . . .
After lunch the cavalcade set out for the center of town where
a vast crowd had congregated. There was no shade and the tropic
sun beat down without mercy, making me squirm, sweat; finally
I put my handkerchief, dampened with water, to my face to keep
from feeling faint.
An African band—composed mostly of drums—played music and
a group of singers chanted a dirge for the dead Kwesi Plange; then
speaker after speaker lashed out at the crowd in Fanti and English.
It seemed that the oppositionist, Dr. Busia, had allowed himself at
some time or other to be quoted as saying that he did not think that
the country was ready for self-government and this was used for
all that it was worth against him. Even if people were not ready to
govern themselves, they certainly would not want to be told so in
such snobbish terms. . . . Nkrumah's orators were no novices; they
were consummate politicians and they played upon the crowd's
emotions with great skill. But from where had they gotten this
art . . . ?
Again, as it had been in Accra, the meeting was a mixture of
tribal ancestor worship, Protestantism, Catholicism—all blended together and directed toward modern political aims. One speaker,
for example, trained his audience to respond verbally by telling
them: "When I say ——, then you say ——!" The speaker then

chanted his words and the audience responded, not knowing where
the seemingly innocent words were leading. It went something like
that game that children play when they recite: "One nis ball, two
nis ball, three nis ball . . ." And ending in: "Ten nis ball. . . ." And
when the crowd discovered that they had been unknowingly led into
chanting a political slogan or hurling a stinging insult at the
opposition, they literally howled their approval. One man, clad in
a toga, rose, lifted his hands skyward; his eyes glazed and dreamlike, he sang out with orgiastic joy:

"What a wonderful life! What a wonderful life!"

Never before had that man had a chance to express himself, or
to hear others state what he felt to be true, and the mere hearing
of someone recount his hopes and dreams was enough to make
him feel free. England was reaping the results of keeping these
people from trying to manage their own lives and now they were
relishing freedom, savoring it, so to speak.

The Prime Minister advanced to the microphone. He was in
form; he was sharp, unyielding in his condemnation of the opposition. He hissed:

"I don't care how many university degrees that Busia and
Danquah have between them! The truth is: they don't know
politics! Why, they are scared of you, as scared of you as the British
are!"

The crowd laughed.

"Danquah ought to be an assistant librarian and leave politics
alone! I'll give him such a job, if he wants it!"

The audience listened, open-mouthed, smiling in agreement.

"Busia? He's a goat! Let him keep to his sociology! As a politician,
why, he's not worthy to stoop down and untie my shoestrings!"

This was hard fighting and the crowd roared their appreciation.

"We prefer self-government with danger to servitude in tran-
quillity!"

"FREE—DOOOOOOOM! FREE—DOOOOOOM!"

The crowd chanted as their dark and emotion-spent faces left the
meeting; wistfully I watched their toga-draped bodies wander off in
the fading light of the setting sun. . . . I sat brooding. How had he

conquered them? He had held them in the palms of his hands; he had poured scorn on the claims of the opposition; he had allowed no mercy for a contrary opinion; and it seemed that that was what his followers wanted. Prolonged British evasion and aloofness had made them ready to embrace certainty, definiteness. . . .

Back in my hotel room that night in Accra I tried to analyze what I'd seen. One could argue that Nkrumah had learned such tactics from observing Communist activities in London and New York, but there was the problem of determining how his aides, in five short years, had developed such a high degree of political dexterity with the masses. I had had enough experience in the Communist Party of the United States to know that what I had seen in Cape Coast had not been Communism. Communism was, above all, ideological; and what I had seen was the quintessence of passion.

My tentative answer was that, with the multitude of revolutionary examples before their eyes to indicate a general sense of direction, Nkrumah and his boys had doped out the rest, had guessed it, had fumbled and found how to organize their people; moreover, back of it all was, I believe, something much deeper and more potent than the mere influence of Marxist thought. It was my conviction that the twentieth century was throwing up these mass patterns of behavior out of the compulsive nakedness of men's disinherited lives. These men were not being so much guided as they were being provoked by elements deep in their own personalities, elements which they could not have ignored even if they had tried. The greed of British business-men and the fumbling efforts of missionaries had made an unwitting contribution to this mass movement by shattering the traditional tribal culture that had once given meaning to these people's lives, and now there burned in these black hearts a hunger to regain control over their lives and create a new sense of their destinies. White uplifters were generally so deficient in imagination that they could never realize how taunting were their efforts to save Africans when their racial codes forbade their sharing the lives of those Africans. . . .

What I had seen was not politics proper; it was politics *plus*. . . . It bordered upon religion; it involved a total and basic response to reality; it smacked of the dreamlike, of the stuff of which art and myths were made. . . . The number of men around the Prime Minister who knew Marxism were few in number, and how could they have instilled so quickly such abstruse ideas into illiterate masses? What I had seen was a smattering of Marxism plus the will to be, a thirst for self-redemption! And I suspected that Nkrumah himself was but an *agent provocateur* to the emotions of millions—emotions which even he did not quite grasp or understand in all of their ramifications. . . .

X I . . .

At last the Prime Minister's political secretary, Kofi Baako, called at my hotel to talk to me. He was a short, brownish-black man, thin, restless, intense, nervous. So well did he know the story that he had to tell that he had no need of notes; he got down to work at once, the words coming fluently from him. I recapitulate his story:

In August of 1947 the leaders of the Gold Coast met at Saltpond and inaugurated an organization called the United Gold Coast Convention, the declared aim of which was self-government. To carry on the work of the organization, a full-time secretary was sought and Nkrumah, then in London, was recommended for the post.

Arriving in December of 1947, Nkrumah defined the political character of the organization as being "the people's nationalist movement," and at once a deep conflict of interests arose. The wealthy Africans in the organization, lawyers and doctors educated in England, did not regard their efforts as representing the aims of the "people." They wanted to rule in *their* name; Nkrumah wanted the widest strata of the *people* to become involved. . . .

Nkrumah set about at once broadening the basis of the organization and his drive coincided with the efforts of Nii Bonnie II, a subchief of the Ga states who had launched a nationwide boycott of imported goods in an attempt to force foreign firms to reduce prices. The boycott terminated in a meeting at which members of the government and foreign merchants pledged to Nii Bonnie II to reduce prices.

But, on the morning of the 28th of February, 1948, when the people went into the stores, they did not find a reduction of prices and spontaneous demonstrations broke out against a score of European firms. In the afternoon of the same day a delegation of ex-servicemen marched on the Governor's castle in Christianborg to present grievances and a clash developed between the ex-servicemen and the police, the latter charging that the demonstrators had deviated from the agreed-upon line of march. When ordered to disperse, the demonstrators refused and the police opened fire and killed three veterans of British campaigns in India and Burma. . . . The news spread and an infuriated populace began a looting of foreign firms; arson and street fighting ensued and, during the following days, violence gripped the southern half of the country. Twenty-nine people were killed and about two hundred and thirty-seven were injured.

These disturbances prompted the leaders of the United Gold Coast Convention to send cables to London petitioning the British to create a commission of inquiry to study the underlying causes of the disorders; they also demanded an interim government. A few days later the leaders of the United Gold Coast Convention, Kwame Nkrumah, J. B. Danquah, Ako Adjei, Akufo Addo, Obetsebi Lamptey, and William Orfori Atta were arrested and banished to the Northern Territories; they were incarcerated separately for fear they would meet and plot.

The Governor declared a state of emergency and a curfew was imposed. Suspicion rose in the minds of the British that the local soldiers and police were not loyal and they imported troops from Nigeria.

The Colonial Secretary in London appointed a commission to investigate the causes of the violence and to recommend constructive measures. The Watson Commission—so named because of its chairman, Aiken Watson—took testimony in April of 1948 and the six arrested leaders were released so that they could give evidence. In June of that year the commission issued a report which declared the old constitution outmoded, urged a new constitution embodying the aspirations of the people, and endorsed a ministerial type of government patterned on those obtaining in the dominions.

But, when the Governor appointed a constitutional committee of forty Africans under the chairmanship of Mr. Justice Coussey, apprehension set in. The committee was composed entirely of upperclass chiefs and lawyers and the younger elements of the population were completely ignored.

When the committee began work on the 20th of January, tradeunionists, students, "mammy" traders of the streets, and the nationalist elements launched a protest against their representatives being excluded. Nkrumah hastily formed a youth committee and sent young men touring the nation to raise three demands: (1) universal adult suffrage; (2) a fully elected legislature with a fully representative cabinet; and (3) collective ministerial responsibility.

The traditional leadership of the United Gold Coast Convention now felt that Nkrumah was deviating from the organization's policies and an inevitable class split developed. Nkrumah was determined that the people should know what the real issues were and, accordingly, on September 1, 1948, he founded the *Accra Evening News*. The split widened as Nkrumah's journal vehemently demanded a democratic constitution. Attempts to bridge the differences between the right-wing old generation and the left-wing new generation served but to sharpen the conflict. Failing to achieve a satisfactory agreement with the leaders of the United Gold Coast Convention on points which he felt too vital for compromise, Nkrumah publicly announced his resignation.

The Convention People's Party took actual shape from that point on and Nkrumah announced his intention of staging positive action based on nonviolence if the people's demand for a democratic constitution was not granted.

The British Government now actively entered the campaign against Nkrumah, filing a series of libel suits. On September 15, 1949, Nkrumah was charged with contempt of court and fined three hundred pounds. This sum was quickly raised by the voluntary exertions of the street "mammies." This incident, more than any single thing else, convinced the leaders of the new Convention People's Party that they had the solid support of the masses of the common people, and they intensified their protests.

Upon the release of the Coussey Committee's report, Nkrumah summoned a monster mass meeting composed of trade-union leaders, farmers' organizations, and other political parties to study the report and to decide to what extent it was acceptable. This meeting took place on November 28, 1949, and the crowd was estimated at over 80,000. . . .

This mass meeting declared immediate self-government as its aim; it objected to the three ex officio members representing British vested interests being included in the cabinet; it protested against the suffrage age limit being set at twenty-five years; it demanded a legislature composed of fully elected members instead of, as the report recommended, some being nominated and others being elected.

The organizers of the Convention People's Party now took to the field and urged the people to prepare for country-wide civil disobedience and nonco-operation if the British refused these demands.

This campaign brought about a conference, on January 5, 1949, between British government officials and the leaders of the Convention People's Party. At this conference the British informed the nationalist leaders that they were studying the proposals and asked that positive action should not be evoked. When, however, the next day, the British announced on the radio that an "agreement" had been reached, Nkrumah felt that the British were merely playing for time and he announced that positive action would begin.

On the morning of January 8, not a train ran; no one went to work; busses and transportation trucks stood still. The nationalist leaders agreed to the functioning of essential services: water, electricity, health, medical care, etc. For twenty-one days, despite threats of dismissal of workers from jobs, numerous warnings and curfews, and the full evocation of the emergency powers of the Governor, positive action continued. When it became evident that such action could continue almost indefinitely, the British ordered the arrest of the leaders of the Convention People's Party. Nkrumah and about twenty others were seized, charged with sedition, and refused bail.

... The trial, which lasted two months, ended with all of the leaders being convicted and sentenced to prison terms varying from three months to four years.

Yet, in 1950, during the imprisonment of the leaders of positive action, elections for town councils took place in Accra, Cape Coast, and Kumasi and the condemned party won majorities in all three cities. It began to look as if the real leaders of the nation were in prison.

In April, 1950, Gbedemah, one of the leaders of the Convention People's Party, came out of prison and became acting chairman of the party and took charge of organizing for the coming general elections, presenting candidates in all of the thirty-eight constituencies. And from the imprisoned leaders came smuggled-out directives as to how the campaign should be conducted! It was in prison that the greeting of "Freedom" and the salute of the elbow-resting-on-the-hip-and-the-palm-fronting-outward was conceived of. . . . Nkrumah himself, in his cell, wrote the party's song which the marching Africans sang: "There Shall be Victory for Us."

On February 8, the Convention People's Party swept the nation, winning thirty-five out of thirty-eight seats. The people of the Gold Coast had elected as leaders of the new government men who were lodged in prison cells and the British had a new headache on their hands.

A few days later the imprisoned nationalists were told to get dressed in civilian clothes, an order that aroused their suspicion, for they thought that the British did not want the populace to see their newly elected leaders being transferred to another prison. . . . But it was freedom, an act of "grace," as the British quaintly called it.

Convoking the national executive committee of the Convention People's Party, Nkrumah made it plain that the party would enter the new government as a representative of the will of the nation. "We are going into the government to show the world that the African can rule himself. We want the chance to fight for the political, social, and economic improvement of the country from both within and without the government." He warned the people that self-government had not been achieved and he described the con-

stitution under which he would be acting as "bogus and fraudu-
lent."

Nkrumah had won the election, but his thirty-five seats represented a minority, for nineteen representatives had been named by
the Territorial Council, and there were seventeen chiefs or representatives of chiefs, and there were also three ex officio British members representing special interests, such as mines, commerce, etc.

Appointed Leader of Government Business by the Governor,
Nkrumah was then elected to the same post by the Assembly in a
vote that carried seventy-eight out of eighty-four voices. His ministerial colleagues, five in number, were also elected by the Assembly.
Three other cabinet posts were filled from three other territorial
councils: one from Ashanti; one from the Northern Territories; and
one from the Colony.

Eight months later, in October, 1951, the Convention People's
Party, through the Legislative Assembly, smashed the old system of
Indirect Rule (Native Authority) which had given the chiefs statu-
tory powers to maintain order, collect taxes, and dispense justice, etc.
In place of Indirect Rule there was erected a system of District,
Urban, and Local Councils elected on the basis of universal suf-
frage. . . . With this one stroke religion was swept out of govern-
ment and the will of the people took its place.

"This, in short, is how the first determined bid of Africans to rule
themselves turned out," Mr. Baako told me. "We know that we're not
through, that victory has not been won. This is only the first step. . . ."

"Suppose the British do not grant full self-government? What
then?" I asked Mr. Baako.

"Our program has the full support of the masses," he told me.
"And the British know it. They have co-operated so far. If they do
not continue, we shall declare ourselves a republic."

After Mr. Baako had gone I marveled how, in one historic leap,
the Gold Coast African had thrown off his chains. Though the conditions of his life were harsh, ridden with fetish and superstition,
he would eventually be free, for he was determined and tough. . . .

XII...

Next morning I resumed my trudging through the winding mazes of James Town's slums. And this time, as each time I sauntered out, I saw something that had escaped my notice before. The streets, doorways, and the little compounds were jammed with able-bodied men lounging the hours away. How was it possible that so many men were idle when ships, filled with manufactured goods from Britain, were docking every hour? Having spied these loafing men, my eyes traveled farther and I saw that men were cooking most of the meals in all the European homes and hotels, that men did all the washing, scrubbing, dusting, sweeping, kindling of fires, and making of beds. . . . These black men did everything except the wet-nursing of European babies. It seemed that it was beneath the dignity of a tribal African woman to work in a European home, and only a declassed woman would do so. Maybe this was the manner in which the African male saved his honor, kept his women out of reach of the Europeans?

As I entered the offices of the United States Information Service to look over the recent newspapers from America, I was stopped by a young lad.

"Dr. Wright, may I speak to you, sar?"

"Certainly. What is it? But I'm no doctor, son."

"I want a camera like that, sar," he said, touching the instrument I held under my arm.

"Well, they are rather expensive, you know."

"But I've an idea, sar," he said. "You see, sar, if you gave me a camera like that, I'd take pictures with it here and I'd send you the pictures in Paris and you could sell them, sar."

I blinked, trying to grasp what he was saying.

"I don't understand."

"You see, sar, when you sell my pictures, I wouldn't want you to send me any money until you had sold enough to get your own money back *twice*. . . ."

It was obvious that he had no intention whatsoever of trying to defraud me; he simply did not quite grasp the reality involved in his scheme.

"That's very kind of you," I told him. "But don't you know that they sell these cameras right here in Accra? Have you any money?"

"I could get the money, sar," he told me. "But they wouldn't sell me a camera like *that*, sar."

I finally understood what he meant. He was trying to tell me that he believed that the British would, say, take out some valuable part of the camera before they sold it to him, an African. He was convinced that every move of the British contained some hidden trick to take advantage of him. (Many Africans, I was told, ordered their goods directly from the United Kingdom and paid duty on them, believing that the goods would be of better quality than those sold by foreign merchants in local stores. And an African boy, wanting a bicycle, has been known to beg a Britisher to buy it for him, feeling that the foreign storekeeper would cheat him, but wouldn't dare cheat the Britisher. . . . A sodden and pathetic distrust was lodged deep in the African heart.)

"Look, I'd like to help you, but, honestly, I don't know how. . . ."

He seemed to be about twenty-one years of age. . . .

"But I'd pay you back; I'd send the pictures to you; I swear, sar," he begged me.

I sighed. I was angry, but I didn't know with whom. I tried to avoid his pleading eyes. I was not angry with him.

"I'd suggest that you go to a school of photography," I advised him.

He looked crestfallen. He did not accept it. But he nodded and allowed me to pass. I sat down to read, but my mind was trying to fathom how these young boys saw and felt reality. The boy had seemed to feel that he had a claim upon me that I could not accept. I was for him, but not in the direct way he seemed to feel that I ought to be. Did he think that I was naïve enough to make him, a stranger whose merits I did not know, a present of an expensive camera? Obviously, he did. But why? I had never in my life dared ask anybody for a gift so exorbitant.

That evening I discussed this boy's demand with an African who had been educated in the United States.

"That boy thinks that you are his brother—You are of African descent, you see," he told me.

"But you don't give expensive cameras to boys even if they are of your color," I protested.

"You don't understand. The boy was trying to establish a sort of kinship with you. In the Gold Coast, a boy can go and live with his uncle, demand to be fed, clothed, and the uncle cannot refuse him. The uncle has a sacred obligation to comply. Tribal life has bred a curious kind of dependence in the African. Hence, an uncle, if he has four or five nephews, can never accumulate anything. His relatives live on him and there is nothing that he can do about it."

"But what right has the nephew to make such claims?"

"The uncle's sister's blood flows in the nephew's veins. . . . Look, if an African makes £100,000, do you think he can keep it? No. His family moves in and stays with him until that money is gone. You see, the family here is more of an economic unit than in the West. . . . Let's say that an African family has gotten hold of a few thousand pounds. They'll hold a family meeting and decide to send Kojo, say, to London to study medicine. Now, they are not giving that money to Kojo; they are *investing* it in him and when he masters his medical subjects, returns home, and starts practicing, the family stops working and goes and lives with Kojo for the rest of their lives. That's their way of collecting their dividends, a kind of intimate coupon clipping, you might say. . . .

"African society is tightly, *tightly* organized. . . . No one is outside of the bounds and claims of the clan. You may never get rich, but you'll never starve, not as long as someone who is akin to you has something to eat. It's Communism, but without any of the ideas of Marx or Lenin. It has a sacred origin—"

"What sacred origin?" I asked.

"It all starts with the sun. . . . Say, you must read Dr. Danquah's book; it's called *The Akan Doctrine of God*."

I jotted down the title of the book, but realized that curiosity in

Africa led one not to any immediate satisfaction, but only toward ever-winding avenues of searching. . . .

Next afternoon Mrs. Hannah Cudjoe, the propaganda secretary of the Women's Division of the Convention People's Party, called upon me at the suggestion of the Prime Minister. She was a pleasant, soft-spoken woman, diffident in manner, slow-moving, coy-eyed, short, heavy, black, with a shrewd, placid face. She spoke English with a slight tribal accent. We sat in a shady spot on the hotel veranda and I ordered two bottles of beer. She seemed ill at ease, kept her knees tightly pressed together, and seemed not to know what to do with her hands. Despite her self-consciousness, I felt that in certain circumstances she would know how to throw herself forward, for there slumbered beneath her evasive eyes a restlessness, a superfluity of hard energy. I questioned her about her work and she laughed, fell silent for several moments and sat in an attitude of deep repose, reflecting, staring off.

I discovered later that this shyness indicated that she was afraid of saying the wrong thing; above all, it meant that she did not completely trust me, did not *know* me. . . . Western "knowing" and non-Western "knowing" were two different things. It was impossible for a European to "know" somebody in the sense that an African "knows" somebody; "knowing" a person to an African meant possessing a knowledge of his tribe, of his family, of the formation of his habits, of the friends surrounding him, of being privy to the inmost secrets of his culture. While Western "knowing" was limited to a more rational basis—to a knowledge of a man's profession, of his ideas, and perhaps some of his interests.

So often had the Africans been deceived that distrust had become enthroned in the very processes of their thoughts. I could feel Mrs. Hannah Cudjoe's distrust of me; it came from no specific cause; it was general. I was a stranger, a foreigner, and, therefore, must be spoken to cautiously, with weighed words. Distrust was in full operation before any objective event had occurred to justify it. A stranger confronting an African and feeling this distrust would begin to react to it and he'd feel himself becoming defensively distrustful himself. Distrust bred distrust; he'd begin to watch for evasion; he'd begin to question a flattering phrase. So, with no basis in immediate reality, both sides would begin regarding the other warily, searching for hidden meanings in the most innocent statements. In the end, what had begun as a stranger's apprehension of the African's wariness would terminate in a distrust created out of nowhere, conjured up out of nothing. This fear, this suspicion of nothing in particular came to be the most predictable hallmark of the African mentality that I met in all the Gold Coast, from the Prime Minister down to the humblest "mammy" selling *kenke* on the street corners. . . .

I had literally to pull Mrs. Hannah Cudjoe's words out of her, so cautious was she; finally, she told me frankly:

"You know, we black people have to be so careful. We don't have many friends. Everybody wants to hurt us. They come here and grin in our faces, and then they go away and make fun of us. . . ."

"I understand," I said. "But you must learn to control your reactions; you mustn't let others see that you are afraid. You must never show weakness, for weakness invites attack—"

"You think so?" she asked me.

"Absolutely," I told her.

She was silent for a few minutes, then she relaxed and began to talk slowly. She told me that she had enlisted in the Convention People's Party in the early days when the party had been young and the going hard. She had stood alone and many of the women of the Gold Coast had reviled her for daring to enter the political field. . . . She had once married one of the top party leaders, but she was now divorced. She worked hard, making four or five speeches a day, always on the move.

"Please, be careful what you write about us," she begged me. "We are poor and we must learn to live the modern way. So many people have hurt us."

Her answers were simple, direct, and factual, but she could not grasp abstract ideas and could not give me broad, coherent descriptions. She related how she had gone into the "bush" and had recruited hundreds of women into the party, how she had taken food to them and had made them feel that others cared about them, how she had shown them how to wash and feed their children.

"Just what is the position of tribal woman today?" I asked her.

"We are chattel," she said frankly. "Under our customs the woman is owned by the husband; he owns even the clothes on her back. He dictates all of her moves, says what she can and can't do. That's why we don't have as many women in the party as we would like. When a woman tells her husband that she wants to attend a political meeting, the husband tells the wife to stay home, that he'll go to the meeting and he'll tell her what she needs to know. A tribalized African simply cannot, will not believe that a woman can understand anything, and the woman alone can do nothing about it. Tribal law is against her; her husband has the right to collect all of the wife's earnings. . . ."

"But, despite that, some of them are joining the party, aren't they?"

"Yes. Slowly," she said. "Almost all the women in our party are illiterate. In their homes, the women cannot speak about politics. But once they join the party, they find that life can be different. So some of our best defenders are women. They give their lives to the party and will stand and fight as nobody else will."

"Listen, Mrs. Cudjoe," I asked her, "do you think that it's possible for me to become a paying guest in an African home? You see, I'd like to get closer to the people, like to know how they live in families. What do you think?"

I watched her face grow thoughtful and I knew that it was not a question of whether she could find an African home that would accept me as a paying guest; the question in her mind was: what would be my reactions to the life I'd see in an African home? She feared my scorning that life, laughing at it; she was afraid of me; I could feel distrust welling up in her. . . .

"I'll ask around," she mumbled without enthusiasm.

And the lame tone of her voice told me that I'd never hear from her about my request, and I never did. What had been done to these people? That they had had and still had a lot of enemies, I had no doubt; but how could they ever win sympathy or friends if they were afraid to honor a simple, human request, if the most casual questions evoked grave doubts? Or were they so childlike as to imagine that they could hide the entire life of the Gold Coast from strangers? With the exception of the work of one or two of their educated men, all the history of their country and the interpretations of their customs had been written by Europeans, and those interpretations had shamed and angered them, but it was only to Europeans that they could talk really, that they could try to communicate.

When Mrs. Cudjoe had gone, I fought against a horrible realization that was seeking to make itself manifest in me: these people could never really trust me. They had a tradition of nearly a hundred years of trusting—even against their will—the British and they had grown used to British authority, so used to it that they kept on trusting the British even when they hated them. For a long time to come it would be only to their British masters that they could really open their hearts. They'd grown used to British snobbery, curtness, aloofness and, even though they loathed it, they missed it when it was absent and felt loose and uncomfortable. I gritted my teeth and shook my head in dismay. Centuries of foreign rule had left their marks deep, deep in the personalities of the people, deeper than the people themselves had any idea of. . . .

The Africans I met knew that I knew something in general of the conditions of their lives, the disorder, the polygamy, the strange burial customs, etc.; these were the things in which they most deeply believed, yet they were ashamed of them before the world. How could one believe in something that one was ashamed of? Perhaps it was because it was all that they had? Western civilization had made them want to hide their traditional lives and yet that civilization had given them no other way to live. . . .

All that the African personality seemed to have gotten from the West so far was a numbed defensiveness, a chronic lack of self-confidence. How could even that which the Africans were ashamed of be changed if they never wanted it shown or talked about? Their contact with the West had been so negative and limited that they could not objectively determine what in their lives they could be proud of or ashamed of. They were uncertain, uneasy, nervous, split deep within themselves. I wondered if the British were sensitive enough to know what they had done to these people? Crimes have been committed in this world of so vast a nature that they have never been recorded in any criminal code.

XIII...

Next morning I paid a visit to the headquarters of the Convention People's Party. It was housed on the second floor of a stone building in a thriving trading quarter of Accra. It looked exactly like any political headquarters of any political party in the world: that is, dingy, humdrum, ill-lighted, and bare. Mr. Kwame Afriyie, the general secretary of the party, was presented to me and at once he said:

"We won in Cape Coast, you know."

I congratulated him. During my entire visit the phone rang; every party member was wanting to know the results of the Cape Coast by-election. Streams of people flowed in and out of the office, asking questions, seeking help in their party work, and offering themselves to be assigned to duties. A chief came in with his "linguist," his umbrella, and all; he was taken into a private room. . . .

"Do chiefs come here too, especially after your party has clipped their political wings?" I asked Mr. Afriyie.

"Oh, yes," he said, laughing.

"But why do they come?"

"They're sensible," Mr. Afriyie told me. "They're adjusting themselves to the new situation. Some of them come here to beg the Prime Minister to address audiences in their local areas. You see, when a chief feels that he is losing prestige, he wants our help. Then sometimes a chief is the president of a local council and he wants our advice on some point or other. And a lot of chiefs are now wanting to become presidents of town councils; you see? We don't bother with the chief's sacred, religious, or ceremonial functions, but we see that he keeps out of politics. The smart chiefs see the handwriting on the wall and are trying to get adjusted to the new social order that is in the making.

"Since we have come to power, the old tribal spirit and cohesiveness have declined. Many of the old chiefs were corrupt, holding their positions by right of the British under a system of indirect rule. Many people were deeply dissatisfied with them. Chiefs pitted their little tribes against other little tribes in senseless disputes, and the resulting debilitating atmosphere was discouraging to the masses who wanted something concrete and practical done. Then many of the chiefs were illiterate and would co-operate with no one. They could understand nothing."

"And did the British try to correct that?"

"Why should they have tried to do that?" he asked me. "It wasn't in their interest. The British wanted things to stay just as they were."

I examined the membership book of the Convention People's Party and saw that the Prime Minister's name headed the list. The party had a membership of about 400,000, the average age being about thirty-five. The rank and file were carpenters, students, clerks, seamstresses, goldsmiths, photographers, tailors, pressmen, watch repairers, printers, chauffeurs, barbers, teachers, building inspectors, electricians, foremen, masons, draughtsmen, traders, nurses, blacksmiths, fitters, mechanics, and storekeepers—essentially a petty bourgeois class.

Tribally they derived from Wangara, Wassaw, Ajumaku, Asdna, Shai, Prampram, Grushie, Ga, Fanti, Twi, Ashanti, Ewe, Akan, Guang, Nzima (the Prime Minister's tribe), Akwapim, Kwahu, Efutu, Demkyira, Anum, Krobo, Adangme, Nkronyo, Ada, etc.

"Tell me, how do you get discipline in the party?" I asked Mr. Afriyie.

His genial smile wavered. I saw distrust flicker across his face. The moment I touched upon some vital question, I could feel the African's emotions running away. . . .

"We follow the Leader," he said evasively.

I knew that it would have been useless to persist. Yet I could sense tense dramas taking place in the life of the party: expulsions, chastisements, factional battles, etc. I was once a Communist and

I knew that those things were inevitable in any vital organization. But all of that was hidden and, so far as I was concerned, would stay hidden. Yet, I could guess at the concealed reality. I studied Mr. Afriyie and could see that he felt that he had fooled me. To have insisted would only have roused his doubts and suspicions of me. I found that the African almost invariably underestimated the person with whom he was dealing; he always placed too much confidence in an evasive reply, thinking that if he denied something, then that something ceased to exist. It was childlike.

I shook hands all around and took my leave. Didn't Africans know that their elusiveness simply whetted people's curiosity the more? The African had a mania for hiding the facts of his life, yet he hid those facts in such a clumsy way that it made others know that he was hiding them. In short, African secretiveness defeated itself by calling insistent attention to what was being secreted.

I wander through the Accra streets. . . . Is it because I see so many men and women urinating publicly, in drains, on the sides of roads, in bushes, behind hedges, that I've begun to think that Africans urinate oftener than other people . . . ? That, manifestly, is not true. Then, what is it? Is it that the African urinates, as it were, so unconsciously that one is forced to the conclusion that he urinates oftener than other people? It cannot be that, as a nation, they have weak bladders; "racially," no such fact could be proved. A woman suddenly pauses at a corner, leans a little against a wall, opens her legs, and urinates, standing up. . . . Then she walks blithely off. Men will squat with their backs to the roadway, their heads turned to watch the traffic or passers-by, and urinate. At cocktail parties the British have an expression for wanting to urinate; they say, mindful of African habits:

"I must go and water the garden."

One wonders what such constant urination does to the plants, flowers, grass, etc.

One evening I accompanied a young, American-educated African to an outdoor dance arena, the Weekend in Havana. The specialty of this establishment, as with all the dance spots in the Gold Coast, was a shuffling, lazy kind of somnambulistic dance step called High

Life. Curiously enough, even here I observed that tendency of the African sexes to segregate themselves. Little knots of women—they all wore European dress to these social affairs—clustered together. I was informed that this avoidance of the opposite sex was but an extension of the rituals of the tribal African family life; in the home men and women slept under different roofs and ate their meals separately, even when they were married. And so ingrained had those habits become that even when they were participating in non-African activities they tended to keep to their fundamental patterns of behavior. Perhaps it made them feel more at ease, quieted a sense of guilt for deserting their traditional ways . . . ?

I compelled myself, out of politeness to my host, to watch the dancing. Nothing could have been more boring to my temperament than such spectacles and I sat with a fixed smile on my face, nursing a bottle of beer, wishing I was somewhere else. I'd seen better and more spirited dancing among the Negroes of New York's Harlem and Chicago's South Side, but since it was expected of me to watch Africans demonstrate that they could imitate Europeans or Americans, I thought that I'd better pretend to be interested.

Then my eyes caught sight of something that all but pulled me up out of my seat. Two young men walked slowly across a corner of the dance floor, each with his arm tenderly about the waist of the other, their eyes holding a contented, dreamy gaze. . . . What was *that?* Had I misjudged the African capacity for the assimilation of Western emotional conditionings? But maybe those two boys were from Oxford or Cambridge . . . ? They didn't look like it. I wanted to question my friend about this, but I feared appearing too indelicate. But, just as I repressed my impetuosity, the two young men glided gracefully out upon the dance floor and moved with all the sexual suggestiveness of a mixed couple to the catchy music. Again I inhibited myself, not wishing to wade too abruptly into such matters with people whose reactions I could never predict. After all, I was a stranger in a strange land. I sat quietly, watching, wondering. Had the British brought homosexuality to Africa? Had the vices of the English public-school system somehow seeped through here? Just as the African had taken inordinately to alcohol, had he taken to this too? Then I was startled to see two more young men, holding hands, walk leisurely across the dance floor, heading, it seemed, for the bar. A deep, calm togetherness seemed to exist between them. Was this more evidence of that innocence of instinct that I had previously observed? I could no longer restrain my curiosity. I leaned toward my host and whispered:

"Look here. What's going on?"

"I don't get you," he said; but I saw an ironic twitch on his lips as he suppressed a smile.

"If what I see happening here tonight between young men happened in New York, the police would raid the place and throw the people in jail. . . ."

My friend guffawed.

"What do you *think* you see?" he demanded.

"I think I see some pretty overt homosexual behavior," I said quietly.

"You *don't,*" he said flatly.

"Then what am I looking at?"

"You're looking at nice, manly tribal young men who love dancing," he explained in a somewhat aloof voice.

"Look, I'm no moralist; I don't care what they are," I said. "But I want to make sure."

"And I'm making no moral defense of Gold Coast boys," he said. "But you don't see any homosexuality. Listen, I wanted you to come here to see this. I could have called your attention to it, but I was waiting for you to notice it—"

"How could I escape it?" I asked him. "Now, why are they acting like that?"

"It's a bit complicated," my host explained as the music jumped all over the dance floor. "These young boys are still mainly tribal. They speak English; they go to school, to church; and they work as clerks, perhaps, in European offices. But their deepest reactions are still basically tribal, not European. Now, in tribal dances men dance with men, women dance with women, or they all dance together, or each person alone, if he wants to. . . . Tribal dancing is not uniquely sexual. Sometimes they dance for a god, to please

him, to coax him, to tell him something. Sometimes they dance to
please each other. Long habituation to this kind of dancing makes
them, when they dance in public to Western tunes and rhythms
which are replete with sexuality, still follow their tribal conditioning. There is no homosexuality here. In most tribal dancing men
get used to touching or holding other men; they think nothing of it;
and they'd be morally shocked, hurt, if they thought that you saw
something perverse in it. So you have here a strange synthesis of
seemingly disparate elements—young boys dancing together, embracing ardently, holding hands, with no thought of sex. They are
brothers."

"I see," I said.

Each hour events were driving home to me that Africa was another world, another sphere of being. For it to become natural to
me, I'd have to learn to accept without thought a whole new range
of assumptions. Intellectually, I understood my friend's all too clear
explanation of why boys liked to hold hands and dance together,
yet the sight of it provoked in me a sense of uneasiness on levels
of emotion deeper than I could control.

Later that evening the dance gradually reverted more and more
to African patterns. The drums in the orchestra took over the tunes
and beat out wild, throbbing notes. Around two o'clock in the
morning there were but a few mixed couples on the floor—mostly
everyone was dancing alone, his eyes half closed, his lips hanging
slightly open, his right hand pressed to his heart, as though lost in
the sheer physical joy of movement. Presumably each person was
dancing for himself or whatever friend or god he felt was near him,
or for whoever wished to observe his ecstasy. The African seemed
to feel that whenever he experienced something vital, he had to
share it; his joy had to arouse joy in others, even though those
"others" were unseen. It was to that which was not present to sight
or touch, sometimes, that the African seemed to want to talk, to
plead, to trust. There was in him a tinge of otherworldliness even
when he danced to sexy jazz tunes; he seemed chronically addicted
to a form of physical lyricism. He spoke with physical movement,

protested with a stiffening of his neck, argued with his legs, cajoled with his arms, said yes with his hips, and no with a slow roll of his head. . . .

X I V . . .

There are no mail deliveries. You went to the post office each morning for your letters; if you lived in Accra, you kept a post-office box, that is, rented one. If you didn't, you asked a friend to receive your letters for you in his box.

When I inquired why mail could not be delivered, the explanation was that the problem of illiteracy made it impractical to assign the delivery of mail to literate men when there were far more important jobs for those literate men to do. It would have been, I was informed, an abuse of the value of the few literate men to impose delivering mail upon them. In banks, stores, and shops there was a desperate need of clerks, and such men could not be spared to sort or handle mail.

The more I probed into the problem of illiteracy, the stranger it became. It was generally stated that there was a 90 per cent illiteracy in the Gold Coast; that is, only 10 per cent of the people could read and write *English*. All of which might well be true. A few of the natives read and wrote their own tribal languages, but such proficiencies were almost useless in the daily business world where English was not only the official language of the country, but the dominant language of the most vital trade areas of the earth.

Yet, despite this vast illiteracy, an average "mammy" who buys and sells staples in the open markets handles, during the course of a year, a turnover amounting to £50,000! But how does she know this, since she cannot read or write? She keeps it all in her head! It's possible that tribal African customs have conditioned her to perform these feats of memory for such a multitude of details.

The great majority of the Africans buy not from the European stores, but from each other, and one feels, when looking at the bustling activity in the market places, that almost the whole of the population is engaged in buying and selling. Just how this strange method of distributing products came about is a mystery. Perhaps it can be partly explained by the manner in which British firms ship their products to the Gold Coast. The British exporting firm generally deals through a certain *one* firm; that firm in turn sells to another, and *that* firm to *yet* another. . . . An African "mammy" finally enters this elaborate process, buying a huge lot of a certain merchandise, which she, in turn, breaks up and sells in fairly large lots to her customers. And her customers now sell directly to the public or maybe to other sellers who sell to the public. African wives are expected to aid in augmenting the income of the household and they thus take to the streets with their heads loaded with sundry items. . . . Naturally, this fantastic selling and reselling of goods drive the prices up and up until finally poor Africans must pay higher prices than a Britisher for a like product! Capitalism here reaches surrealistic dimensions, for even an ordinary match gains in value if it must afford profit to each hand through which it passes. This frantic concentration of the African mind upon making a profit out of selling a tiny fragment of a bar of soap or a piece of a piece of a piece of cloth is one of the most pathetic sights of the Gold Coast.

Of late there has been an effort to establish co-operatives to eliminate this senseless and self-defeating trading, but a casual glance at Accra's market places reveals that the whole process of buying and selling is anarchy calling for the sharpest wits imaginable. Haggling over a penny enlists the deepest passion, and you have the impression that the African trader is dealing in life-and-death matters. One wonders if such a manner of trading could have grown up in any society other than an illiterate one. It's likely that traditional tribal customs can account to some degree for this seeming preference for direct cash dealing on the part of the African, for his passion for visible, tactile methods of exchange of goods; I don't know. . . . All I know is that the African seems to love a petty financial game of wits and he'll ask you ten times the value of any object he's selling without batting an eye. Of course, the true explanation might be much simpler; the African might have learned all of this innocent chicanery from the Europeans during five hundred years of trading with them. The Portuguese, the Danes, the Swedes, the Germans, the French, and the English had some pretty sharp and unsavory methods of trading cheap trinkets for gold dust, a transaction which allowed for a wide leeway of bargaining. . . . But I leave this question of accounting for the "economic laws" (I don't believe that there's any such thing!) of the Gold Coast to other and more astute minds.

And yet a smart "mammy" will let a moneylender cheat her. . . . Since an African, when he is short of cash, thinks nothing of borrowing as much as he needs to tide him over, the Gold Coast moneylender will charge two, three, or four hundred per cent interest. I was told of a case in which a cocoa farmer borrowed money on his farm and pledged the yield of each year's crop as interest; of course, since his farm did not bring him any income, he could never pay off the principal!

Marriage and adultery too operate on a "cash and carry" basis. Tribal Africans do not like to admit that they buy their wives, but obtaining a wife amounts to no more or less than just that. And if your wife commits adultery, you can be compensated for it. There exists a regular fixed scale of fines to be paid by those either trapped or caught in the act of adultery. Or if your wife runs away, you can claim from her family—that is, the ones from whom you bought her —the return of your money. I'm reliably informed that some chiefs urge their many wives to commit adultery so that they can collect large sums of money by fining the culprits gullible enough to commit fornication with them.

The following is a list of fines leveled against all sections of society in a given Gold Coast area for the crime of adultery:

	£	S.	*Plus*
Any Akan man or indigene	5	5	1 bottle of gin
The wife adulteress	2	2	2 fowls
Any clerk	7	4	1 bottle of whiskey
All artisans, carpenters, blacksmiths, etc.	7	4	1 bottle of whiskey
Linguists for divisional chiefs	7	4	1 sheep and 1 bottle of gin

As the delinquents rise in the social scale, the fines increase. For example, men high in the tribal hierarchy, members of royal families, etc., are fined for adultery as follows:

Divisional chiefs without stool	10 —	2 bottles of gin
Divisional chiefs with stool	25 —	2 sheep and 2 bottles of gin
Divisional chiefs	100 —	3 sheep and 1 case of gin
Divisional chief's wife	7 4	2 sheep and 1 bottle of gin

The most severe penalty is meted out to royalty. For example, an Omanhene's adultery fee is fixed at

200 — 7 sheep and 2 cases of gin

It is reckoned that the committing of adultery with an important person's wife amounts to a defilation of his stool and those of his superiors, hence sheep are slaughtered to sanctify the stools or fetishes. A person's ultimate importance to the state, in the Akan tribal society, is judged by the amount of his adultery fee. The above amounts of fines are in force as of this moment in the Gold Coast, having been enacted by a state council (which will remain unidentified) on the 12th of May, 1953.

Marriage fees are likewise fixed. (This does not refer to what the man pays to the family for his wife.) The following prevails today:

NEW MARRIAGE	£ 1.10/
SECONDHAND MARRIAGE	£ 1. 2/

Every woman should give her husband one fowl at a new marriage

When a man marries a new wife, he should pacify his old wife with 8/.

Funeral expenses are also fixed by the state; it was decided that at the death of a man, all women should pay 6d. and men 1/. But when a woman dies, all women should pay 3d. and men 6d. When a young man dies, the chief should pay 3d. and the men 6d. When an adult dies the chief should pay 4/.

These rules were made in an attempt to keep down the cost of funerals, for it has been known for funerals to plunge families in deep debt for years. The motives for spending so much money on funerals are simple: the deceased is about to enter the other world and he has to go there in style, with dignity, etc. One costly item for funerals is alcohol; most funerals are occasions for an inordinate degree of drinking. Attempts are being made to limit the drinking to palm wine, which, God knows, is potent enough. Some chiefs. influenced by Christianity, are actually arguing for lemonade. They constitute a "still small voice" as yet. . . .

So great is the propensity of Africans to celebrate death that many local councils have sought recently to impose drastic time limits upon funerals. For example, in an unnamed but prosperous Gold Coast state, the local council has decreed that:

A. Funerals for young men should be strictly limited to one week.

B. In the case of a child, there should be no funeral. (This is a rather involved and metaphysical point, for when a child dies it is assumed that the child did not wish to stay in the world of the living. It is said that the child's ghost mother in the other world has persuaded the child to return. In the old days the dead child was actually beaten and punished for not wishing to stay.)

C. Funerals for adults should be strictly limited to two weeks.

Funerals for chiefs, etc., are special occasions and the local council determines the duration of the funeral; the expenses are arrived at by a consultation between the chief's subjects and the chief's family. After the funeral the amount spent is shared among all the chief's subjects.

Adultery fines meted out to Gold Coast people of different religious persuasions often involve odd and incongruous items. For example, a Mohammedan caught in adultery is fined:

£5.5/–, 100 kola nuts and 1 piece of white shirting material.

Further items relating to marriage state:

To the woman he marries, a man owes: £1.10/–, plus a pot of palm wine, 3 headkerchiefs, 2 good cloths, 1 ordinary cloth, 1 hoe, 1 cutlass, 1 wooden tray and also a £2 dowry.

Any marriage contracted after that, the man owes the new wife £1.2/–, plus 1 pot of palm wine, 3 headkerchiefs, 2 good cloths, 1 ordinary cloth, 1 hoe, 1 cutlass, 1 wooden tray and also £2 dowry.

The codification of marriage rules, expenses, etc., runs into fine detail. Nothing is left to chance. For example, the seduction of a young girl who does not go to school is reckoned in terms of fine at £7. But if the girl is in school, the fine is fixed at £50. (Missionary influence?) If a man lives with a young girl as man and wife and refuses to marry her, he can send her off with £5. But if the girl refuses to marry the man, she can send him off with £7.

There is no sighing, longing, or other romantic notions in a young African seeking a wife; kissing is not a part of courtship, and is unknown except among chaste Christians. A man regards a woman as an economic investment; she must be sturdy, able to do a hard day's work, bear many children, and, above all, obey. . . . He may aid her in the heavier parts of her field labors, but his aid is limited to providing certain essentials for the household, such as meat which he obtains by hunting. The basic drives reveal themselves not as romance or love, but children and crops.

What desperate coping with nature dictated the African's concentration upon these elements? Maybe we will never know. Some of his greatest festivals center, until this day, around celebrating the harvest of yams. Another deep regard of the African heart is toward water, for it was water that kept his fields growing. Around ponds, lakes, rivers, and lagoons are likely to be found many myths and legends, and any untoward event occurring in connection with water is at once enshrined in memory. The whole of tribal life is pitched on a sacred plane, and the imposition of any other religion is likely to give them not more but less religion.

This dense illiteracy and the astonishing oral tradition—transmitted from generation to generation—upon which it feeds, its roots sunk in tribal memory, has formed a barrier, has erected a psychological distance between the African and the Western world and has made it increasingly difficult for the African to be known. This distance has not lessened with the passage of time; indeed, it has widened, for the tempo of progress of the West has qualitatively made the difference between the Western and non-Western world almost absolute. The distance today between tribal man and the West is greater than the distance between God and Western man of the sixteenth century. Western man could talk to his God in those days; today illiterate tribal minds are numbed when they hear of the atomic weapons of the Western world; and even when those tribal people revolt against the West and its technical mastery of the earth, they oftime find themselves, ironically, more dependent upon their white masters than before they launched their nationalistic revolutions. . . .

A Westerner must make an effort to banish the feeling that what he is observing in Africa is irrational, and, unless he is able to understand the underlying assumptions of the African's beliefs, the African will always seem a "savage." And yet the African too is struck by what seems to him the irrational nature of the world that is non-African, for he too does not often know the assumptions of that non-African world. And when those assumptions are revealed to him they are just as fantastic to him as his are to the West.

In such areas of compounded involvement the chances for self-deception are enormous. For example, the African fondly believes that there is another world beyond this world, and he predicates his most practical actions upon its validity. Therefore Westerners who live or work among Africans, for religious or business purposes, cannot escape lending a degree of recognition to the nonexistent world that the African projects in his living, thereby adding weight to the African's delusions.

Conversely, the Western assumption of the inferiority of the African compels the Westerner to constrict the African's environment; so, in time, African psychological attitudes and conditions of life come to reflect the West's assumptions. And the African, anchored amidst such degrading conditions, cannot help but reinforce them by accepting them; and what was, in the beginning, merely a false assumption, becomes a reality. Men create the world in which they live by the methods they use to interpret it. . . .

Even the astute men of the British Colonial Office, classic imperialists though they are, are no exceptions to this involved process of self-deception. Indeed, after holding the Gold Coast in their complete power for decades, having had access to the entire life and customs of the people, they reacted until very recently to the beliefs of the Africans more or less on the same basis that the Africans themselves reacted.

For example, in March of 1900, Sir Frederic Hodgson, Colonial Secretary of the Gold Coast, addressing the King of Ashanti and his chiefs and aides, asked for the surrender of the Golden Stool in the following words:

". . . Where is the Golden Stool? Why am I not sitting on the Golden Stool at this moment? I am the representative of the paramount power; why have you relegated me to this chair? Why did you not take the opportunity of my coming to Kumasi to bring the Golden Stool, and give it to me to sit upon? . . ."

The Africans had sunk the harpoon of their own indigenous assumptions deep into the Englishman's heart! The Golden Stool, of course, was not a seat to be sat upon; not even the King of Ashanti did that. Says W. E. F. Ward, in his *A History of the Gold Coast,* (London: Allen and Unwin, 1948, p. 304): ". . . It [the Golden Stool] contained the soul of all Ashanti; and the Ashanti could no more produce it to be sat upon by a foreigner than a Christian bishop in the Dark Ages could be expected to invite a barbarian conqueror to feast off the communion plate at the high altar of his cathedral . . ."

It seemed that Sir Hodgson believed in the magic of the Golden Stool, that is, in the mystic power presumably inherent in its possession, as much as the poetic Africans did, and his rash demand brought war between the English and the Ashanti in its wake. . . .

It was in 1923 or thereabouts that Capt. R. S. Rattray, an English anthropologist, uncovered some of the complex meanings of the Akan rituals and ceremonies and gave English governors and civil

servants an inkling of the nature of the beliefs of the Akan people;
but, by the time that that knowledge had shed some belated clarity
upon the nature of Akan customs, Gold Coast lives and institutions
had been so mauled and truncated that the knowledge was all but
useless, and any *healthy* revivification of Akan customs in whole
or part was beyond hope.

The Ashanti, being thus conquered, had to dilute his indigenous
religious customs with Christian ones, had to pretend to be Christian in order to live and be left alone. . . . And the pattern of evasion,
doubt, and distrust was set.

Hence, no one was more surprised than the British, in 1948, at
the sudden and violent upsurge of nationalist feeling in the Gold
Coast, for it contradicted not only the observations of the trusted
civil servants on the spot, but its existence found no explanation or
support in British academic circles. Until the coming of Nkrumah,
the Gold Coast had been referred to as the "model colony," that
is, a place from which a fabulously high return could be gotten on
modest investments without a need to fear native unrest or reprisals.

Informal conversations with the Gold Coast Information Service
officials elicited the following facts: At the very moment when
Nkrumah was launching his positive action program that would
paralyze the economic life of the colony, a British professor of anthropology in London was briefing a group of civil servants bound
for the Gold Coast. He spoke to them somewhat as follows:

"The Gold Coast is a kind of colonial Eden. You'll find the natives
gentle, satisfied, and deeply grateful for what we have done for
them."

But when the shipload of civil servants docked at Takoradi, they
could hear gunfire raking the streets and they were informed that
violence had gripped the entire colony. . . . It seems that imperialists
of the twentieth century are men who are always being constantly
and unpleasantly surprised. The assumption of the inferiority of
the African, which gave the British the courage to conquer them,
was now the very assumption that stood in the way of their seeing
what was actually taking place. To enforce docility, they had

rammed down African throats religious assumptions which they themselves believed in more deeply than the Africans ever did, and the basic mood of the Africans, of course, always eluded them.

X V ...

One afternoon, after lunch, I walked down to the seashore where the stevedores were unloading freighters. I had to identify myself and get a pass before being allowed into the area where swarms of half-naked men were carting huge loads upon their heads. The nearer I got to the men, the more amazed I became. I paused, gazing.

Coming toward me was an army of men, naked save for ragged strips of cloth about their hips, dripping wet, their black skins glistening in the pitiless sun, their heads holding pieces of freight —parts of machines, wooden crates, sacks of cement—some of which were so heavy that as many as four men had to put their heads under them to carry them forward. Beyond these rushing and panting men, far out on the open sea, were scores of canoes, each holding twelve men who paddled like furies against the turbulent surf. Save for the wild beat of the sun upon the sand of the beach, a strange silence reigned over everything. I had the impression that the tense effort of physical exertion would not permit a man to spare enough breath to utter a word. . . .

The wet and glistening black robots would beach their canoes filled with merchandise and, without pausing, heave out the freight and hoist it upon their heads; then, at breakneck speed, rush out of the sea, stamping through soft, wet sand, and run; finally, they would disappear over a dune of sand toward a warehouse. They ran in single file, one behind the other, barely glancing at me as they pushed forward, their naked feet leaving prints in the soft sand which the next sea wave would wash away. . . . On the horizon of the sea, about two miles away, were anchored the European freighters and between the shore and those ships were scores of black dots—canoes filled with rowing men—bobbing and dancing on the heaving water.

Another canoe came toward the beach; the men leaped out, grabbed its sides to steady it until it touched the sand; again I saw that wild and desperate scrambling for the merchandise; again they lifted the boxes or crates or sacks or machine parts to their heads and came rushing toward me, their lips hanging open from sheer physical strain. My reactions were so baffled that I couldn't tell what I felt. What I saw was so useless, so futile, so inhuman that I didn't believe it; it didn't seem real. I felt no protest; I was simply stunned, feeling that someone had snatched back a curtain and I was contemplating half-human men as they had labored in the hot sun two thousand years ago with the threat of death or physical torture hanging over them. But I saw no whips or guns; a weird peace gripped the scene. . . .

The harbor here, I was told, was much too shallow to allow ships to dock; they could dock, of course, at Takoradi, 170 miles away, but that would mean that the various shipping companies would have to send their freight by rail to Accra. That was why this beastly work had to take place; it allowed a higher profit to be made on the merchandise.

Each of the twelve men in each canoe held a short, splayed oar with three prongs; each man had to dip and pull this oar through the water sixty times a minute if the canoe was to keep afloat and move through the raging current, and each stroke of each man had to plunge into the water at the same time. There were some children working too, but not in the canoes; they waited at the water's edge and helped their fathers or friends or brothers to lift the heavy loads to their heads.

Nearby was a young black clerk dressed in Western clothes; he held a sheet of paper in his hands, and, as each canoe came in, he checked it off. I went up to him.

"Do they make much money working like that?"

"Each boat earns twelve shillings a trip; that's a shilling for each man, sar."

"How many shillings can a man make a day?"

"If he works hard, sar, he can make seven."

"But why do they rush so?"

"It costs a ship a lot of money to stay out there, sar."

"When do they start work?"

"At daybreak. Not much sun then, sar."

"Do you have trouble finding workers?"

The young man looked at me and laughed. Then he turned and pointed to a far crowd of half-nude men huddled before a wooden stairway leading up to an office.

"Do you lose many men in the sea?"

"Oh, no, sar! Those men are like fishes, sar. But we do lose merchandise—the company and the ships can stand it, sar. They're insured. Oh, sar, if you saw the beautiful automobiles that go down in that sea—"

A man passed with a sack of something lumpy upon his head, running . . . .

"That looks like a sack of potatoes," I said.

"It is, sar."

"Why aren't they grown here?"

"I don't know, sar."

"Is seven shillings a day considered good pay?"

"Well, sar, for what they buy with it, it's not bad."

He wandered off, jotting down figures on his sheet of paper. I'd seen men tending machines in frantic haste, but I'd never seen men working like machines. . . . I'd seen River Rouge and it was nothing compared to this hot, wild, and hellish labor. It was not only against exploitation that I was reacting so violently; it frightened me because the men did not seem human, because they had voluntarily demeaned themselves to be spokes in a wheel.

I walked toward the exit, then paused and stared again at the fantastic scene, seeing it but not believing it. I felt no hate for the shipowners who had contrived that this should be; there was something here amiss deeper than cheating or profit. . . . My reactions were elementary; the ships could have remained at anchor until they rotted, I wouldn't have cared. There are circumstances in which human life is no longer human life, and I'd seen one of them. And for this particular barbarity I had no answer, no scheme; I would not have gone on strike if I had worked there; I simply would not have worked there in the first place, no matter what. . . .

I returned to my hotel and lounged in my room. Water seemed to stand in the air. I got up and went into the bathroom and picked up my nail file. Good God. . . . It had turned red. I looked farther. All the metal in my toilet kit was a deep, dark red. I rubbed my fingers across the metal and a soft mound of wet rust rolled up. What a climate. . . . What could last here? Suppose the Gold Coast was cut off from the Western world, for, say, ten years? Would not the material level of existence be reduced to that which existed before the coming of the white man? Practically nothing, under British colonial policy, was manufactured in the Gold Coast. Indeed, the only ostensible difference between the environmental conditions of the bourgeois blacks and the tribal blacks consisted in the possession by the upper-class blacks of a mass of imported British products in their homes. The British argument until now has been that the climate ruled out industrial production, but I was convinced that this was a British "rationalization" to keep down potential industrial competition. I was sure that if the British *had* to industrialize the Gold Coast, they would have found a way of doing it. . . . Until some effort was made to preserve metal against corrosion, this place was under a sentence of death. And I realized that whatever history was buried in this hot and wet earth must have long since decayed, melted back into the red and ravenous clay. No wonder that archeologists, no matter how long and earnestly they dig, could find little or nothing here. Throw the whole of Detroit into this inferno of heat and wetness, and precious little of it would be left in a hundred years.

Restless, I wander again into the streets and am struck by the incredible number of mere tots engaged in buying and selling. I've begun to feel that, as a whole, there is no period of "youth" here in Africa. Here, at one moment, one is a child; then, almost overnight, at the age of eight or ten, one assumes the status of an adult. Children toil at minding smaller children, cooking, carrying water on their heads, trading in the market place, assuming responsibilities long before the children of the West. Perhaps "youth" is a period of luxury which middle-class Westerners alone could give their children?

Maybe that was why one so seldom encountered what might be called "idealism" in Africa? Perhaps there was no time for dreaming—and how could one get the notion that the world could be different if one did not dream? Though the African's whole life was a kind of religious dream, the African scorned the word "dream." Maybe the plant of African personality was pruned too quickly, was forced to bear fruit before it had a chance to grow to its full height? What would happen to a romantic rebel in an African tribe? The African takes his religion, which is really a waking *dream,* for reality, and all other dreams are barred, are taboo.

In the late afternoon a rainstorm broke over the city; it had been threatening for some hours and when it did come, it came down with a violence that made you feel that some malevolent being was bent upon harm. Nature here acts with such directness, suddenness, that the mind, in spite of itself, projects out upon natural events animistic motives. After the first cloudburst the rain settled down to a long, steady downpour. The air was still; I could almost feel the moisture enter my lungs as I breathed. It was not until after ten o'clock that the sky cleared and the stars could be seen, distant, mingled with clouds.

Again I poked about the alleyways of James Town. Now that the rain had stopped, the gregarious natives were returning to the streets. At corners women were lighting candles and huddling themselves beside their piles of staples. Plantains were being dropped into cauldrons of boiling fat. Finding myself out of cigarettes, I paused in front of a woman.

"A can of cigarettes," I said, pointing.

She stared, then opened a can and took out one cigarette.

"No; I want to buy a can," I said.

She turned and called, summoning help. Cigarettes were sold in round tin cans of fifty each and they were vacuum-packed against the moisture. A young girl came; she and the woman chatted.

"No; she sell you *one.*" The girl was emphatic.

"Why won't she sell me a can?"

"She can't." Again she talked to the woman in tribal language, then she turned to me once more. "She sell can for one pound."

A tin can of cigarettes cost but seven shillings. Was she trying to cheat?

"That's too much," I protested.

"You can buy *three*; that's all," the girl said.

I finally understood the crisis that I'd brought into the woman's life. In this poverty-stricken area rarely did a native buy more than one cigarette at a time, and I had confronted her with a demand for fifty, which was wholesale business!

I pushed forward in the dark, down lanes of women sitting besides their boxes, their faces lit by flickering candles. As I strayed on I heard the sound of drums. Yes; I'd find them. . . . Guided by the throbbing vibrations, I went forward until I came to a vast concrete enclosure. The drums were beating behind that high wall. . . . Could I get in? I went around the wall until I came to a narrow opening. Discreetly, I peered through and saw, far back in the compound, a group of people dancing to drums; kerosene lanterns lit up the tableau. Ought I go in? They were black and so was I. But my clothes were different from theirs; they would know me for a stranger.

A young man came toward me; he was about to enter the compound. He paused and asked:

"What do you want?"

"Nothing," I said, smiling at him. "What's going on in there?"

"You're a stranger, aren't you?"

"Yes; I'm an American."

"Come on in," he said.

I followed him in, noticing as I passed a row of dim-lit rooms that in some rooms only men were seated and in others only women. . . . We came to a swirling knot of men and women; they were dancing in a wide circle, barefooted, shuffling to the demoniacal beat of the drums which were being pounded by a group of men near the wall. The ground was wet from the recent rain and their bare feet slapped and caressed the earth.

"Why are they dancing?" I asked the young man.

"A girl has just died," he told me.

There was no sadness or joy on their faces; they struck me as being people who had to go through with something and they were doing their job. Indeed, most of the faces seemed kind of absent-minded. Now and then some man or woman would leave the ring and dance alone in the center. They danced not with their legs or arms, but with their entire bodies, moving slowly, undulating their abdomens, their eyes holding a faraway look.

"Why are they dancing?" I asked again, recalling that I'd asked the same question before, but feeling that I hadn't had an answer.

"A young girl has just died, you see," he said.

I still didn't know why they were dancing and I wanted to ask him a third time. An old man came to me and shook my hand, then offered me a chair. I sat and stared. The lanterns cast black shadows on the wet ground as the men and women moved slowly to the beat of the drums, their hands outstretched, their fingers trembling. *Why are they dancing . . . ?* It was like watching something transpire in a dream. Still another young man came and joined the two who now flanked my chair. They mumbled something together and then the young man who had brought me in stooped and whispered:

"You'd better go now, sar."

I rose and shook hands with them, then walked slowly over the wet earth, avoiding the rain puddles. *Why are they dancing . . . ?* And their dancing was almost identical with the movements of the High Life dancing that I'd seen in the outdoor dance hall. . . . At the entrance I paused and looked back; I was surprised to see that the young man had discreetly followed me.

"You say that a young girl has died?"

"Yes, sar."

"And that's why they are dancing?"

"Yes, sar."

I shook his hand and walked into the damp streets, my eyes aware of the flickering candles that stretched to both sides of me. Jesus Christ, I mumbled. I turned and retraced my steps and stood again in the entrance to the compound and saw that the men and women were now holding hands as they circled round and round. The young man stood watching me. . . .

"Good night!" I called to him.

"Good night, sar!" he answered.

I walked briskly and determinedly off, looking over my shoulder and keeping in the line of my vision that dance; I stared at the circling men and women until I could see them no more. The women had been holding their hands joined together above the heads of the men, and the men, as though they had been playing London Bridge Is Falling Down, were filing with slow dignity through the handmade arches. The feet of the dancers had barely lifted from the ground as they shuffled; their bodies had made sharp angles as they moved and I had been surprised to see that they were moving much quicker than I had thought; they had given me the impression of moving slowly, lazily, but, at that distance, there was a kind of concentrated tension in their gyrations, yet they were utterly relaxed. I had been looking backward as I walked and then the young man pulled the wooden gate shut and it was gone forever. . . . I had understood nothing. I was black and they were black, but my blackness did not help me.

XVI...

One heard the word "palm" all day long; you were invited out for "palm chop," that is, a meal cooked with palm oil. Or you were offered a drink of palm wine or palm gin. I began inquiring into the uses to which the palm tree had been put, and here's what was revealed: The palm tree bears red berries called palm kernels which, if boiled and cracked open, yield a red and white oil. The red oil is used for cooking and the white oil for the making of many kinds of pomades, soap, etc. The red oil is called palm butter.

Many of the articles sold by the "mammies" on the streets are wrapped in palm leaves, and the plaited palm leaves are used in erecting fences and screens to keep out the prying eyes of strangers. Roofing of a sort is made from the leaves, and so are decorations, toys, and dishes. The stems of the palm leaves are used to make a short kind of broom with which the African women sweep their houses and yards.

When a palm tree is cut down, the heart of the palm is eaten and is considered a rare delicacy. Palm wine is made by fermenting the whitish fluid which the tree yields; also palm gin is made, though both palm wine and palm gin are declared illegal, for their alcoholic potency is considered dangerous to health. The tree's wood itself is used for fuel or building.

I sat at the table in the hotel's dining room, eating lunch, staring moodily out of the window. In the distance I saw a bright, shining object moving erratically. It looked like a brass pipe or pole; then I became aware that there was a mass of people clustered about the gleaming brass object. What could it be? Sounds of drums, of shouting, of shooting came to my ears. Was there a political disturbance? I rose and ran to the balcony; the mass of people was drawing near and the shooting and the drums sounded sharp and clear through the bright sunshine. A businessman, a German who stayed in the hotel, joined me.

"What is it?" I asked him.

"A funeral," he said. "And it's a big one. Must be for a chief."

"But why are they shooting?"

"They always do that. . . . Say, you'd better get your camera and go down—"

"Yes!" I said, tearing off to my room.

When I returned to the balcony, a wave of flowing robes, red, yellow, brown, scarlet, and russet was rolling down the street. Huge drums were being pounded by men who sweated and whose faces were tense. Men bearing vast red umbrellas marched and behind them came men holding red flags aloft, then more flags. Men and women came rushing madly from all directions. My eyes darted, trying to encompass the many things that were happening all at once. The men, dressed in red, formed a huge circle in a vacant lot and began firing the muskets they held. A funeral? How was that possible? It seemed more like an advertisement for a circus. Another round of firing into the air made a pall of light blue smoke drift over the field and the acrid scent of gunpowder smote my nostrils. The procession flowed on below me; then my eyes looked to the left. My mouth dropped open. A group of men bore aloft on their shoulders a brass coffin, gleaming and polished until it glittered in the sun. The coffin went round and round. . . .

"Is that really a coffin?" I asked the German.

"It sure is."

I was afraid that the coffin would fall and smash against the concrete pavement, but, evidently, the men had had long experience bearing whirling coffins on their heads and the coffin spun slowly, the men rushing with it seemingly at random from spot to spot. For example, they'd run to a corner, stop, twirl the coffin, then, amidst shouting, singing, chanting, they'd turn and race with the coffin spinning above their heads in another direction. . . .

I ran from the balcony; I had to see this at close range. Some ritual whose significance I could not understand was taking place. A thousand questions popped into my mind and no answers could even be imagined. I reached the street just as a young chief, borne aloft on a palanquin decorated in brightly colored silks, came by on the bare black shoulders of his carriers. Above him was the usual vast umbrella being twirled by a panting and sweating boy. Now the brass coffin came again, the black men running as they turned it round and round on their heads, and this time I noticed that in front of the men bearing the brass coffin was a half-nude woman, wearing a skirt made of raffia; she had a huge black fan made from feathers and she was swishing that fan through the air with hurried, frantic motions, as though trying to brush away something invisible. . . .

The parade or procession or whatever it was called was rushing past me so rapidly that I feared that I would not get the photograph I wanted; I lifted my camera and tried to focus and when I did focus I saw a forest of naked black breasts before my eyes through the camera sight. I took the camera from my eyes, too astonished to act; passing me were about fifty women, young and old, nude to the waist, their elongated breasts flopping loosely and grotesquely in the sun. Their faces were painted with streaks of white and sweat ran down their foreheads. They held in each of their hands a short stick—taken from packing boxes—and they were knocking these sticks furiously together, setting up an unearthly clatter, their eyes fixed upon the revolving coffin of brass. . . .

Then came another palanquin upon which sat a young boy about nine years old; his face was sad, solemn, and over him too was held a wide, spinning red umbrella. There followed a long stream of women dressed in native cloths, most of them bearing babies strapped tightly to their backs; they sang some weird song in staccato fashion. . . . Again came the turning coffin of brass and this time I noticed that it too had an umbrella of its own, that a man was rushing and trying to keep up with it, to hold the umbrella over it to shade it from the sun. . . .

The men in red were firing muskets again, and blue, thin rings of smoke hung in the sunlit air. I tried to keep up with the procession, but the men carrying the coffin changed their direction so abruptly and so often that I gave up and stood feeling foolish and helpless in the hot sun, sensing sweat streaming down my face.

I had understood nothing, nothing. . . . Why were they rushing so quickly and seemingly at random with that brass coffin? The funeral still flowed past me; there must have been five thousand people in it. I looked closer and saw that the faces of the women and children were marked with a reddish paint on the left cheek. . . . My mind reeled at the newness and strangeness of it. Had my ancestors acted like that? And why?

The men rushing with the turning coffin ran past me again and I stood aghast. I was nervous, feeling that maybe the poor dead man would fall out of the coffin, and I could imagine his being there jolted and bumped as they tossed the coffin round and round. . . .

These people were acting upon assumptions unknown to me, un-felt, inconceivable. Slowly I mounted the steps of the hotel and stood again on the balcony. The funeral was far away now, but I could still hear the vast throng shouting, the muskets firing, the women chanting. . . .

I found myself standing next to an African dressed in Western clothes.

"That's some funeral, all right," he said.

"But who's dead?" I asked.

"It's a chief," he told me.

"I can't understand it," I confessed.

"It's not simple," he said.

"Why do they fire those muskets?"

"Who knows? Some say that they got that firing of muskets from the Europeans during the fifteenth century," he said. "They have forgotten, maybe, just where they got it from."

"But the dead man, won't he fall out of that coffin?"

"There's no dead man in the coffin," he said.

"What? It's *empty*?" I asked, dumfounded. "Then why are they rushing about with it like that?"

"The coffin has the dead man's hair and fingernails in it," he explained. "The body is buried somewhere in secret, that is, after the brain has been taken out—"

"Why bury it in secret?"

"So no one will find it."

"But why would anyone want to find it?"

"Well, there are several reasons. . . . You see, a chief's body is sacred. . . . If somebody finds it, they can use it, take its power and use it—"

"Then why don't they stand guard over the body?"

"They've *got* to hide the body; they're hiding it from the man's spirit—"

"But the man's *dead*," I protested.

"Yes; but they claim that the man's spirit is hanging around, wanting to re-enter the body. . . . The spirit doesn't want to leave; you see? The body's the home of the spirit. If the spirit can't find its home, it'll keep on traveling—"

"And the man's brain. . . ? Why do they take the brain out of the skull and hide it?"

"Because they believe that the brain's the seat of the man's power. They hide the brain for fear that the dead man's enemies will get hold of it and take over the role that the dead man played in life. . . ."

"And the hair and fingernails in the coffin?"

"They are substitutes for the body. By putting the hair and finger-nails in the coffin, the spirit is fooled. When the spirit seeks the body and can't find it, it then finds the fingernails. . . . It knows then that the body is gone. . . ."

"And why were those women beating those sticks?"

"That's to scare the spirit on its way. . . . And to announce to the spirit world that the spirit is coming."

"And the running and twirling of the coffin? What does that mean?"

"It's the same thing. . . . It's a kind of farewell that they're giving to the dead man, you see. But they are trying to fool the spirit away at the same time. Now, they take the coffin, running with it, back to all the places in the city where the dead man had enjoyed him-self. The dead man is paying his last respects to his relatives, his friends, and so forth. Now, when they turn, change their direction, zigzag this way and that—that's to lose the spirit which is supposed to be trying to keep up with the body. The man's spirit, of course, will haunt the houses of the man's friends. So, when they rush up like that, spin the coffin, and then rush off, going from left to right, the spirit becomes confused. . . . You understand?"

Yes; if you accepted the assumptions, all the rest was easy, logi-cal. The African's belief in the other world was concrete, definite. If there was another world, then the African was about the only man really believing in it; and if there was no other world, then one could maintain an attitude of indifference toward the idea. But if there was one, then evidently one should do something about it. The African sincerely believed that there was another world and he was desperately trying to do something about it.

The tropic night fell suddenly and there was complete darkness; then, after a bit, the sky turned a pale, whitish color and the moon came out, a glowing yellow sphere. My room was damp, hot; I tried to sleep, my mind filled with tumbling brass coffins. I awakened the next morning feeling more fatigued than when I had gone to bed.

It was Sunday and the idea occurred to me to visit a Christian church and see, for the sake of contrast, how the followers of

Jesus behaved themselves. The word "pagan" was beginning to have a real meaning for me now; it was against these desperate pagans that St. Paul had fought. . . . I could understand a Christian service; I knew its assumptions. In my wanderings I'd seen a Wesleyan Methodist church and I was determined to go there.

The service was under way as I entered rather timidly. I didn't know if they had any special rules or not, so I stood discreetly at the back. A preacher was talking in a tribal tongue, quietly, with no gestures, no passion. To my astonishment the congregation was segregated: men sat on one side and women on another; young boys sat together and young girls did the same.

An usher showed me to a seat. I saw that the congregation wore their native clothes. The church was built of stone, but it had no panes in the windows; there was no need for any, for it never got cold here. The interior of the church was dim and I noticed that the ears of the women glowed softly with gold earrings. What a contrast to paganism! At the forefront of the church was the Cross, the symbol of Christianity, just as the Golden Stool was the symbol of the Akan religion. I recalled that frenzied pagan funeral I'd seen and I was kind of surprised that Protestant religion still existed. There was no fierce joy here, no dread, no anxiety; everything was taken for granted. The preacher's voice droned on sedately, mildly. If religion partakes of the terror stemming from the proximity of human life to eternity, to an absolute otherness, then there was, by a hell of a long shot, much more genuine religion in that barbaric pagan funeral than I could feel in this quiet, bourgeois Christian church!

The choir rose and sang and I was disappointed. There was none of that snap and zip (and a little sexual suggestiveness!) which American Negroes manage to inject into their praises to God. The tones and volumes fell flat, and the singing was namby-pamby, singsongy, nasalized. The mood of their worship was a longing to be socially correct, and I felt that it was a crime to take a vital and earthy people like these and thwart and blunt their instincts—instincts which they sorely needed in their struggle to live against the odds of nature *and* the British! Even though the men and the women wore their native clothes, it was easy to see that they were striving to be middle class. Why was it that Christians always seemed to have money and comfort, when the symbol of Christ, half naked and bleeding on the Cross, evoked a sense of suffering in the world?

Being areligious myself, I preferred the religion I looked at to be interesting, with some of the real mystery, dread, and agony of existence in it. I'd much rather have heard the kind of singing that Paul Laurence Dunbar described in his poem: *"When Malindy Sings"*:

> *She just opens her mouth and hollers,*
>   *"Come to Jesus," 'til you hear*
> *Sinners' trembling steps and voices*
>   *Timidlike a-drawing near;*
> *Then she turns to "Rock of Ages,"*
>   *Simply to the Cross she clings,*
> *And you find your tears a-dropping*
>   *When Malindy sings.*

But that Gold Coast hymn evoked in me merely a cough of embarrassment behind my cupped palms. . . .

Of course, the pastor no doubt would have unctiously told me that there was no need now to suffer, that Christ had felt it all for us, had suffered the supreme penalty and had set us free by an act of grace. But was there not somewhere in such a rationalization a sneaking evasion, a dodge? How the Christians had their cake and ate it too! O poor pagans who lived the naked terror of life, spurning all the symbolic substitutions, without steady incomes, without comfortable clothes! They had no Christ to die for them; they had to sweat and suffer it all. My sympathies were with the pagans; the pagan was my kind of a Christian, the kind that the Christians hated and feared. . . .

I left the church and got out into the sinful streets where naked little boys confronted you, begging for pennies. It would be to these that the future would have to look, these whose souls had not been stunted, whose sense of earthly pride had not been intimidated, and in whom the will to live still burned with undiminished fervor.

Religion has been only one aspect of the means by which the Gold Coast has been maintained as a captive nation for more than a hundred years. Just as the early Portuguese traders had sought to keep out sundry strangers, so the British have not been unmindful of stray foreigners or alien ideas knocking about in a domain so rich in gold. This isolation of even the Gold Coast intellectuals from the currents of modern thought has kept them from realizing how universal were their predicaments. With the exception of Nkrumah, the actions of their politicians were not informed by lessons drawn from other peoples and other countries; and, until the coming of Nkrumah, there was no attempt on the part of the British government officials to dramatize or publicize local events and enlist the comment or scrutiny of interested outsiders.

Another means by which the Gold Coast African had been led astray was by the British insistence, almost to the point of absurdity, upon the highest possible academic standards and qualifications for all kinds of work. This in itself, of course, was not at all bad; but the manner in which it was used was more a means of control than a means of enlightenment. Prior to 1948, education in the Gold Coast was not even remotely related to practical accomplishment or functional efficiency, or even to a comprehensive grasp of life; it smacked more of status, manners, class standing, "character," and form. . . . The African leaving Oxford or Cambridge found all doors in Africa open to him; in an illiterate society, he was at once at the top of the heap; he did not have to accomplish anything to merit his position; it was his by right of his having absorbed certain acceptable qualifications. . . . Education therefore assumed a kind of religious tone capable of conferring upon its devotees, like the act of conversion, all the boons of life, of civilization. The result was that the psychological distance between the educated and uneducated became almost absolute in character, and among the illiterates there developed an attitude toward education that reeked of yearning, of pathos, of a ludicrous waiting. . . .

Conditioned to give as little of himself as possible when working for the British, living amidst a prodigious jungle abounding in great heat and humidity, the Gold Coast African has never been too strong an advocate of manual labor; and the British stress of "education" and "qualification" tended to reinforce in him the feeling that the most humiliating thing that could possibly happen to him was that he would have to work with his hands for a living. One of the first lessons that Nkrumah had to drive home was that technical education was not only respectable, but that it was one of the indispensable conditions for national freedom.

Of the value of the teachings of the missionaries as a technique of colonial control, Mr. W. E. G. Sekyi, president of the Aborigines' Rights Protection Society, said explicitly:

"I've no way of telling what the average individual missionary was thinking when he preached his white paganism to us. All I can tell you is that such teaching and preaching supplemented and complemented the schemes of the merchants and the men of the colonial office. Its effect was to break the military traditions of our tribes. The missionaries used to inveigh against 'Black Christmases,' human sacrifices, etc., but they knew that our society was one organic whole, and that if you broke one part of our customs, you influenced them all. Their aim was to destroy our capacity for self-defense. Wherever the seeds of the Christian doctrine fell, the will to resist was weakened. And the missionary was careful in propounding his 'glad tidings' to us; he never went so far as to instruct us in regard to the concrete steps that we could take to become self-sufficient. His propositions dealt with the soul and obedience. Always he stopped short of imparting that kind of information that would lead to activities that made for self-reliance and the independence of our people. . . ."

XVII...

My money is melting under this tropic sun faster than I am soaking up the reality about me. For two days now I've moped about my hotel room with no visitors or telephone calls. In the newspapers are items telling of monster mass meetings, of vast educational rallies; I'd have liked to have attended those events, but I hear of them only after they have taken place. My frequent visits to the Convention People's Party's headquarters do not elicit any information about what is transpiring, and I cannot escape the feeling that my seeking information has somewhat frightened the African politicians.

I'm of African descent and I'm in the midst of Africans, yet I cannot tell what they are thinking and feeling. And, without the help of either the British or the Africans, I'm completely immobilized. Africa sprawls far inland and my walking jaunts about Accra are no way to see this life. Yet, I cannot just take a train or a bus and go; the more I ask about jungle conditions, the more I'm dismayed. The general state of affairs in the country is not conducive to the safety of wandering tourists. There are but few hotels in Accra, Takoradi, and Kumasi, and their accommodations are of a sort to discourage the heartiest of travelers. Trekking into the interior can only be done with the aid and consent of the government, for, without it, one does not have access to the government resthouses that are stationed at intervals in the jungle. Beyond that, one must depend upon the willingness of the Africans or the British to put one up in their private homes! This does not mean that the British would forbid anyone's going off alone into the jungle to trust his luck, if he was fool enough to want to do it. . . . Neither do I say that this has been expressly arranged; it just works that way.

Each time I entered a store, the Indian or Greek or Syrian merchant wanted an account of my opinions. I suspect that my attitude caused a lot of background talk, for my reactions were open and direct and I could not order them otherwise. When something struck me as being strange, I erupted with questions; when something seemed funny, I laughed; and when I was curious, I dived headlong to uncover the obscurities. . . . Moreover, being obviously of African descent, I looked like the Africans, but I had only to walk upon a scene and my difference at once declared itself without a word being spoken. Over and above these liabilities, I had a background steeped in Communism, yet I was no Communist.

My thought processes were of interest even to the British banker who cashed my travelers' checks.

"Well, sir, what do you think of all this?" he asked me.

"You know, I've only been here a few days," I tried to evade him.

"I mean, don't you think that the people are happy?"

"I've seen so little—"

"Don't you think that we've done a lot for them?"

"I haven't seen very much of life here yet," I stalled.

He knew damn well what I thought, but I was determined not to give him the satisfaction of letting him hear me say it. He leaned forward as he spoke and his tone was low, urgent, confidential:

"You American chaps are three hundred years ahead of these Africans. It'll take a long time for them to catch up with you. *I* think that they are trying to go too fast, don't *you*? You see, you American chaps are used to living in a white man's country, and these fellows are not."

In his attempt to influence my attitude, he was using the old tried and trusted British technique of divide and rule.

"I don't know about that," I said, smiling at him.

He counted out my pound notes through the barred window.

"Thank you," I said.

"Good morning, sir," he sang out.

"So long," I said.

There was no room for jockeying or making tactical moves in a colony; the European was at close grips with the native who was trapped in the European net of trade and religion. Every casual remark of the dubious stranger had an implied bearing upon policy. Whether you danced or not, whether you were interested in a given scene or not, whether you laughed or not—all of these items were weighed, examined, and filed away in the minds of the upper-class African or British civil servant. A sort of living dossier was kept on you: what you said casually at Mr. So-and-so's luncheon table was discreetly and questioningly served up to you at Mrs. So-and-so's dinner table on the evening of the same day. It was check and double-check.

So far my random observations compel me to the conclusion

that colonialism develops the worst qualities of character of both the imperialist and his hapless victim. The European, on duty five hundred miles from the Equator, in the midst of heat and humidity, can never really feel at home and the situation breeds in him a kind of hopeless laziness, a brand of easygoing contempt for human life existing in a guise that is strange and offensive to him. Outnumbered, he feels safe only when surrounded by men of his own race and color. Since, for questions of policy, he cannot live with the native, he develops an indifference for the land that grows the food. *His* food is transported over vast distances and at great cost for which the native must pay in the form of taxes. Hence, the European tries without success to convince himself that he is worth all of this bother and care, but he never quite can. His basic concerns are centered upon the wealth of the country, upon doing his job so that no crass criticisms will be heaped upon his head. The social setting produces a chronic suspiciousness about the ultimate meanings of the most ordinary ideas and remarks of the natives, and there is a continuous undertow of concern about the possibility of the native's developing a mood of rebellion, for, at bottom, no matter how jaunty the European pretends to be, he cannot rid himself of the idea that what he and his kind are doing is stealing. . . .

And the native, when he looks at the white man looming powerfully above him, feels contradictory emotions struggling in his heart; he both loves and hates him. He loves him because he sees that the white man is powerful, secure, and, in an absentminded and impersonal sort of way, occasionally generous; and he hates him because he knows that the white man's power is being used to strip him slowly of his wealth, of his dignity, of his traditions, and of his life. Seeing that there is nothing that he can do about it, he loses faith in himself and inwardly quakes when he tries to look into the future in terms of white values that are as yet alien to him. Charmed by that which he fears, pretending to be Christian to merit white approval, and yet, for the sake of his own pride, partaking of the rituals of his own people in secret, he broods, wonders, and finally loses respect for his own modest handicrafts which now seem childish to him in comparison with the mighty and thunderous machinery of the white man.

In the end his own land lies fallow, his skills waste away, and he begins to prefer menial jobs with white families which will enable him to buy tinned food shipped from Europe. He no longer fishes for herring; he buys them in a can; he no longer burns local fats; he depends upon kerosene; he abandons his weaving and buys cloth from Lancashire; he goes to mass and learns to cross himself, and then he goes to the Stool House to propitiate the spirits of his long-departed ancestors.

This afternoon, after taking a nap, I went upon the veranda to escape the humidity of my room. A young African boy was there, wrapped and bundled in his cloth, stretched upon a bench; he glanced at me, then leaped quickly to his feet and hurried off. He turned his head and stared at me as he went around a bend of the veranda. . . . Why had he been so apprehensive? I sat and looked about; the veranda was empty. I had forgotten my cigarettes and went inside my room to fetch them; when I returned the young African was there upon the bench again. Seeing me, he rose at once and walked quickly off. There was no doubt about it; he was afraid. . . . He had thought that I was a European and would be offended at his presence. But what could I say to him? Merely to speak to him might well frighten him even more. . . .

XVIII...

I decided to try something on my own; I'd rent a taxi and start making short trips out of the city and into the neighboring villages. Good God, whoever heard of seeing Africa by taxicab?

I knew that barging out into tribal villages alone in a taxicab was rash. Being alone and with no knowledge of the language, I'd miss a lot that I'd want to know, but, being alone, unannounced, with no guide or interpreter, I'd catch the native African without warning; he would have no chance to dress up or pretend; the chiefs would have no opportunity to get out those big and ridiculous umbrellas. The idea appealed to me.

Wearing a sun helmet and a T-shirt, with a camera slung over my shoulder, I ambled out to a line of waiting taxis at the hotel entrance. The drivers began honking their horns, trying to attract my attention. I went to an elderly man, feeling that he would think twice before trying any tricks or cheating. . . .

"What's the nearest village that's worth looking at?"

"Don't know, Massa."

"You know some villages. You live here, don't you?"

He scratched his head and eyed me speculatively.

"There's Labadi, Massa."

"What kind of a village is it and how far is it?"

"Three miles, Massa. It's where the beach is. . . . And they fish there. Cost you two pounds, Massa."

"What do you think I am?"

He guffawed and his eyes avoided me.

"Three shilling an hour and one shilling a mile, Massa."

"All right," I agreed. "Let's go."

Labadi lay athwart the highway to Tema, the big port that was under construction. The driver raced along with a carelessness that made me wonder if he saw the cars coming in the opposite direction. Before I knew it, he was pulling up alongside rows of wooden huts with rusty tin roofs.

"Labadi, Massa."

"Lock your car and come with me," I ordered him, expecting him to demur. But he didn't. I found that that was the only way to get any consideration out of a native; he'd been conditioned by the British to being ordered and would obey only when ordered.

Labadi was a small fishing village and was a mixture of the primitive and the modern. The houses that fronted the highway were mostly of wood or cement, but when I poked behind them I came across the usual mud hut crowned with thatched straw. I walked as though I knew where I was going and the taxi driver followed me.

"Massa know somebody here?"

"No. Why?"

"Better see chief, Massa," he advised me.

"Why?"

"Always see chief, Massa."

"Where is the chief?"

"Don't know, Massa."

I knew that his counsel was sound, but I decided to ignore it. I pushed on and saw compounds alive with black men, women, and children. They glanced up at me, pausing in pounding their *fufu*, grinding pepper, or mending fish nets. Sheep, goats, turkeys, guinea hens, and pigs mingled with the naked, dirty children. Here the women did not bother to cover their breasts; they must have thought that I was an African schoolteacher or some government worker. I walked down winding paths bordered by tall weeds.

"Any snakes around here?"

"Yasa, Massa. Snakes all round here—"

I paused, hearing a droning, dashing sound.

"Is that the sea I hear?"

"Yasa, Massa."

I headed for the sea, not knowing where I was going, but not wanting to give the impression that I was wandering. I noticed that the men stared at me long after I had passed. Then suddenly, a voice yelled:

"Hey, sar!"

I turned and a brown-skinned boy ran up to me.

"Where're you going, sar?"

His voice had a hard, direct quality. He confronted me with purpose.

"I'm just looking around," I said.

"Oh," he said, studying me. "Are you an American, sar?"

"That's right."

"Oh, sar. What do you want to see?"

"First, I want a drink of coconut milk from one of these coconuts on that tree," I said.

He was taken aback for a moment, then he turned to one of the crowd of men who had gathered behind him. He spoke to them in

his tribal language and one of the boys ran toward a coconut tree
and scaled it, monkeylike.

"Where did you learn such good English?" I asked him.

"At missionary school, sar," he said proudly.

"Do you work?"

"Yes, sar. I'm an electrician," he said.

A mass of shy black children began crowding about. Playfully,
without attempting to take a picture, I pointed the lens of the
camera at a boy and he shuddered, burst into tears, and ran off
screaming.

"What happened to him?" I asked the young electrician.

"Nothing, sar. He's just scared."

"How many people are in this village?"

"I don't know, sar."

"You live here?"

"Yes, sar. With my mother and father."

I noticed that many of the children's entire heads were gripped
with sores and that yellow matter streamed from their eyes.

"What are those sores on their heads?" I asked.

"Yaws, sar," came the prompt reply.

"Are many of them like that?"

"Yes, sar. Most all of them, sar."

"Are they being treated?"

"They are talking about it, sar."

"How many babies die here during the first year of their lives?"

"I don't know, sar."

(I was afterward informed, in Accra, that the infant mortality
rate was more than 50 per cent during the first year of life.)

"What's your nationality?" I asked him.

"Fanti," he said proudly. "Oh, sar, here's your coconut."

"Aren't you a Gold Coast man?" I asked pointedly, accepting
the coconut. "Thank you. . . ."

He grinned at me; he knew what I meant. At no time did I hear
an African identify himself as other than belonging to a tribe. It
was only after I had prodded him that he would identify himself
as a Gold Coast citizen. They wanted their country to be free, but

the idea of a national identification was too new to have sunk home in their minds so that they could give an automatic reply.

"What's your profession, sar?" he asked me.

"I'm a writer," I said.

"You write for the newspapers, sar?"

"Sometimes. But mostly I write books."

"Do you think somebody in America would give me a scholarship, sar?"

"Perhaps; but you have schools here."

"But I want to go to America, sar."

"What makes you think they give scholarships in America?"

"They're rich, sar."

"I was born there and nobody ever gave me one," I told him.

He stared, then looked off. He turned to me with a timid smile.

"But you are rich, sar; aren't you?"

"No. I'm not. I was born as poor or maybe poorer than you are now," I told him. "I'm not rich."

"But you went to a university, sar?"

"No."

"Then how did you become a writer, sar?"

"Because I wanted to be a writer."

He could not understand that. He yearned for an education, but he did not associate personal will with it. He felt that only the generosity of somebody else could open the door to education for him.

"You can study right here in Labadi and be anything you want to," I told him.

He shook his head and smiled doubtfully.

"What kind of mission school did you attend?"

"Methodist, sar."

"Did you like your teachers?"

"Yes, sar. They were very kind."

"May I see where you live?"

"Oh, yes, sar," he said eagerly. "Come along, sar."

I told the taxi driver to go back to his car. I followed the boy, and a swarm of black children trailed eagerly after me. We went past stagnant lagoons that stood but a few yards from thatched mud huts.

"There are a lot of mosquitoes here, aren't there?"

"Oh, yes, sar."

"Why don't they fill in these lagoons?"

He stared a moment before answering. I suspected that the reason was that some god was connected with the lagoons. . . .

"I don't know, sar," he said.

"Is there much malaria and yellow fever here?"

"Yes, sar. We have it all the time. But there's not so much right now."

I noticed that the children's bellies looked like taut, black drums, so distended were they. Almost every child, boys as well as girls, had monstrous umbilical hernias. We came to a broad lagoon across which a few rotting logs had been placed as a bridge. He walked surefootedly across and I hung back, going slowly, balancing myself. The children, for some reason, stopped at the water's edge. We skirted a small pond in which men and women were bathing, their black skins streaked with white lather.

"Tell me, in school did they tell you not to worship fetish?"

"Oh, yes, sar," he said, his eyes round with seriousness.

"And if they caught you doing fetish, what did they do?"

"They whipped you, sar."

"And would they put you out of school for it?"

"No, sar. I don't think they ever do that."

"Your family—Is everybody Christian?"

"We're all Christians, sar," he said emphatically.

We were now passing between swish houses. The yards were of red clay and clean-swept. Women sat pounding that inevitable *fufu*. . . . I paused and watched a mother dart her black and gnarled fingers in and out of a huge wooden mortar into which her daughter rammed a long wooden pole, pounding boiled yams, cassava, plantains. They both looked at me and smiled; the daughter glanced down each time she sent the end of the pole plunging into the soft, yellowish mass of *fufu;* but the mother, confident that her hand would never be crushed, stared at me and then burst into a laugh, hanging her head.

"How many times a day do they make this *fufu*?" I asked.

"In the middle of the day and at night, sar."

"Now, look—you are an electrician. Why don't you invent a machine to pound that stuff?"

His mouth dropped open and he stared at me, then he tossed back his head and laughed.

"I'm serious," I said.

He spoke hurriedly to the two women and they laughed so heartily that they had to abandon their work. The daughter lifted her cloth to her mouth and yelled, then ran away, laughing hysterically. But the mother quickly grew solemn; her supper was being delayed. She called sternly to her daughter and the pounding began again, but the daughter continued to giggle.

"What are they laughing at?" I asked the electrician.

"They say machines can't make *fufu*, sar," he told me.

"Do you believe that?" I asked him.

It was evident that he did believe it, but he was too polite to want to contradict a stranger.

"You'll have to believe it before you can invent the machine," I told him. "We make bread in America with machines."

"Really, sar?"

"Of course. And *you* can make *fufu* with a machine," I said.

There was silence. I felt that it would be a long, long time before machines made *fufu* here. It was not that the young electrician could not make the machine, but I felt that the women would surely have had none of it. . . . Making *fufu* with a machine would have been the work of evil spirits. As we moved along, the boy was pensive. I turned and tried imitating that queer, African hand wave and the people waved back at me, smiling, their fingers trembling. Women passed, carrying those huge tins of water on their heads, their necks straight, their eyes proud, somber, and bold, and their lips ready to give vent to an embarrassed giggle. Yet no movement of their bodies so much as caused a tremor of the huge tins of water, which must have weighed thirty pounds. . . .

We were passing a magnificent woman who sat nursing a fat black baby. The long red rays of the setting sun lit her ebony torso to a soft distinctness. I requested the boy to ask her to let me take a picture. He spoke to her and she nodded her head.

"Penny, Massa," she said, extending her hand.

I fished a shilling out of my pocket and gave it to her. She rose, laughed. I tried to focus my camera and she lunged past me, holding the baby with one hand under its belly, and made a beeline for the mud hut; she was out of sight before I could utter a word. A howl of black laughter echoed through the compound. I stood looking like a blundering fool. She had outwitted me. I laughed too. She had won.

I walked past compounds filled with black life, naked, dirty, diseased, shy, friendly, curious. . . . Was it possible that Great Britain had had the power to rule here for 104 years? Three generations had passed and things were like this? Obviously, no one had really tried to do anything. I felt that these people could have created conditions much better than this if they had been left completely alone. It couldn't have been worse. Yet, from the soil of these people had come an untold fortune in gold, diamonds, timber, manganese, bauxite. . . . Truly, Nkrumah had a job to do. . . .

We reached the top of a hill and I stared down at a cluster of compounds. The sky was gradually darkening, but there was still enough sun to light up the black bodies, to make the rusty tin roofs distinct, and to outline the sleepy lagoons. And suddenly I was self-conscious; I began to question myself, *my* assumptions. I was assuming that these people had to be pulled out of this life, out of these conditions of poverty, had to become literate and eventually industrialized. But why? Was not the desire for that mostly on *my* part rather than *theirs?* I was literate, Western, disinherited, and industrialized and I felt each day the pain and anxiety of it. Why then must I advocate the dragging of these people into my trap?

But suppose I didn't? What would happen then? They would remain in these slavelike conditions forever. . . . The British would continue to suck their blood and wax fat. Of that there was no doubt. Yet, there was an element of sheer pride in my wanting them to be different. With what godlikeness we all thought of the lives of others! I yearned for them to break away from this and master machines, dig the minerals out of the earth, organize themselves, grow strong, sovereign. . . . And why? So that the British would not exploit them, so that they could stand equal with others and not be ashamed to face the world. I wanted them to redeem themselves. . . .

But was not this, my yearning for them, predicated upon the premises of the British? Was it merely for that that I wanted their lives changed, their beings altered? Well, their lives had been already altered; the faith of their fathers had been taken from them. True, they'd not been admitted into the world that had decreed that their past lives had not been good, and they had played no part in the world that had condemned theirs as being bad. And their participation in that world was what I was hungering for. . . . Why? Was it just my pride? Just to show the British that these people could do what the British had done. . . ?

But, if not that, then what? I didn't know.

I brooded over the young electrician who walked ahead of me. In that boy lay answers to questions. But could he tell me what he felt?

"Look, you want your country to be free, don't you?"

"Oh, yes, sar," he answered, amazed that I should ask.

"Did the missionaries ever tell you to dedicate your life to freeing your country?"

He looked at me thoughtfully, then shook his head.

"No, sar."

"But they taught you to read, didn't they?"

"Yes, sar."

"And after they had taught you to read, you read, didn't you? And when you read you found out that the British had taken your country? Is that it?"

"I think so, sar," he said slowly and evasively. "I know the history of my country, sar. We were conquered."

"Did the missionaries ever tell you that you were conquered?"

"No, sar."

"Did they ever tell you to fight for your freedom?"

"They didn't talk about that, sar."

"But the reading that they taught you, you used it to learn about freedom, didn't you?" I hammered at him.

He was beginning to understand. He had understood it before I spoke to him about it, but he had just never put it into words, into ideas.

"We'll be free some day, sar. We'll drive them *all* out," he said grimly, under his breath.

His footsteps had slowed. His eyes were wide and unblinking. Over and over again I found that same reaction: the Gold Coast African loved the white missionaries as long as he thought of them in the category of their teaching him to read and write, but when the same reading and writing brought home to him a knowledge of what the British had done to him, a knowledge of how his country and his culture had been shattered and exploited, he felt a rising tinge of resentment against the missionaries. Unwittingly, the missionaries had placed themselves in a strange position, a delicate position in the minds of the African people. Toward the European missionaries the African held that somewhat ambivalent attitude of love and hate that he held toward almost everything Western. It was easy to love and hate at the same time, but it was hard to talk about it.

When we came to his home, which was a tin-roofed swish house whose outer walls had been covered with a coating of cement, he introduced me to his mother, then to his grandfather, an old man who was partly blind. His father—the boy was almost tearful about it—was absent. I stood and waited, for no one spoke English but the boy.

"Who makes the money to pay the bills?" I asked.

"My father and I work, sar," he said.

I longed to go inside the house and look at the rooms, but I felt that I would have been trespassing. One room, he told me, was a kitchen in which his mother washed and cooked when it rained; otherwise, she worked out of doors. I saw that she had finished her *fufu* and it was laid out in earthen dishes in round yellow balls covered with palm leaves. Everything was neat here; all tools and utensils could be accounted for. The little short broom —made from the veins of palm leaves—was lying against a wall near a pile of rubbish. The *fufu*-pounder—I never did learn the name for it—was washed and lying atop the tin roof. Zinc washtubs were turned upside down in one corner of the yard. Nearby was an orderly okra patch. Farther out was a garden of tomatoes which had not yet begun to ripen and each plant was tied to a stake driven into the earth.

"How old is your grandfather?"

"Seventy-eight, sar."

"Have you any brothers and sisters?"

"No, sar."

"Just you, your mother, father and grandfather?"

"Yes, sar."

"What kind of electrical work do you do?"

"I'm an apprentice, sar."

"And what do you make?"

"£2. 10/- a month, sar."

"Is that all?"

"Yes, sar. And I pay 15*s*. a month for transportation, sar."

I wanted to stay here and learn this life, to feel it, to try to find out the values that kept it going. But I didn't like prying out the details. The African had been violated often enough in the dark past. And I had a taxi waiting. The light of the sky was growing darker.

"Your grandfather, does he remember a lot of history?"

The grandfather was consulted; when he understood what I had asked, he laughed loudly and nodded his woolly head. The boy translated:

"He says, sar, that he's seen a lot of things. Wars and fighting, sar."

"You've been very kind," I told the boy.

I gave him some shillings and shook hands all around. I started back toward the taxi.

"I'll come with you, sar."

The compounds were noisier now; it seemed in Africa that the days were quiet, but, as night drew on, a clamor set in, increasing as the hours passed. Even the children, who had been somewhat listless all day, now began their games. Was this because of the heat?

"Tell me: is there any difference in the way the pagans and the Christians live?" I asked the young electrician.

"I don't understand, sar."

"Do pagans and Christians live together? Or separately?"

"Oh, we all live together, sar."

"How does one tell a Christian from a pagan?"

He was silent for a moment, looking at me, puzzled.

"We all live together, sar. Christians go to church on Sundays—"

"Do *you* follow pagan ceremonies?"

"Oh, no, sar!"

"But when you have holidays, you enjoy them with the pagans, don't you?"

"Yes, sar. We do that, sar."

I walked slowly beside the boy in the dying light. The swish houses of the landscape were now bathed in soft purple shadows. A candle flickered here and there. So this was the White Man's burden that England had been so long complaining about? How cleverly the whole thing had been explained to the outside world! How wrapped up and disguised in morality had this lust for gold become!

"Sar, perhaps you could come and see my father?" the boy asked me shyly.

I promised him that I would try. When we reached the roadway he was a little downcast that I was leaving him.

"Study hard," I told him.

"Yes, sar," he said.

I could see the wistful smile on his shy, tight little brown face as my taxi pulled off into the deepening night.

Well, paganism and Christianity were all mixed up, blended. It seemed that being a Christian didn't mean giving up all of one's former outlook. Then I wondered how a pagan could really surrender all of his paganism when the community in which he lived was still basically pagan. It was a halfway world, all right. There were in both religions elements that the people needed in their lives; the only way paganism could really vanish would be for the total pagan environment to be transformed, and that was manifestly impossible. It would have been demanding of the pagan something that even the Christian had not demanded of himself.

The more I reflected upon the work of the missionaries, the more stunned I became. They had, prodded by their own neurotic drives, waded in and wrecked an entire philosophy of existence of a people without replacing it, without even knowing really what they had been doing. Racial pretensions had kept them from sharing intimately the lives of the people they had wanted to lift up. Standing outside of those lives, they had thrust their doctrines into them, gumming them up, condemning them, and yet they had failed to embrace those pagans who had turned Christian and who now yearned so pathetically to follow them into their world. . . .

What would happen when the native began to realize all of this clearly? Some were already doing so, and they felt a deep and sullen anger that was almost speechless in its intensity. I recalled Nkrumah's having told me with suppressed emotion that the missionaries had been his first political adversaries.

For centuries this sugared duplicity had held forth; and, because there were so many European national philosophies to justify it, so many European interests involved in it, there had been no one to come forward and call the deed by its right name. Indeed, so intertwined was Christianity with this getting of gold and diamonds that it was not until now that any real crime has been felt—and even by a *very* few—to have been committed! In Sunday schools all over the Western world little boys and girls were giving their pennies to help save the "soul of the heathen"!

Yet, as I saw and felt it, the looting of the country of gold and diamonds and slaves had not been the greatest crime that had been committed against these people. Diamonds have no great value when weighed in the scales against human life; and gold, though it figured symbolically in the Akan religion, could be done without and the Akan people haven't suffered mortally from losing it.

The gold can be replaced; the timber can grow again, but there is no power on earth that can rebuild the mental habits and restore that former vision that once gave significance to the lives of these people. Nothing can give back to them that pride in themselves, that capacity to make decisions, that organic view of existence that made them want to live on this earth and derive from that living a sweet even if sad meaning. Today the ruins of their former culture, no matter how cruel and barbarous it may seem to us, are reflected in timidity, hesitancy, and bewilderment. Eroded personalities loom here for those who have psychological eyes to see.

And even when, as Nkrumah's valiant efforts are directed now, they did finally rebel and strive to throw off the psychological shackles of foreign misrule, they were compelled to attempt it in terms of the values and on the moral grounds of their conquerors . . . ! In a certain sense, even if the Gold Coast actually won its fight for freedom (and it seems that it can!), it could never really win. . . . The real war was over and lost forever!

I do not say that the impact of the missionary was deliberately made to coincide with the military and commercial conquering of the Gold Coast people, or that the missionary was a conscious hand-maiden in subjecting them to the yoke of economic imperialism. Frankly, I doubt if the oldtime English mercantile pirates were that smart or foreseeing. Their aims, I suspect, were much more limited when they struggled so desperately for a foothold on the Guinea Coast.

However synchronized or not were the motives of the missionaries with those of the imperial financial interests, their actions could not have been more efficient in inflicting lasting psychological damage upon the personalities of the Africans who, though outwardly submissive, were never really deeply converted to a Christianity which rendered them numb to their own dearly bought vision of life, to the values for which they had made untold sacrifices.

XIX...

My next taxi sortie took me to Tema where a modern port was being built. The government, I was told, has great plans for the transformation of this all too sodden place.

I got out of the taxi and threaded my way between dark yellow swish huts with thatched roofs. The fishermen had just brought in a huge catch and wherever my eyes fell I saw herring neatly laid out in rows to dry: on roofs, on the red earth, on planks, on stretches of cement. Everywhere were huge black iron vats three or four feet in diameter; across the tops of these vats were stretched metal slats or screens which held herring being smoked, a process that caused a blue mist to rise through the blinding sunshine and hang over the entire village. The stench of fish mingled with the odor of urine and excrement that flowed in an eroded gully down through the center of the village. Flies, satiated, buzzed in lazy clouds. Naked children, gripped by disease, followed me for a mile as I walked to the seashore and looked at the gray and misty Atlantic. . . .

Returning through the village, I came across a huge black woman sitting in front of her hut; she was obviously ill, her eyes cloudy and her head bent forward. At her side was a bottle of patent medicine and a bottle of gin, both imported from England. I spoke to her through my taxi driver.

"Is it your stomach that's bothering you?"

"Yasa, Massa."

I picked up the medicine bottle and examined the label which read: BILE TONIC. . . . The woman's stomach was enormous and she was no doubt suffering from some liver complaint.

"Why do you drink?"

"It helps me, Massa."

"Is it your liver that's bad?"

"Yasa, Massa. Doctor say so. Bad liver."

I sympathized with her; alcohol was good, but not for what was ailing her. I gave her a few shillings and left. Time and again I had

154

to choke back feelings of compassion in these mudholes. If one allowed one's feelings to become identified here, one could no longer see anything; in fact, one could no longer think.

I came across a tiny wooden structure which, I learned, was the village school and church. The children were out at sports and the schoolroom was deserted. I entered and found that clothes had been discarded hastily and thrown upon desks. Desks? I stooped low and examined the strange objects. They were made of soapboxes, had rough, jagged edges, and the sides and ends of the boxes still bore the name and address of the English manufacturer stenciled in black letters. Most of the boxes were about 18 inches in length, about 6 inches high, and about 2 feet across; some of them were so arranged that the opened side ran lengthwise, facing the child, and thus provided storage space for books, etc. Nailed to the bottom of these boxes were four slats of wood chopped from the same kind of packing cases.

Such a "desk" must have given a child a great deal of discomfort. The remainder of the seating accommodations was comprised of chairs, but chairs not as we know them. The seats were about nine inches from the floor and the backs were so sloping that they could give little or no support to the back of any child optimistic enough to expect it. These chairs were miniature in every respect, and just how the children managed to adapt their limbs to the whims of these desks and chairs is difficult to imagine.

Hovering over this evil-looking litter of a schoolroom was a swarm of slow-moving flies. . . .

At the head of the classroom was an altar set upon a dais and rising above this was a heavy, gilded cross. . . . I saw no books, no evidence of this being an educational institution other than a soiled sheet hanging on a wall with a few clippings from illustrated journals pinned to it. Under these clippings was a timetable that showed that the children received one-half hour of religious instruction each day.

Outside of the school building, about a hundred yards away, a group of about thirty children sat in rows upon benches. Their average age seemed to be about six years. I stood discreetly to one

side while an African man conducted the class; with a pointer he
indicated the following words which were chalked in white upon
a blackboard:

I go
I go up
I go so
I no go

Beside each expression was the vernacular equivalent. I couldn't
believe it, but there it was.

This, of all things, was a church mission and, as such, I wondered
just what the mission thought it was doing. . . . Saving the heathen?
In my opinion it would have been far better to have left those children alone; either one gave them a decent education or none at all.
I would have preferred to have seen them retain their tribal heritage
intact than to have had drilled into them this travesty of a Western
education. These children, when they grew up—if they could possibly survive amidst this appalling filth—would come in time to
hate what had happened to them, especially if they turned out to
be intelligent and had the capacity to reflect.

It was, of course, the European traders who first brought the
missionaries to the Gold Coast and helped to establish these
churches; those traders were the Portuguese, the French, the
English, the Dutch, the Swiss, and the Germans, in short, most of
western Europe. From about 1687 to 1820, companies ruled the colony and had the final and decisive say in everything, including the
education of the natives. In 1843, with the aid of some West Indians, the missions became firmly established and began to work
closely with the government, and, by 1848, a girls' school had been
established. At Akropong, in the same year, a seminary was set up
for catechists.

In 1876 the Methodists opened a high school for boys in Cape
Coast; this was followed by the establishment, in 1909, of Mfantsipim Secondary School, which was a union of the Wesleyan Collegiate School and the Fanti Public School. In 1880 the Roman

Catholics began religious teaching at Elmina, and by 1900 the Catholics had opened six or seven schools. . . . The government aided these schools somewhat, but it must be remembered that it was not until 1900 that fighting between Britain and Ashanti ceased and allowed some steady and continuous progress to be made in educational work.

In 1924 the Methodists opened a college at Kumasi and thereafter the government became active in opening trade schools for artisans; but it was only in 1930 that "national" schools came into existence. These schools represented the efforts of native rulers, chiefs, etc., and were administered by Africans. In 1924 the government established Achimota College. . . . Education in the Gold Coast has been a slow, torturous business. Indeed, "business" itself—gold, diamonds, timber—fared far better than education, and, though businessmen exploited the Africans, I believe that their impact, in the final analysis, was far less detrimental to the personalities of the Africans than that of the religious teachings of the missionaries.

The conducting of mines and timber camps brought the African into contact with the most progressive and dynamic aspects of the Western world and, though it cheated him, at the same time it roused his sense of achievement, challenged him to emulate the undertakings of white men and free himself. Those African leaders who today fight courageously and without stint for their country are those who have been impressed by the techniques of Western exploitation, by the manner in which the West produced. It was not what Nkrumah learned about God in his Catholic mission school that urged him to struggle for the liberation of his country, but his grasp of the role played by economic forces in the modern world that launched him on his path to grapple with the British, and when he did come to grips with them, he knew the exact spot where they were most vulnerable; that is, he knew how to paralyze the economic life of the colony. It was an economic vision rather than a metaphysical one that had organized the personalities of the young men I met in the Convention People's Party.

On the other hand, the religious teachings of the mission schools, though it did impart the three R's to a few hundred thousand in a hundred years, tended to develop quietism in the African personality. More detrimental to the personality of the African than the religious instruction *per se*, perhaps, was the strange, neurotic temperament of the missionary—kind but impersonal, near but aloof, anxious but superior; in brief, it was a relationship calculated unconsciously to arouse hatred and jealousy. Few or no really independent African personalities emerged from the nervous ministrations of these missionaries who, because of racial feelings which even religion could not help them to overcome, could never actually identify themselves completely with the people.

It seems that the world cannot leave Africa alone. All of Europe is represented here in Africa, to kill or save Africa. The businessman, the missionary, and the soldier are here, and each of them looks at the question of the meaning of human life on this earth when he looks at Africa. The businessman wants to get rich, which means that African suffering to him is an opportunity. The soldier wants to kill—for the African is "different" and is, therefore, an enemy. The missionary yearns to "save," that is, to remake *his* own image; but it is not the African that he is trying to save; it is himself, his sense of not belonging to the world in which he was born. . . . (No one should be allowed voluntarily to enter Africa; one should be *sentenced* there to service. . . .)

One does not react to Africa as Africa is, and this is because so few can react to life as life is. One reacts to Africa as one is, as one lives; one's reaction to Africa is one's life, one's ultimate sense of things. Africa is a vast, dingy mirror and what modern man sees in that mirror he hates and wants to destroy. He thinks, when looking into that mirror, that he is looking at black people who are inferior, but, really, he is looking at himself and, unless he possesses a superb knowledge of himself, his first impulse to vindicate himself is to smash this horrible image of himself which his own soul projects out upon this Africa.

In the future men will die, as they have died in the past, about the meaning of Africa; the only difference in that future fighting and dying will be that the Africans themselves will be wholeheartedly involved in the fighting and dying from the beginning, for they too have now caught a sense of what their problem is; they too have seen themselves reflected in the mirror of their misery and they are aroused about the meaning of their own lives. The European white man made Africa what he, at bottom, thought of himself; it was the rejected and the self-despised of Europe who conquered and despoiled Africa. But today Africa is not alone in her misery. She is keenly aware that there are others who would solve their problems at the expense of her misery. . . .

To ask if Africa can be changed is to ask if man can be changed. Africa must and will become a religion, not a religion contained within the four walls of a church, but a religion lived and fought out beneath the glare of a pitiless tropic sun. The fight will be long, new, unheard of, necessitating a weighing of life in terms that modern man has not yet thought of.

Life in Africa must handle life; life here is just bare, sentient life; life is all that life has in Africa. This might sound strange to Western ears, but here it is so plain and simple and true. No wonder men killed and enslaved others in Africa; no wonder they sacrificed human beings; no wonder they invented fantastic religions—they did these things because they were really reacting to themselves, their sense of themselves.

Africa, with its high rain forest, with its stifling heat and lush vegetation, might well be mankind's queerest laboratory. Here instinct ruled and flowered without being concerned with the nature of the physical structure of the world; man lived without too much effort; there was nothing to distract him from concentrating upon the currents and countercurrents of his heart. He was thus free to project out of himself what he thought he was. Man has lived here in a waking dream, and, to some extent, he still lives here in that dream.

Africa is dangerous, evoking in one a total attitude toward life, calling into question the basic assumptions of existence. Africa is the world of man; if you are wild, Africa's wild; if you are empty, so's Africa. . . .

These were the thoughts that ran through my mind as I bathed and dressed the next morning. I felt tired, as tired as when I had gone to sleep. I was gripped by an enervation that seemed to clog the pores of my skin. I was about to pull on my shoes when I discovered, to my horror, that my clothes were getting mildewed, that my shoes were beginning to turn a yellowish green color. I scraped at it; it was mold. I called the steward and asked him what caused it.

"That's the heat and the sea water in the air, Massa."

"Well," I sighed, "try and do something about it."

"Yasa, Massa. I put clothes in sun."

"Okay."

I took a taxi to the Prime Minister's office to see if I had any mail there. The Prime Minister's secretary looked at me and asked:

"How are you getting on?"

I felt depressed. She knew what was happening and I resented her asking me to tell her what she already knew.

"I feel like the Africans have put their *juju* on me," I muttered, trying obliquely to let her know that I was dissatisfied.

She whirled in her swivel chair and stared at me.

"You must be careful of *that*," she said in a deadly serious tone.

"What?" I exclaimed, coming fully aroused now.

"There's something to *juju*," she said to me sternly.

I wanted to howl with laughter, but a Prime Minister's office was not the place to act like that.

"You're kidding," I said.

She shook her finger solemnly in my face and said:

"Watch it!"

"My God, *you* don't believe that," I said.

"There's more to it than you think," she snapped.

I sank weakly into a chair and stared at her. I'd met this cool, intelligent, and efficient woman in London and Paris and we'd had long discussions about the state of the world; and I had respected her opinions. And now, here in this heat and humidity, she was hinting to me that *juju* was real and not just a psychological delusion.

"What do they do to people down here?" I asked her. I walked slowly out of the office, feeling defeated. Lord, *juju* . . .? Let 'em bring on their *juju*. . . . If you didn't believe in it, it could never influence you. . . . And that *juju* was real was being hinted to me in the Prime Minister's office! Oh, no! Oh, no!

I hailed a taxi and climbed in. Just as the taxi got under way, I saw a tall, well-dressed black girl running wildly toward the car, waving her hand at me.

"Hold it, driver," I said.

The girl came panting to the car window.

"Say, please. . . . Give me a ride into town with you?"

"Why not?" I said.

She got into the taxi and settled into a seat. She was dressed in stylish European clothes, high-heeled shoes. She was deeply rouged and her hair was piled high on top of her head, like that of a woman who was imitating photographs of European women in fashion magazines.

"Where would you like to be dropped?" I asked her.

She looked at me and smiled slowly. I felt *juju* coming; but it was not that of the Gold Coast or anywhere in Africa. It was as old as mankind; the Africans could not claim it. . . .

"Where are *you* going?" she asked me.

"To my hotel. Why?"

She still continued to smile at me. The sun flickered through the taxi window as we sped past tall trees and I could see that her hair was soaked in grease. She edged closer to me and I felt her naked arm touching mine. Here it comes, I thought. They have this in Africa too. I sat still and stared determinedly out of the window. Then I glanced at her and she laughed. She grasped my hand. I pulled away from her.

"Look, what is this?" I asked her.

"It's *me*," she said.

"Are you working for the government?" I asked.

"No. I'm a social worker," she said.

"And are you now performing a part of your duties?"

She giggled.

"Do you live in Accra?" I asked her.

"No. Not now. I was born here. But I've been in school in Cape Coast. I'm leaving shortly for England to study."

"I see. I doubt if England has anything to teach you," I told her.

She took hold of my hand again, holding it tightly now, glancing at me out of the corners of her eyes. I looked full at her and she bent over laughing.

"Did someone send you to my taxi?"

"No."

"Then why did you pick *me* out to ask for a ride?"

"I just liked the way you looked," she said simply.

The taxi bumped along in the hot sunshine.

"Where are you going *now*?" she asked me again.

"I told you. To my hotel—"

"Take me there—"

"I can't. I've an appointment—"

"Later, then," she insisted.

"No. Really, I'm busy today."

I wondered how long she had been practicing this kind of approach to men; and, above all, where she had learned it? She could not have been over twenty-one and her English was fluent.

"Are you a Christian?" I asked her.

"Of course," she said.

Asking a person if he were a Christian or not in Africa does not mean what it does in the West; it is asking if the person belongs to a certain social status. It has little or nothing to do with morals, ethics, or metaphysics.

"You live with your family?" I asked.

"Yes."

"You like movies, don't you?"

"Yes," she said, surprised. "How did you know?"

"Oh, I know," I said.

I could not tell her that she was acting like a very bad movie. Again and again in Africa I found natives trying to imitate American movies, but, having no idea of the distorted context of life in which Hollywood actions take place, they vulgarized those actions, making them even more fantastic, which was no mean accomplishment. She was accepting a shopgirl's escape dream as a realistic vision of life!

"You know," I said seriously, "you are young and you ought to be careful. You'll get into trouble, maybe, if you do anything like this in London."

She was suddenly sober; I had made her a little doubtful, but not for long; she still believed in her goal but was searching for new means. She looked yearningly at me and tried to talk convincingly.

"I need a friend," she said. "I've never had a friend."

"Do you say that to all the men you meet?"

She laughed, surrendering her tactic. But undismayed, she switched to another one.

"I've spent so much money buying things for my trip," she explained. "Four days ago I had seventy-five pounds. Today I've only three pounds."

"What did you do with your money?"

"I bought a trunk and a winter coat. . . . They say it's cold in England. . . . God! If I had a friend, I could have some money."

"Do all of your girl friends have friends?"

"All of them except me."

"Where did you get seventy-five pounds?"

"My family."

"And why won't they give you more?"

"They haven't got it. I need forty pounds."

"That's a lot of money," I said.

"Well, twenty pounds, then."

"How did you get the idea of asking for money like this?" I asked her. "It was from a movie, wasn't it?"

She looked at me and giggled again. And I knew that it was from either a movie or a novel that she had gotten the notion.

"What school did you go to in Cape Coast?"

"The Methodist Mission," she said.

Well, Christianity had changed her. Before professing Christ, she might have slept with a man for the sheer physical pleasure; now, she still wanted to sleep with a man, but she wanted to be paid, and, moreover, being out of touch with reality, she had placed a fantastic overestimation upon herself.

"You're selling and I'm buying, is that it?" I tried to shock her.

She brushed it off. Her eyes moved frantically as she thought of ways and means.

"Haven't you got a friend who'd be nice to me?"

"I have no friends in Africa," I told her.

"Come home with me."

"But aren't you with your family?"

"My aunt. But she'll leave if I ask her to."

"Listen, this is no way to study social work," I argued.

"Can't you let me have ten pounds?"

"No."

"Five pounds?"

"No."

"Would you take me to the movies tonight?"

"No, no. This is no way to live, sister."

"I'm trying to go to school," she explained.

That justified it all. I desisted. I could see nothing in her that I could appeal to. She was using tribal methods in order to latch herself onto the twentieth century. . . . She was somehow terribly innocent, and, at the same time, hotly and crassly determined to put her life on a cash-and-carry basis to buy an education. Hers was a mixture of Christian and tribal values.

"Do you smoke?" she asked me.

"Yes. Pardon me. Do you want a cigarette?"

"No. I don't smoke. Do you drink?"

"Yes; sometimes. . . . Do you?"

"No; I never drink," she said.

She looked off in wonder. She was trying to become quickly acquainted with the most elementary things of life.

"Your family and the teachers at that mission school watched you pretty closely, didn't they?" I hazarded.

"Yes; but all that's over now," she said.

I looked at her and she hung her head and giggled, then she lifted her knuckles to her lips, thinking intensely.

"I have a sister in America," she said suddenly.

"And you want to go there?"

"If I can."

"You go to the movies too much," I said.

"But I like movies," she said defensively.

The taxi spun round curves. The hot sun splashed on the rickety houses and the crowded streets where young black women, wearing native cloths, carried unbelievable burdens upon their heads. The taxi stopped; I got out and held the door for her.

"Won't you come in, please?"

"I can't, really."

"Meet my aunt, won't you? She's there."

"I'm sorry, little lady."

Her eyes were baffled. She turned suddenly and walked off across the street and entered a vacant, littered lot; she paused and looked back at me, laughing nervously in the hot sun. The taxi driver stared at me, waiting.

"Come in for a moment," she begged.

I shook my head, forcing a wry smile.

"Good luck to you and be careful," I called to her.

She stood still. I moved backward toward the open door of the taxi. Then she turned and ran; she reached a corner of a cement house and paused again, standing a little sideways; she smiled, laughed, then beckoned me with her finger. I shook my head, filled with pathos. She ran out of sight.

I climbed into the taxi and settled down. The driver sat, not moving.

"To the Seaview," I told him.

"Massa no go with girl?" he asked me.

"No," I said.

He laughed and started the motor.

"Mary, she want too much money, hunh, Massa?" he asked, wagging his head.

"Do you know her?" I asked him.

"Oh, naw, sar!" he said.

"Then why do you call her Mary?"

"They all named Mary, Massa," he told me, and he laughed until his shoulders shook.

Late that afternoon I visited, in the company of some young

Africans, the famous Korle Bu Lagoon, a center of legend and fetish worship situated on the outskirts of Accra. The lagoon was a wide stretch of gray, stinking mud over which a modern concrete highway ran. You could smell the lagoon's awful stench a few moments before your car reached it, and you also believed that you could smell it for an hour afterward when you were miles away, so nauseating was its odor.

"But why don't they do something to cover the thing up?" I asked of my companions in the car.

"Oh, that's a problem," I was told.

"Won't the government act?" I asked.

"Oh, yes. If they could—"

"It's a simple job. Isn't there money enough for that?" I asked. "At least they could cover all that slime with a coat of thick oil and mosquitoes couldn't breed in it. That stagnant water causes typhoid and yellow fever and malaria. . . ."

"We told you that there's a story—"

The story I heard went something like this: Years ago, according to legend, the Fanti tribe was fighting the Accra tribe. The Fanti tribe, so went the story, advanced with a powerful army to the edge of the lagoon but, since it was nearly night and they were tired, they decided to camp and rest till morning. . . . The Accra tribe, seeing that their enemies, the Fanti, had given up hope of launching an attack, took heart, mobilized their forces, made a few sacrifices, called on their gods, and attacked and won a smashing victory. . . . And, of course, that victory, according to the calculations of the tribal mind, had come from the helpful spirit of the lagoon which had confounded and confused the Fanti and prevented them from fighting! Since that day the Korle Bu Lagoon has been held in deep reverence; it is thought that a god resides in it. So, when the government decided to drain the lagoon, a crowd of thousands of angry and terrified Accra people gathered, headed by the fetish priests and priestesses, and dared the government authorities to act! And, so far, the government authorities have not acted. . . . And this reeking lagoon lies within a stone's throw of the most modern tropical hospital in all West Africa!

XX...

On the tenth of July the Legislative Assembly convened, presided over by the brown-skinned, wigged, robed, and spectacled Sir Emmanuel Quist, distinguished lawyer and elder statesman. The Prime Minister, clad in a smock of the Northern Territories, submitted a motion calling for drastic modifications of the constitution —modifications which would eventually mean a large measure of self-government for the people of the Gold Coast.

The session was impressive, colorful, but restrained. Most of the Convention People's Party members of the Assembly wore their tribal costumes; the opposition members were dressed strictly in Western style. Nkrumah, as well as all of his aides who had been imprisoned with him for sedition, wore peaked white caps, the same kind that they had been forced to wear when behind bars; and on the front of those caps was printed in red letters for all to see: P.G., meaning: Prison Graduate.

The high-ceilinged room in which the Assembly met had been consciously modeled on the British House of Commons and the mood that prevailed was more British than the British themselves could have provided. Most of the speakers droned in voices so low that I could barely hear one half of what was being said.

At once I was aware of the contrast between this prim atmosphere, this staid gathering, this chaste room and the screaming and dancing crowds that I'd seen in Accra and Cape Coast. Would these men fulfill the hopes of those hopeful people? I was not doubtful or cynical; I was just wondering and skeptical. I was for these men and I found myself hoping that the British, uncannily politically astute, had not already snared this revolution in a net of politeness and parliamentary maneuvering. . . .

All around the grounds outside of the Assembly were thousands of Gold Coast citizens clad in their native togas and waiting behind long cordons of Northern Territory police. Every time a car rolled up bearing some Convention People's Party functionary, the crowd would let out a long roar of applause. These were the masses; they had put Nkrumah in power and now they were waiting to see if he would fulfill the mandate that they had given him.

Inside, with the help of an African newspaperman, I spotted the key Britishers who held the decisive cabinet positions and the balance of power for Britain. There was Sir Charles Arden-Clarke, the Governor of the Colony: short, stumpy, aloof, detached, hiding his tension. There was broad-browed, spectacled R. H. Saloway, the Minister of Defense and Foreign Affairs. There was P. Branigan, Minister of Justice, Queen's Counsel, tight-lipped, sharp of features, partly bald, and with the subdued air of a detective. And there was R. P. Armitage, the Minister of Finance, a wisp of hair dividing his bald dome, reserved, determined. . . . These four Britishers had the armed forces, the money, the administration of the courts, and the foreign affairs of the colony in their hands. The rest of the power was in the hands of Africans. It was truly a delicate balance.

In the galleries there were almost as many Europeans as Africans and that reminded me that Nkrumah, so far, has had to rely, ironically enough, mainly upon the British for the burden of administering most of the departments of government. The black intellectuals from Oxford and Cambridge were, almost to a man, with the opposition and were, therefore, unacceptable. In coming to power Nkrumah had to import more Britishers to serve in technical capacities than had ever been in the Gold Coast before; the drive toward self-government had not lessened but increased the number of British officials. . . . If Nkrumah had not followed this line, his new and varied programs of social reform could not have gotten under way so quickly; in short, he'd not have been able to keep the many promises that he and his party had made to the masses. . . .

As the preliminaries began, I mulled over the strange facets of this political situation: had the British, having faced many similar situations of revolt in other lands with other people, known the exact moment when to call these black boys into power? There was no doubt but that Nkrumah's acceptance of responsibility in the government had been to demonstrate to the world the African's capacity to shoulder the burdens of office. But had he accepted these responsibilities too *soon?* Might not the famous British gesture of an "act of grace," the releasing of Nkrumah and his aides from prison, have concealed a knowledge on the part of the British that the new political party and its leadership were not yet quite *ripe* to rule, and that they would have to depend upon the British? The British would not have been able to rule the Gold Coast without force had they not invited Nkrumah and his party into the government as partners. But the black brother who had been invited into partnership was a weak one, inexperienced. . . . In other words, the victory of the Convention People's Party, as astounding and unheard of as it was, had not been really and truly decisive. The British, having their hands upon the money and the police, and having the right to say who could or could not enter the colony, could bottle up the country any time they wanted to. And, though they were quiet about it, the mining, timber, and mercantile interests, all foreign, had their own ideas about what was happening.

Nkrumah's speech petitioning Her Majesty's Government to enact the necessary legislation for Gold Coast self-government was calm, competent, and calculated to appeal to the traditional British pretensions of self-rule for colonies. His most telling point came when he stated that as long as the British ruled the Gold Coast, all the mistakes of the Africans could be laid at British doors. He said nothing to frighten foreign capital; he expressed a desire to remain within the Commonwealth; and I could not escape the feeling that the speech implied an almost formal understanding with the British. . . . There was nothing inherently shameful in that; any smart politician would have done it. But I could not help but ask myself if it should have been done *now*—with the national front broken, with the most able men of the country sulking in their corners . . . ? I did not disagree with Nkrumah; I simply and honestly feared for him and his people.

At the conclusion of the Prime Minister's speech, prolonged applause broke forth and the Prime Minister was taken outside and lifted upon the shoulders of his comrades and paraded to and fro. The surging crowds behind the cordons of police cheered and chanted:

"FREE—DOOOOOM! FREE—DOOOOOM!"

Their faces streaked with white clay as a sign of victory, decked out in wild and gay colors, the women did that slow, snakelike dance, shuffling their feet over the ground, their fingers lifted and trembling in the air, chanting songs, clapping their hands in off-beat rhythms. But I was apprehensive about a reality that lurked behind the reality I saw. I could feel the fragility of the African as compared with the might of the British, the naïveté of the African when weighed against the rancid political insight the British possessed, the naked plea of the African when pitted against the anxieties of man holding the secrets of atomic power in their hands. . . . And a phrase from Nietzsche welled up in me: the pathos of distance. . . . The Africans were grappling with a new and different kind of god that could be propitiated only with raw materials: uranium, bauxite, gold, timber, and manganese. . . . It was not what Nkrumah had said but what he had left unsaid that induced in me a mood of concern, of uneasiness.

How would the black bourgeois opposition handle this? I'd heard a lot about Drs. Danquah and Busia. I'd been told that they were able men when it came to handling words and this was pre-eminently a battle in which words were the decisive weapons.

While waiting for the opposition speakers to get under way, I wondered if it would not have been wiser for Nkrumah to have refused to share power with the British, to have allowed the black bourgeois opposition to rule while he enlarged and strengthened his party. . . . In a nutshell, what was bothering me was the manifest shallowness of the African foundation for the efficient exercise of power. If Nkrumah could have postponed his entering the government, he could have had, when he did come to power—as he inevitably would have!—a power that would have been *African* power, a control over the country so complete that he could have ruled in the name of his party until he could have trained a new legion of like-minded young men to help him.

The disruption of the class and social relations of a tribal country that has long been under the fumbling tutelage of a Western imperial power throws up a variety of possibilities, the crux of them being: for whose benefit will the turnover in power be made?

There could have been a narrow, nationalist revolution made for the benefit of the chiefs, the intellectuals, and the not too numerous black middle class. Such a realignment would have been a restoration, at a higher level, of the tribal power which the British had once smashed, and this power would have had to depend upon foreign mercantile interests. Under such a regime the masses of the people would have fared no better than they had fared before.

Yet, another revolution could have been made in the name and for the benefit of the Gold Coast and the whole of West Africa; such a revolution, of course, would have been attacked at once by the combined forces of both Britain and France; but, if such a revolution could have maintained discipline within its geographical boundaries and denied the exploitation of its natural resources to foreigners, it would eventually have been able to deal with the Western powers on a new basis. Such a revolution would have been difficult, costly in human life, would have entailed great sacrifices; but, in the end, whether it won or not, the entire black population of West Africa would have been forever committed to the new course, and the fetish-ridden past would have been killed beyond recall. . . .

Africa needs the West and the West needs Africa; the problem is: How can this exchange of values, services, and materials between Africa and the West be made on a basis that will not outrage the African sense of justice, a basis that assumes the equality of needs on both sides?

The revolution that was actually made was for the benefit of British capital, the interests of the Commonwealth interlaced with the interests of the Gold Coast; and this revolution necessitated a sharp ability on the part of the participating Africans to know where their interests _began_ and where those of the Commonwealth _ended_. Already the clash of interests, the ceaseless bickering over definitions of power was a lawyer's paradise!

The British-educated, black bourgeois opposition opened with an attack delivered by Dr. J. P. Danquah, lawyer, philosopher, politician, dramatist, and long-time nationalist leader. Short, slow-moving, he rose, shuffled his pile of notes; then, in a well-modulated baritone, he charged Nkrumah with converting the Gold Coast into another Malta. He pecked away at Nkrumah's motion without ever once getting beneath the surface of the situation. It was evident that he was innocent of the meaning of the twentieth-century industrial world. His concepts were dragged from the nineteenth century and hell and high water were not going to shake him loose from those prepossessions. England had laid her hand upon his spirit and, in spite of himself, he hated England but could not tell how England had grabbed hold of him. . . . He had no idea how hard and cold were both the white and black men with whom he was dealing, men who were professional politicians and who labored at their craft every waking hour. . . . (Dr. Danquah gave only his spare time to politics!) He argued as though he were exhorting, say, on behalf of Shell Oil. Not once did he indicate that he felt that the fate of millions of his fellow countrymen was at stake, that they had passionately asked for something for which they were willing to die, that they actually were massed and waiting out there in the hot sun to hear their aspirations put into words.

I left the Assembly before Dr. Danquah finished his speech.

After lunch I recalled that I'd noted many American movies being shown in the city. I'd come across the influence of Hollywood so often in the mentality of the Africans that I was curious to see how they absorbed these artificial dreams. I took a taxi and went to the biggest movie house in Accra. One entered the theater from the rear; I suppose that was necessary because of the absence of sidewalks in front. I bought a ticket for the gallery, for I wanted to be close to the side of the black boys and girls whom I'd seen on the streets.

The interior was vast, barnlike, undecorated. To find a seat you had to grope your way forward in the dark, bumping into walls and colliding with other people until your hands encountered vacant space. Smoking was allowed and the air was stale. I sat and became aware that an uproar was going on about me and I looked at the screen to see what was causing it. An advertisement was being projected; a bottle of beer was leaping and jumping on the screen as a British voice extolled its merits. The beer bottle tilted and foam gushed from its neck, demonstrating the beer's wonderful qualities of nourishment, and the audience howled with laughter. Then a black boy was shown drinking from a bottle and the audience hooted and yelled. They seemed amused no end to hear an alien voice telling them about something that was a daily familiarity in their lives.

This quality of uproarious detachment continued when the main feature was projected. Indeed, the laughter, the lewd comments, and the sudden shouts rose to such a pitch that I could not hear the shadowy characters say their lines. I could not follow the story amid such hubbub and came to the conclusion that they could not either; it soon became clear that the story was of minor interest to them. It was upon each incident that they were concentrating with such furious noise. If a man accidentally fell, they screamed with delight. If a love scene was portrayed, they hooted:

"Take her! Take her!"

And when a frustrated man rested his head tenderly upon a woman's breast, they jeered:

"Don't break 'em! Don't it hurt!"

It was a Western movie, packed, as they say, with action. In the Legislative Assembly the Africans had made believe that they believed in Western values; here, in this dark movie, they didn't have to pretend. Psychologically distant, they mocked at a world that was not their own, had their say about a world in which they had no say. . . . When a cowboy galloped across the scrubby plains, they shouted in chorus:

"Go, go, go, go, go . . . !"

During stretches of dialogue, they chatted among themselves about the last explosion of drama, waiting for the action to begin again. It was clear that the African was convinced that movies ought to move. . . . A fist fight took place and each blow that landed brought:

"Swish-um! Swish-um!"

Throughout the film the audience commented like a Greek chorus, and when the heroine was trapped I was sure that they wanted the villain to violate her. They applauded when the hero rushed his panting horse to the rescue; but their applause was not because they were concerned about the poor girl's virginity, but because his horse was beautiful and fast and strong. I dare say that these boys must have wondered, years ago when these films were first being projected in the Gold Coast, why the hero rushed so in such cases. . . .

And it did not matter too much whose hands held the smoking guns—the hand of the law or outlaw—for they helped to speed the bullets on their way with:

"boom! boom! boom!"

When a character made his reappearance, they greeted him like an old friend. (The same film is shown over and over again, for the audiences derive great joy from seeing the same action performed time and again!) Scenes filled with suspense caught them up totally; a thunderous drone would fill the air until the moment of climax and then, as the net closed tighter and tighter about the hero, or as the villain moved in for the kill, they went wild. . . . Elements of surprise delighted them; when the hero's bullets had run out and the trigger clicked on empty chambers, the tongues in the audience went:

"Click, click, click. . . ."

The impossible made them stand up and cheer, as when the hero, stealthily creeping around the villain in the semi-darkness, climbed a tree, waited for the villain to lift the blond virgin in his arms, and then plunged headlong down upon the villain—the pandemonium that erupted drowned out the soundtrack.

Not a little dazed, I made my way back to the hotel and tried to sort out what I had seen and heard. It was quite obvious that the African's time sense was not like our own; it did not project forward in anticipation; it oscillated between the present and the past. And at once I knew why there had been no literature in the Gold Coast, no novels or dramas even from those who had been educated in England. (Mabel Dove has written some short stories and Dr. Danquah has written a drama; but I've not read them.)

The great adventure of the Western world, the rise out of feudalism of a new bourgeois class that thirsted to explore experience, that felt that it had a future that had to be ransacked for sensations, had not touched these people.

The African did not strain to feel that which was not yet in existence; he exerted his will to make what had happened happen again. His was a circular kind of time; the past had to be made like the present. Dissatisfaction was not the mainspring of his emotional life; enjoyment of that which he had once enjoyed was the compulsion.

I did not regard this as wrong; it was just different. By implication, it could make for a deep sense of conservatism. That which had occurred was holy, right, just, natural. . . . Why not? It was human. One did not leave the past behind; one took it with one; one made the past the present. I could not get beyond that, for it was alien to me; it was intriguing, but beyond the bounds of my feelings. I could understand it, but I couldn't experience it.

XXI...

As detached and resistant as I try to be, I find myself sometimes falling heir to the reaction pattern which lingers on here as a kind of legacy of British imperialism. One morning I wanted to take a batch of film to the Photographic Section of the Gold Coast Information Service and I got into a taxi and told the driver:

"Photo Section of the Gold Coast Information Service."

"What, Massa?"

"The Photo Section on Boundary Road," I said.

"Yasa, Massa."

He set his car in motion and drove for some time. I noticed that he had taken a route that was not familiar to me.

"Where are you going?" I asked him.

He stopped the car and looked at me, his face flashing a white grin.

"Where Massa wanna go?" he asked me.

"I told you the Photo Section. It's on Boundary Road."

He drove off again; then once more he slowed the car and said to me:

"Massa, tell me where it is. . . ."

"What are you doing?" I demanded. "You drove off like you knew where it was—" Houses have no street numbers in Accra.

"Yasa, Massa," he said, picking up speed.

What was wrong with the guy? The taxi sped past buildings that were strange to me; soon I saw the green landscape of the suburbs of Accra.

"Say, boy! Where're you taking me?" I yelled at him, leaning forward.

"Massa, I don't know where it is," he mumbled, slowing the car.

"Then why didn't you *tell* me? Why are you driving about aimlessly?" My voice was so sharp that he winced; the heat and the humidity held me in a grip. I noticed the lazy, relaxed manner in which he sat slouched behind the wheel and I was suddenly angry. "For God's sake, ask somebody where the Photo Section is," I directed him. "It's somewhere on Boundary Road. You know where that is, don't you?"

"Yasa, Baas."

He drove on. I sat back and swabbed sweat off my face, chiding myself. I oughtn't to speak to a boy like that. . . . The car rolled on and I watched for familiar landmarks. I saw none.

"Where are you taking me?" I begged of him.

"I don't know, Massa," he said and stopped the car.

"I want to go to the Photo Section on Boundary Road," I said, talking slowly, making sure that he heard every word.

"Yasa, Massa."

He started the car up again and sped off. The landscape was still strange. But perhaps he's taking a roundabout way to get back into the city? I held myself in. But, no; the city was getting farther and farther away. . . .

"Where are you going?" I asked him.

"I don't know, Massa," he said, slowing the car.

"Ask somebody," I told him.

We went forward slowly and, at the sight of a policeman, he

stopped the car and spoke to him in his native tongue. The policeman pointed elaborately and again we were off. I waited, tense,
sweating. I looked at my surroundings and saw a huge sign that
read:

BRITISH MILITARY COMMAND FOR WEST AFRICA

"Boy, stop!"

The car skidded to a halt, the tires screeching on the concrete
pavement.

"Turn this car around!"

He turned the car.

"Now, take me back to my hotel!"

"Massa wanna go back?"

"Yes!"

He started off. I relaxed. I'd get another taxi and start all over
again. Jesus. . . . The British might have thought that I was trying
to spy on them if they had found me wandering amidst their military
installations. . . . A good five minutes passed and when I looked out
of the window of the car I saw the Photo Section of the Gold Coast
Information Service as we were speeding past it. I'd found it by
accident!

"Stop!" I yelled. "There it is!"

He jammed on his brakes and I went forward against the back of
the front seat. I got out and told him to wait. Ten minutes later
I emerged and told him to drive me to the Seaview Hotel. At the
entrance of the hotel, I got out.

"What do I owe you?"

"Eighteen shillings, Massa," he said, his face averted.

That did it. I got mad. I felt that I was dealing with a shadow.

"Don't be a fool, man! Tell me what I *owe* you!"

He looked at me and grinned shyly.

"Fourteen shillings, Massa."

"Talk sense," I muttered, feeling sweat running on my face.

He waited a long time, scratched his head, looked at me out of
the corners of his eyes, his brows knitted, weighing me.

"Twelve shillings, Massa."

"Are you charging me for taking me out into the country? That was your fault—"

"Ten shillings, Massa." He was still bargaining.

"What was the actual price of my trip? You charge a shilling a mile, three shillings an hour, don't you? Did you drive me nine miles?"

I was determined not to be cheated. He looked at me fully now, grinned again, and said imperturbably:

"What Massa wanna give me?"

"Here are eight shillings," I said; I felt that that was too much, but I was willing to settle for that.

"Thank you, Massa," he said, bowing and smiling.

I stood watching him, wanting to tell him that was no way to act, that he should have been honest with me. He looked at me and burst into a wild laugh, a laugh of triumph. I was on the verge of cursing him, but I controlled myself. Suddenly I too laughed, lifted my arm in the Convention People's Party salute, my elbow resting on my hip, the palm of my hand fronting him.

"FREE—DOOOOM!" I roared at him.

He jerked to a surprised attention, gave me a salute in return, shouting:

"FREE—DOOOM!"

I spun on my heels and went to my room. More than once did I find myself slipping into the pattern left here by the British. The Africans had been so trained to a cryptic servility that they made you act a role that you loathed, live a part that sickened you.

XXII...

At midday when the tropic sun weighs upon your head, making you feel giddy, you discover that there are no parks in Accra, no water fountains, no shade trees, no public benches upon which one can rest from a weary walk. There are no public cafés or restaurants in which one can buy a cup of tea or coffee; there are, of course, a few private clubs, but they are either far from you when you need them or you have to be a member to use their services.

This lack of amenities stems from two sources: first, the habits of African tribal life do not call for these tiny, civilized services; second, the British administrators retire to their homes for refreshment and relaxation. There are but a few hundred Britishers in a city like Accra and they do not feel that the city in which they are living temporarily or the country from which they draw their profits or salaries will be the place where their children will stay and grow up.

I strode into the bourgeois section of Accra and passed home after home of rich blacks; they were huge structures, pale pink, light blue, pastel shades of brown, cream, yellow, and red and they were enclosed by high concrete walls the tops of which held barbed wire and jagged shards of glass to keep out intruders. Each house stood a great distance from the others and was surrounded by a wide expanse of ground which usually was overgrown with weeds or was bare or littered with rubbish. Not once did I observe an attempt at making a garden or landscaping. The entire section had about it a garish but bleak air. A little attention would have converted the area into a park, but, even though many of the wealthy Africans of this section had once lived in England, they evidently didn't care for that sort of thing.

I left the paved streets of the rich African section and, leaping over the ubiquitous open sewage drains, wandered into the dusty compounds alive with the usual clutter of children, goats, sheep, and chickens. I stepped cautiously around sedentary but ever-busy women. . . . What could they be doing all the time . . . ? Their housework was no doubt easy; there was no dusting to be done; no floors to scrub or wax; no washing of windows; no lace curtains to be laundered. . . . I peered discreetly into interiors as I passed and only here and there did I see a bed or a cupboard. The windows were square, gaping holes. A roll of straw represented a pallet for the body when placed on the floor at night. And, as closely as I could observe, there didn't seem to be any set time, any scheduled hour for anything; one ate, slept, cooked when one felt like it, and there was no reason for the keeping of rigid hours.

My prying walks ranged as far as the suburbs and, one afternoon, I found myself in Christianborg, an outlying upper middle-class quarter in which both Africans and Europeans lived. While rounding a corner I saw the ruins of a huge building facing me. I stopped, interested. From the atmosphere of settled decay that lay upon the heaps of crumbling stone, I guessed that the structure must have dated from the early nineteenth century. All of its upper floors had long since caved in and a greenish mold clung to the jagged masonry. I climbed upon some rocks and peered over the edge of a rotting wall and saw fallen columns lying athwart mounds of debris, stone stairways that halted abruptly in mid-air, vacant spaces that terminated in masses of rubble.

I sought an entrance into the ruin and was amazed when I came to a vast doorway. A man emerged and, seeing me, he came forward.

"You know what this is, sar?" he asked me.

"No; what is it?"

"It's the Old Slave Market Castle, sar."

"Does anybody live here now?"

"Oh, yes, sar. It's full, sar. Come along. I'll take you to Mr. Hagerson."

"Who's he?"

"He's the head man of the compound, sar."

I looked up at the top of the entrance and saw a faded inscription that read: 1803. . . .

"You live here too?"

"Yes, sar. I'm Mr. Hagerson's assistant, sar."

The interior was more spacious than I had thought. The ruins extended over the area of a city block. At the edge of the mounds of crumbling stone and against the thick walls were crudely constructed rooms in which people lived, cooked. . . . As I penetrated farther I became aware of scores of black families quietly going about their duties. Through the debris were narrow dirt paths that skirted many rooms in which stooped women prepared meals over charcoal fires. . . .

Mr. Hagerson was a brown-skinned man of seventy-odd, clad in a pair of baggy trousers and a frayed shirt. He was barefooted and it seemed that a part of the flesh of his toes had worn away. He stretched out a shaking, skinny hand, greeted me with a smile, obviously delighted to meet a stranger.

"Glad to meet you, sir," he said, lifting a gnarled walking stick to help him stand.

He led me toward his room, hobbling, turning his head now and then to point out a wall or a place where some large room had once existed. I entered his sleeping quarters which were dirty and musty. Pushing the only chair to me, he sat himself upon the edge of a box. On an old sun helmet to my left an eighth of an inch of dust had gathered. Had Mr. Hagerson been a bit taller, he could have been my grandfather. He had the same angular features, the same proud bearing, the same patient dignity that my grandfather had had.

"I'm interested in this place, Mr. Hagerson. Could you tell me a little about it?"

"Be glad to," he began cheerfully.

I wondered why he was so eager to talk. Most Africans are not very communicative unless it's for material reasons. I learned later that Mr. Hagerson was presenting "his case" to me.

"There was a man named Henry Richter," he began leisurely enough. . . .

It seemed that in the early days of the Gold Coast there lived a Dutch family of Richters. One member of that family had been governor for a while; when he left the governorship, he went into the slave trade, took himself an African wife by whom he had several children, mulattoes. When the old man died, he left his mulatto children a fortune in gold dust which they had used to build the Slave Market Castle on whose ruins we now stood. . . .

"Were slaves quartered here?"

"Oh, yes. They sold many, many slaves to America."

"Were any records kept?"

"Yes. But they are hard to find. You see, there are people here in the Gold Coast with records of the sale of slaves in their possession.

But nobody likes to show such things. Nobody likes to say that their family dealt in slaves. . . .

"The people who now live here in this ruined castle are the descendants of John Richter, the son of Henry Richter. He too had an African wife. Now, John had a brother, Bob. John and Bob had a dispute and finally John drove Bob out. John continued to live in the castle until his death. The slave descendants put in a claim to the effect that they owned the castle, and the brother, Bob, who lived at that time in Accra, put in a counterclaim. The slave claim won in the courts."

"You are a descendant of John Richter, Mr. Hagerson?"

"Yes."

"But your name is not Richter?"

"My name comes from my mother's side. We have a matrilineal system, you know," he told me.

I was baffled. The men and women I had seen moving about in the compound had been all black and the descendants of the Richters had been mulattoes. So how could these people, 150 years later, after marrying far and wide, claim to be the descendants of the Richters? And what had become of the white blood?

I learned that in the ruins of this Slave Market Castle lived a compound tribal family of some forty-odd men, women, and children, that Mr. Hagerson, the family's only literate member, had been elected some three years previously as its head and spokesman. Though governed by tribal law in secular matters, the family had divided its religious loyalties among Presbyterians, Anglicans, Church of England, and Catholics; a substantial majority were pagans.

The Castle is regarded as being "owned" by this family; no rent is paid; and the government tax rate is met by a communal pooling of funds. All of the children are being sent to mission schools, but the adult pagans follow the instructions of their fetish priest. Reckoning kinship in African tribal terms, Mr. Hagerson told me that, though only a part of the actual family lived here, many outstanding Gold Coast citizens had their family roots here, that no less than

Sir Emmanuel Quist, the Speaker of the Legislative Assembly, came from the original family of this compound. . . .

"Who was head of the compound before you?" I asked him.

"A Mr. Cochrane. . . . But he's been set aside by the family."

"Was there a dispute?"

He did not answer. I sensed that he did not want to go into the disposition of Mr. Cochrane and I did not press the matter. I was resolved to see Mr. Cochrane later.

"Now, when do you call a meeting of this compound family?"

"Whenever cases arise."

"What kind of cases? Crimes? Marriages?"

"Oh, no. Crimes are handled by the police. Marriages are under the customs of the tribal people. Christians marry in church. I call a meeting when land has to be leased. For example, we own the land on which the petrol station is operating across the street. The people who own that station leased that land from us and pay us rent.

"Now, Mr. Hagerson, suppose a pagan girl here wanted to get married. Or a pagan boy, for that matter. . . . What would happen?"

"With the boy," Mr. Hagerson said, "it's simple. He goes and lives with his wife. But the girl's case is different. If a man falls in love with a girl living here, he must send two of his relatives to the girl's parents to ask if the girl is free, that is, if she's engaged or not. In coming, they must bring a guinea apiece with them, that is, two guineas. If the girl's family says that the girl is free, the two relatives leave and go back and when they return, they bring four guineas and a ring with them. . . . If the girl happens to be engaged, they leave and they forfeit the two original guineas they had brought. . . . If the girl is free and the two relatives have left the additional two guineas apiece and the ring, the bridegroom has to send the following:

    6 guineas
   30 shillings for the mother and father
    2 bottles of gin
    2 bottles of whiskey
    1 dozen bottles of mineral water
    1 dozen bottles of beer

"These are gifts from the bridegroom and his family and they are given to the family of the bride. But the parents of the bride give back to the bridegroom's family a shilling out of each guinea which has been given. The womenfolk change a pound into penny pieces and they send these to all the members of the bride's family with this message: 'Here is drink. Your niece or granddaughter is engaged.'"

"What politics do the members of your family believe in, Mr. Hagerson?"

Mr. Hagerson and his assistant tilted back their heads and roared with laughter.

"Convention People's Party, sir," Mr. Hagerson told me.

I gave Mr. Hagerson some shillings for "drink" and made my way past Christianborg Castle to the home of Mr. W. T. Cochrane. It was a gaunt structure enclosed by a stone wall. Mr. Cochrane was a man of sixty-odd, tall, mulatto, gracious. I told him that I wanted to ask about the Slave Market Castle and he regarded me with caution.

"What do you want to know about it?"

"You were the former head man there," I said. "Why aren't you the head man now?"

"You've talked to Mr. Hagerson?"

"Yes."

Finally Mr. Cochrane cleared his throat and said:

"You see, there's a fight going on in our family. There's a case in the courts—"

"What's it about?"

"Well, you see, it's a fight over the ownership of the land there. These people, who were once slaves—that is, their ancestors were— think that they own that land. They are fighting us about it. They are contesting the ownership of the land in court—"

"Who is 'us' in the case, Mr. Cochrane?"

"Well, *our* side of the family—"

"The mulatto side?" I ventured cautiously.

"I wouldn't put it that way," he said quickly.

Mr. Cochrane was staring thoughtfully before him. I had at last put my finger on the heart of the problem. The black side of the family was fighting the white side of the family for possession of the land. That was not an unusual thing, but the manner of the fight, as Mr. Cochrane revealed it to me, was unique. Convinced now that I, a stranger, had no part in the fight, he talked freely.

"Those people think that because they've lived there all these years, they own that land," he argued. "It's a hang-over from slavery. They argue their claim under tribal law. They say the land is theirs just because they are on it. But they can't prove it in court—"

"And what would constitute proof in court in a case like this?"

"Records and testimony," he said.

"Are there records?"

"There are some," he said slowly.

It was the old war of race and class being fought all over again in a new guise; it was Europe against Africa, Christianity against paganism; freedom against slavery; law against custom; white against black; the rich against the poor; individuals against the tribe. The black side of the family had been born in slavery (that is, their ancestors had been), and they were now contending that they, by custom and traditional right, owned and controlled the land; and the mulattoes were contending that the documents and legal instruments in their hands gave them the clear right to the land. . . .

I couldn't guess who would win that fight, but, in a sense, it was the same fight that Nkrumah had made in the Legislative Assembly a few days before. Nkrumah had had no legal right to the land in which he had been born; he had pled that since his people had been living for centuries on that land, they had the right to rule it. . . . That fight, that claim, that plea went straight through the heart of all black Africa.

XXIII...

I spent the afternoon visiting the newspaper offices. There are about twenty daily and weekly newspapers in the Gold Coast but none of them, with the exception of one—the *Daily Graphic*—is a newspaper in the sense that the West uses that term. They are broadsheets, badly printed, dingy, smeared, horribly written, with atrocious layouts and unreadable editorials. The two official papers of the Convention People's Party, the *Ghana Evening News* and the *Ashanti Sentinel,* though suffering from being printed under primitive conditions, are at least coherent and militant, reflecting the basic moods and hopes of the people.

The printing shops are tiny and cluttered; many of the presses are hand-powered; the staff, in terms of quality, is extremely poor; and the salaries of the reporters are unbelievably low. Sometimes when a press breaks down, the paper does not appear on the streets for days. . . .

It was Nkrumah who founded the *Ghana Evening News* (formerly the *Accra Evening News*) in 1948, and it has a circulation of more than 15,000; it is the most influential single newspaper in the Gold Coast. Then there is the *Daily Graphic,* owned by the West Africa Graphic Company, a subsidiary of the *London Daily Mirror,* the British Labour Party paper. Launched in the fall of 1950, the *Graphic* has evoked intense local African opposition which dubs it the "white press." It is technically the best newspaper in the Gold Coast, having a circulation of more than 40,000. It is equipped with linotype machines and has a number of Europeans on its staff.

The most influential of the opposition press is the *Daily Echo,* one of the two publications of the Independent Press, Ltd. Its editor in chief is Daniel George Tackie, a member of the royal family of James Town with the title of NII Arde Nkpa. Other Gold Coast papers are the *Spectator,* the *African Morning Post,* the *Ghana Daily Express,* the *African National Times.* . . .

Nothing short of a miracle gets these papers printed at all. In one shop I talked to the editor and his co-workers; I asked them why many of the city's papers did not merge their resources and circulation, etc., and try to lift up the standards of the Fourth Estate. I was informed that such co-operation among educated Africans was impossible, that each African was fiercely independent. I countered by reminding them that the Africans were reputed to be communal-minded. . . . Well, it seems that newspapers here are generally owned by families, and these families in turn are tied up with tribal interests, politics, etc.

Strictly speaking, there is no independent press in the Gold Coast; each paper is violently partisan and libel suits are many and ludicrous. One of the devices for squeezing out unwelcome competitors is to sue, and the one to whom the court decision is awarded has the right to seize the press of the loser!

Here is a short news item taken from the *African Morning Post* (Wednesday, September 16, 1953):

ODIKOR'S DEATH BEING
INVESTIGATED

> The Kedwai Police are invest
> gating the death of the Odikor of
> Senfi near Bedwai Nana Kwami
> Booba who was fou d dead in the
> bush recen ly with a gun shot on
> his chest
>   It is said that the Odikor left
> home early i the morning with a
> gun to see his animal traps in the
> evening when it was discovered that
> the chief had not r t   ed a search
> party was organized He was found
> lying dead in the bush

The government, trying to aid the press, has suggested that a national printing press be set up on which all of the newspapers can run off their editions. Such a press would seek to teach the basic essentials of the modern newspaper, how to increase circulation, how to devise a strict libel code, etc., but, so far, the African editors will have none of it. They feel that the opposition would have an opportunity to learn what they were printing and would, therefore, steal their news if all the papers were printed on a common press. . . .

The Gold Coast press differs sharply from the press of the Ameri-

can Negro. If one ignored the names, one would never know that
the press was giving news of black people. Words like discrimination, lynch, race, Jim Crow, white people, etc., are conspicuously
absent.

Most African papers carry no foreign news at all; the *Daily
Graphic* usually devotes two or three paragraphs to "World News."
The Gold Coast African feels that he is at the center of the universe
and a conversation about world affairs is likely to elicit silence. The
African newspaper, like the African himself, is a local thing. African
ideas and culture do not fare well on alien soil, and the African has
no hankering for foreign parts.

X X I V . . .

I was invited by the Gold Coast Information Service to hear Mr.
Gbedemah, the Minister of Commerce, deliver a talk upon one of
the pet schemes of Nkrumah's government. The scheme, known as
the Volta Project, is to be launched with the creation of one of the
world's largest inland lakes. There is a vast basin, sparsely populated, in Ashanti; this basin is surrounded by hills and if the Volta
River were dammed up at a certain point, a lake, in about three
years' time, would rise, making a body of water some two thousand
square miles in area.

The main object in creating this lake would be to obtain cheap
electric power with which to manufacture aluminum. Fabulously rich
Ashanti has not only timber, gold, and diamonds, but also deposits
of bauxite estimated at 200,000,000 tons. . . . Enough to last for two
hundred years! The trapped waters of the Volta River are expected
to turn turbines and generate enough electric power for the production of aluminum cheap enough to be sold on world markets.

At present the Gold Coast Government, the British Government,
and the Canadian Aluminum Company are trying to find a formula
to pool their joint funds and build the dam, control the flow of

water, and produce 600,000 kilowatts of electricity per year. Of these 600,000 kilowatts of electric power, 500,000 will be earmarked for the production of aluminum, and 100,000 will be allocated to the Gold Coast for industrial and agricultural purposes. Hence, there is expected to spring up on the Accra plains a light industry under African leadership. Also experiments are being made to determine if the arid coastal plains will grow quantities of food if sufficiently irrigated. . . .

The British are asking the right to buy aluminum from such a project at rates prevailing in the dollar areas of the world. It is estimated that many thousands of workers will have to be moved from their present living sites and this will entail a vast job of re-settlement of people who are not used to leaving the lands of their ancestors. It is also hoped that the edges of this great lake will provide marshes in which rice can be grown. This last item sounds attractive inasmuch as the Gold Coast now imports much of its rice supply from Liberia. It is also contended that the new project is needed to balance the economy of the Gold Coast, for at present the mainstay of the farmers is the one-crop system of cocoa. If one year the cocoa crop should fail, the Gold Coast would face famine or worse and the country would be engulfed in economic chaos.

All of this sounds wonderful, but for whose ultimate benefit is it? If the Africans are able to swing such a mammoth project with the British and the Canadians, and if the British civil servants can be trusted not to try to be civil masters, it would be a step toward the twentieth century for the Gold Coast. But does not this Volta scheme sound as though the British were exchanging political for economic control?

After I'd left Mr. Gbedemah's lecture, I was talking with a group of young Africans about the fantastic wealth of the Gold Coast, and one of them told me that some Americans were skeptical of such wealth. I told him that I saw no reasons for American skepticism in such matters, and that I was certain that he was mistaken. He then showed me the following document, laughing uproariously as he handed it to me.

It read as follows:

Faith in God!   Hope in Immortality!   Charity to All Mankind

OFFICE OF
UNITED AFRICAN MISSIONARY ALLIANCE
747 EAST 62ND STREET
CHICAGO 37, U. S. A.

July 5, 1952

The British Embassy
3100 Massachusetts Ave., N.W.
Washington, D. C.

Honorable Sir:

The United African Missionary Alliance is interested in purchasing the British Gold Coast Colony in West Africa as a homestead for those of our members in the United States who are desirous of going to Africa to do missionary work.

Please inform your government at London immediately of our intentions, and if your government is willing to sell this territory to us, please notify the United African Missionary Alliance at once. Tell us how much money your government will accept in exchange for this territory. We will pay your price, if it is reasonable.

Looking forward to hearing from the Embassy just as soon as you can get a reply from your government.

Yours truly
United African Missionary
Alliance
(signed) Rev. J. H. Edmondson

JHE:mc
Encl-DP

All of which indicated how remote America was from Africa, from colonies, and the realities that govern the lives of the people who live in them. The gentleman who showed me the above letter was a responsible man and he obtained the document from government

files. I have no way of gauging the intentions of this particular
organization to buy the Gold Coast and send missionaries to lift up
the poor African to something lower; I can only hope that the
Africans can be spared more interference of that kind.

When I awakened one morning, damp and enervated as usual,
the steward came to tell me something and I could not understand
him; then and there I took my first lesson in pidgin English and
found that it consisted of a frightful kind of baby talk.

The first principle was that the African never referred to the
European in the second person; it was always the third person that
he had to use. For example, "Massa go now?" Never: "You go now?"
When an African houseboy is asked to fetch something, he replies:
"I go bring 'em, Massa." A child is always called "piccin," which is
short for pickaninny. Lunch, dinner, eating, a meal, and food of all
kinds are designated by the word "chop." The word "little" must
have caused them great pains, for it has been replaced by the word
"small." Everything that is little is "small"; something very little is
"small small." It is used in a great variety of ways. For example,
instead of saying, "Wait a little," one says "Wait small." If one does
not wish much whiskey to be poured into one's glass, one says:
"Small whiskey. . . ." If one does not wish to eat much, one says:
"Small chop." "Dash me, Massa," means, "Give me a tip, sir." If you
call, asking for the master, and he has gone upstairs, you are supposed to understand when the houseboy tells you: "Massa, he catch
topside, sar." The stewards have been drilled into a clownish form
of exaggerated politeness. "Yes" is always said as, "Yes, please. . . ."
"No" is uttered as: "No, please. . . ." If a steward dares give a European a bit of information, he must not be so presumptuous as to
speak it straight out, but he begins with: "Excuse me, please, to
say . . ." One hears the word "pass" all day long and all night long;
that one word takes care of the entire range of comparatives, material or psychological. For instance: "I like this pass that . . ." A man
who is more important socially than another "passes" him. A building that is taller than another "passes" the other building. A young-
ster who is impertinent to an older person is trying to "pass" that
older person. To look for something is to "catch" it. Thus, if you

ask for the master of the house, the houseboy will tell you: "I go catch 'im." And if the master is not in, you are supposed to know that fact from the following sentence: "Massa, I see Massa, but he not there." The first time I heard a boy say that I thought he was trying to talk religion. . . .

It was amazing how much one could communicate by juggling these simple words. I suspected that the African had adopted these words on a basis that rested in his own language, Twi, which is fundamentally tonal, and one word can mean many things, depending upon how it is said, its context, etc.

I was still in the dark as to how the African mind functioned and I wanted to come to closer grips with it. I appealed at last to a white missionary, Lloyd Shirer, telling him that I wanted to ask an African, a cook or a houseboy, his beliefs. Mr. Shirer worked for the Department of Welfare in the Northern Territories and knew the Gold Coast well, having spent some thirty years in the "bush." He told me that what his cook could tell me would relate only to his cook's part of the country, that is, the North, but that the basic psychological reactions were mostly the same everywhere. Since Mr. Shirer spoke the language, he promised me a word-by-word translation.

"Come to dinner tonight, and after we've eaten, I'll call in the cook and you can ask him anything you want," he said.

I went to dinner and, after we had eaten, Mr. Shirer called in his cook. He was a tall man of about forty, jet black, slightly bald and skinny. Mr. Shirer told him that I was an American of African descent, that I'd come back to see the land of my ancestors, that I wished to ask him about his life. He had been a little nervous, but now he smiled, sat on a little stool, and nodded.

"Black man's country mighty sweet, sar," he told me; Mr. Shirer was translating.

"Where are you from?" I asked him.

"The North, sar."

"Why are you in Accra now?"

"I'm cooking for Mr. Shirer, sar."

"You are away from your tribe. Do you miss your sisters and brothers?"

"Oh, yes, sar! It's hard to be away from my tribe. But I go back as often as I can. This is *not* my home, sar! My home is with my tribe."

"What do you do to keep up your spirit while you are away from your tribe?"

"I observe all the customs, sar. I sacrifice a sheep or a goat at times of feasts or celebrations and I implore my ancestors to watch over me. If I die, I want to be taken back to my tribe and buried with my ancestors."

I questioned him about his dying so far from the land of his ancestors and his expression darkened. It was obvious that it was something that distressed him acutely. He told me:

"A stranger died far from home, sar. We buried him, but not like we bury our own. We dug a grave in a pathway pointing toward his home. Then we sacrificed a sheep and let the blood drip on the grave and we said a prayer to the spirits. We said:

" 'Spirits and gods, this man had every intention of going home to die. You can see that, for his grave points in the *direction* of his home.' So you see, sar, his ancestors must forgive him. He wanted to do right, but he didn't have a chance."

"And do you think that that prayer fixed everything?"

"Oh, yes, sar."

"Now, tell me . . . Do you ever think of going far away, to America, for example?"

"Oh, no, sar! Never!" he said, shaking his head slowly. "I couldn't leave the land of my ancestors. There is land here for me to cultivate and watch over."

(As he spoke I wondered what terror must have been in the hearts of the slaves who had been, through the centuries, shipped to the New World? It is highly possible that the psychological suffering far outweighed the physical!)

"Now, suppose a great calamity overcame a man? What would that signify?"

His eyes widened and he shook his head, staring at me as though he thought that I was mad.

"Why, sar, it means that a witch has got 'im," he told me with conviction. "And he'd have to go to a witch doctor and get something to counteract the evil eye."

"So when someone dies, it is caused by someone else?"

"Of course, sar. If he is old and has had many children, then he dies a natural death. But if he is young, it is certain that someone has killed him, done something to him. For a young man or a young woman, there is no natural death. It is only when you are old and have had many children that your ancestors call you to join them."

"What do you think happened to the millions of your black brothers who were sold into slavery and shipped to America?"

He was thoughtful for a long time, then he answered, speaking slowly:

"They were being punished, sar. Their dead fathers had no thought for them. Their ancestors did not afford protection for them, abandoned them, did not defend them as they should have—"

"Why?"

"It's hard to tell, sar."

"Is there anything that those slaves could have done to avoid being sold into slavery?" I asked him.

"Oh, yes, sar!" he said, brightening. "Listen, sar, if you are bound in chains, helpless, and if you swear an oath, your ancestors will turn into lions or tigers or leopards and come to your aid. Why, you could ride one of those lions or tigers or leopards six hundred miles in one night. Now, sar, these lions or tigers or leopards that your ancestors turn into are not the kind of animals that a hunter shoots at in the forest. No, sar. . . . They are *magical* animals. . . . You can't see them. But you can hear them crying at night. And if you hear one of those magical animals crying at night, it means something bad will happen. It might even mean that the fetish priest will die."

I next asked him:

"Now, look at me. You can see from the color of my skin that I'm of African descent. Now, after all of these years, why do you think I've come back to the land of my ancestors? Do you think that they called me back for some reason?"

Again the tall, serious cook was deeply thoughtful; he scratched his head and said soberly:

"It's hard to tell, sar. Such a long time has passed." He looked at me and shook his head pityingly. "I'm afraid, sar, that your ancestors do not know you now. If your ancestors knew you, why, they'd help you. And, of course, it may be that your ancestors know you and you don't know them, so much time has passed, you see, sar. Now if, by accident, you happened to go back into the section where your ancestors are buried, they'd perhaps know you but you wouldn't know them. Now, if, while you are in Africa, your ancestors should recognize you, then something strange will happen to you and then, by that token, you'd know that you were in touch with your ancestors."

"What sort of strange thing would happen to me?"

"It's hard to tell, sar," he said.

I gave him a few shillings for "drink" and told him good-bye. I sat brooding. Mr. Shirer watched me and then broke into a soft laugh.

"Does that interview satisfy you?"

"Yes," I told him. "Is he typical?"

"Quite typical," he said. "You see, in my work in the Department of Welfare, I have a lot of trouble with beliefs of this sort. This concern with ancestors makes it difficult for the government to launch schemes of resettlement. For example, if, in a certain region, the land is poor and if it's thought that it's better for a tribe to move into a new area, the people will resist, because they do not want to leave the ground on which their ancestors lived and died. To the grave of his ancestors a man will go each year and kill a chicken and drop the blood on the earth, hoping that this will appease his ancestors, hoping that his ancestors will rest in peace and not come into this world and take him to keep them company in the world of spirits. The ground in which his ancestors are buried is charged with spirits whose influence is both good and bad. Therefore, to leave a spot in which ancestors are buried creates terror in some African tribes. . . . They feel that they are leaving their very souls behind them. It is only after making many sacrifices to the earth, to the dead ancestors, that they are able to leave at all."

The illiterate cook had given me, by implication, answers to many questions. It was now obvious why Africans had sold so many millions of their black brothers into slavery. To be a slave was proof that one had done something bad, that one was being punished, that one was guilty; if one was guilty, one was a slave; if one was not guilty, one would not be in the position of a slave. . . . To be sold into slavery meant that your ancestors had consigned you to perdition! To treat a slave harshly was a way of obeying the spiritual laws of the universe! Hence, he who has misfortune merits it. Failure is a sign of badness; winning is a sign of goodness and indicates that the man who wins has a good cause. If you take something from a man who has lost, whom luck has deserted, you are doing right and adding to your own power and goodness. . . .

"I wonder," I said to Mr. Shirer as I sipped my coffee, "what would happen to that cook if he died here in Accra?"

"Let's see what he has to say about that," Mr. Shirer said. "I'll ask him; I'll call him back—"

"Oh, don't bother—"

"He'll be glad to tell you," Mr. Shirer said, rising and going to the door and calling the cook.

He entered again, wiping his hands on his apron. The question was put to him by Mr. Shirer and the cook answered:

"Oh, that's easy, sar. My son would take me back and bury me in the land of my ancestors."

"But what if your son were not here?" I suggested relentlessly.

That one bothered him. He studied the floor for some minutes, and then he said:

"Then my friends would bury me and then they'd watch my grave for those black ants who are called God's slaves. Now, you take one of those ants when he is crawling over my grave, wrap that ant in a bundle of three stones, and then take that bundle to the land where my ancestors are buried and bury it and and my soul will be there. I'll be with my ancestors then."

These, of course, are but dreams, daylight dreams, dreams dreamed with the eyes wide open! Was it that the jungle, so rich, so fertile, was it that life, so warm, so filled with ready food, so effortless, prompted men to dream dreams like this? Or was it the opposite? These dreams belong to the African; they existed before the coming of the white man. . . . One thing was certain: their sense of reality was but a dream. It may be, of course, that dreams are the staunchest kind of reality. . . . It may be that such beliefs fit the soul of man better than railroads, mass production, wars. . . . And the African is not alone in holding that these dreams are true. All men, in some form or other, love these dreams. Maybe men are happier when they are wrapped in warm dreams of being with their fathers when they die . . .?

X X V . . .

Upon my return to my hotel, I found an invitation to visit Dr. Ampofo of Mampong. After being in Africa for a month, this was the first invitation I'd received from the black bourgeoisie. I was anxious to meet Dr. Ampofo, for his personality was of a kind that evoked extreme reactions; there were those who liked him and those who felt that he embodied something evil.

Half an hour's drive up the escarpment through dense forest brought me to a neat village where, for the first time, I saw flowers blooming. . . . Dr. Ampofo's home could be seen a hundred yards away: a design of stone and serried windows, long lines, terraced landscape, trees, color. . . .

Dr. Ampofo was forty-five years of age, black, short, nervous, thin, alert of body and agile of mind. He smiled quickly, *too* quickly, as he shook my hand. And he laughed. . . . I was beginning to wonder about that African laugh; it did not stem from mirth, as many people have erroneously thought. It was to bid for time, to hide one's reactions, to reflect, to observe, to judge, to make up one's mind! He was most gracious and showed me his beautiful new home which, he said, had been designed and built by his wife. He next showed me a collection of his wood carving which he himself had carved. He had a medical degree; he was the head of a huge African family;

he had acted in the movies; and he conducted a thriving business in timber. . . .

With drinks at our elbows, the doctor and I got to work at last. "Do you mind talking about yourself?"

"Not at all," he said.

He'd come to Mampong in 1919 after four years of schooling in his father's village; he had lived in Mampong until 1922, then he'd attended boarding school at the Annum Presbyterian Senior School until 1926. He related how he and his friends had had to walk for three days and nights to reach this school, for there was no transportation in those days. His schooling continued at Cape Coast in the Mfantsipim's Boys' Secondary School. In 1930 he got a scholarship to study art for his B.A., but, halfway through, he gave it up for science. He won a competitive scholarship for study in England, and in 1932 he went to Edinburgh and completed his studies, obtaining his medical degree in 1939.

Touring Europe, he was caught in Sweden by the outbreak of war; he was forced to remain in Stockholm until February, 1940, at which time he returned to Africa. . . .

"Doctor," I began, "I want to ask you about life in the Gold Coast. I came here because of the reputation of the Convention People's Party. It's the one thing here that seems somewhat familiar to me; it's a modern political movement and operates in terms of concepts that Westerners can understand. Now, this movement is not Communist, for the Communists are opposed to it; they have branded it as 'corrupt, bourgeois nationalism.' Yet, when I try to account for this national liberation movement, I'm baffled. Some aspects of this movement seem to partake of Leftism; other aspects are almost religious in their emotional expression. Sometimes one must use Marxist ideas to aid one in trying to grasp what one is looking at, but Marxism cannot satisfactorily account for this. . . . You don't have in this country a great deal of industrialization which would have created a rootless mass of men ready for such a movement. Neither do you possess a great deal of class consciousness out of which such a movement could be created. The race consciousness here is not as sharp as that of the American Negro. Yet you have a rip-roaring political movement. How did it happen?"

He hesitated, then laughed.

"It has a background. It's not only Nkrumah, I tell you. These things do not just burst out of the blue. There's a creative energy in these people, the Akan people. The Akan is a stubborn and proud man. There is in him a consciousness of national humiliation and there is a deep race consciousness, deeper than you think. . . ."

"How does this race consciousness manifest itself?" I asked. "Both Britishers and Americans have assured me that no such thing exists here—"

"It *does* exist." He was adamant. "The men who organized our people into nationalistic organizations were educated abroad. It was in foreign lands that they learned the meaning of what was happening to our people. The men who went to America and to England came back and injected, and rightly so, the concept of our subjection and the concept of race consciousness into our lives. It came from without.

"The prime event that spurred us to action was the fall of the price of cocoa in 1940-43. Cocoa was so plentiful, the market was so rigged, that the farmers were burning it; there was no good price for it. Cocoa was withheld to lift the prices, and during the war the world market was bad. . . .

"Then the Europeans made a move that brought violence. . . . A group formed a monopoly which was known as the Association of West African Merchants. They aimed to buy cocoa as cheaply as possible from us and sell it as high as possible on the markets of the world. These same merchants sold us imported goods at terribly high prices. We were trapped. . . .

"This led to the events of 1948 when the national boycott was launched and white business firms were looted and burned. . . ."

"So far, it's clear," I said. "But that does not explain the Convention People's Party. Why did it arise in the Gold Coast? I've attended political meetings and I've seen some strange things. I've seen chiefs pouring libations; I've heard prayers, both Christian and pagan; I've heard oaths of personal loyalty taken by vast throngs of people to obey and serve the Leader—"

"You saw oaths administered?" he asked me quietly, seriously.

"I'd not lie to you. Why should I? I saw it on two occasions."

"Yes. It happens," he said, sighing.

"What does it mean?" I asked him.

He looked at me and laughed.

"You're touching on something—"

"An oath in Africa is a terrible thing, I'm told," I said, trying to urge him on.

He laughed again, rose, walked the floor, then scratched his head and whirled to me. He shook his finger at me, saying:

"When you talk of oaths, you're touching on *juju*—"

"Oh, come now," I said.

"You don't believe in *juju?*" he asked.

"Hell, no! You're a doctor. You *can't* believe in such; not literally," I said.

He studied me and wagged his head.

"There's something to it," he said solemnly.

"It's purely psychological," I said.

"I've seen it work," he told me.

"It works only for those who believe in it," I said. "It's a psychological problem."

He was silent again, looking at me and then looking off.

"You're strong-minded," he said.

"Oh, no. It's just common sense. If the African had any damned *juju*, he'd have used it a long time ago to free his country," I said.

"I've seen men who had been sentenced to death by *juju*," the doctor said. "And they died."

"They believed that they would die," I said. "It's suggestion, self-hypnosis, that's all."

"Yes; if you keep in mind that it's psychological, you can escape it," he conceded. "But it gets a lot of people. . . ."

"I've found evidence of that," I agreed. "Now, this business of the compound family and the head of that family to whom the members owe loyalty. . . . Does that have anything to do with the foundations

of the Convention People's Party? *Juju's* out of the way; let's talk
sense. Tell me what you think."

He still walked restlessly about the room, glancing at me now and
then. Then he gave another laugh. I did not know him and he did not
know me; and I *was* breaking in on him rather unceremoniously.

"Look, don't be afraid of me," I tried to reassure him. "I want to
get at the bottom of this reality. But each time I've tried to talk a
little, when I begin pressing questions, the Africans—"

"They close up like clams," he said.

"Exactly. But they ought to know that I know that something is
being hidden here. . . ."

"What do you want to know?" he asked me, sitting suddenly.

"The official line is that this is just pure and simple nationalism," I
resumed. "It is, but it's more than that. Yet it's not Communism. I'd
know it if it was. . . . Now, explain this to me in terms that I, a
Westerner, can understand, can grasp."

His wife entered the room at that moment. She was a tall, handsome woman, poised, Western in her manner. I congratulated her
in her taste in the building and furnishing of her home and she was
modest and polite. She and her husband spoke briefly in their native
tongue and she invited me to lunch. I accepted, but warned her that
African pepper was too much for my stomach. She promised that
the lunch would be mild and simple. . . . When she had gone, I
turned again to politics.

"I see the great influence of the tribe in politics," I said. "But how
is it done? How does the party latch onto the tribal life?"

"All right. . . . We live in a queer way in Africa," the doctor began
his explanation. "Our inheritance is matrilineal, coming from the
mother's side of the family. When a man takes a wife, he cannot
leave the family and live with her; he has to bring her into his
family. She becomes a daughter in his family in addition to being
a wife. She comes under the authority of the family. The family is
supreme in Africa; its authority is unquestioned. That is why no
European girl can fit into our families. They are acceptable, but they
find it impossible. . . .

"When a head of the family joins the Convention People's Party,

the entire family joins. And families in Africa are large. The head
of the family has the final say; his word is law. If a chief is Convention People's Party, then the entire town is Convention People's
Party. . . . Say, did you know that Nkrumah is a Tufuhene . . .?"

"A *what?* What's that?" I asked.

"It's a Fanti term. . . . It means Warrior Chief."

"But that's just an honorary title, isn't it?"

"No."

"It's serious?"

"Of course it is," the doctor said. "Now, the origin of the Convention People's Party came from the Gold Coast Youth Organization,
which was led by Gbedemah, Ako Adjei. . . . Nkrumah was the spirit
of the group. He knew how to set off herd reactions, and the clan
and the family formed the basis for his drive for power. His aim is
to replace the chiefs entirely, and eventually the British also. . . .

"I believe that Nkrumah believes in the same qualities that he
arouses in others. I've tried to question him about these things, and
when I did, he evaded me, he hemmed. He has seen clearly the kind
of life we lead and he is out to organize it. . . . He has learned how
to sink roots into this tribal life and he intends to rule. He is on his
way to wipe out the identity of people like me. . . . It's not
democracy. I know he has the masses with him, but it's not democracy. The real center of power in our society was in the hands of
the chiefs, but Nkrumah has smashed all that. . . ."

"Why are you opposed to this, Doctor?"

"I'm not a political man, but I'm opposed to it."

"Why? Why don't you serve the people? The people need you,
men like you. . . ."

"It's not right," he said.

"What are you saying?" I asked him. "Whatever power there is in
the Gold Coast, they'll need men like you. They are your people;
serve them—"

"The people must be educated—"

"Granted," I agreed. "But why not let them be free first? It would
have taken a thousand years to educate them at the rate the British
were going. The Americans were once a colonial people too. But

they didn't wait until all of their people were educated to make their bid for freedom. They took their freedom and then educated their people. This is a question of power. . . . Either you feel that you ought to be free or you do not."

"Educate the people and then let them be free," he said and laughed.

And I knew that that laugh was to cushion the shock of his attitude.

"What do you think's going to happen here, then?"

"There'll be a blowup, a sudden change," he argued. "This cannot go on. You cannot build anything solid on a basis of mass hysteria."

"In what way will it blow up?" I asked. "It's certain that the country's united against the British. The British have no roots or parties here. Therefore, if there's to be a blowup, it'll have to come from either African opposition or British-supported African opposition. You know that the African opposition's too weak to act alone. Would bourgeois Africans fight Nkrumah for the British?"

"I don't know how it's going to happen; but it won't last," he reiterated. "This is no way to build a nation—"

"Doctor, my mind is open about that," I told him. "You know what happened in Russia. Ideology aside. You know what happened in Germany. In Spain. In Italy. In China. In Argentina. Those were not accidents or the actions of evil men. And a lot more is involved than the problem of education. People are tired of the old, traditional forms of living. All about them they see and sense the possibility of change. The people who should make that change—men like you— do not make it. Then along comes someone who sees that it can be done and he does it. You cannot expect a vacuum to remain unfilled. Don't blame Nkrumah. I'm not partisan. I'm objective. Nkrumah's doing what should have been done long ago; that's why he was able to do it so quickly and easily. The cost of that kind of social change comes high; many things go by the board. . . . This seems to be the reality of the twentieth century. . . . Now, since other nations have proved that the masses can absorb education quickly, why not the masses of the Gold Coast . . .?"

"I'm willing to admit that the masses can absorb technical education quickly. . . ."

"Isn't that decisive?"

"What about the values—?"

"The old values go," I argued. "The new ones are created as men
strive to live, as men's needs prod them forward. . . . I'm not so much
for Nkrumah as I am for the right of the masses of people to cut
loose from the past, and since Nkrumah's leading them from the
past, I'm for him. Man, I've looked at your villages. They and the
people in them are rotting. . . . It's a living death. Only when men
break loose from that rot and death and plunge creatively into the
future do they become something to respect. Life then becomes a
supremely spiritual task of molding and shaping the world according to the needs of the human heart—"

"That's not going to happen in Africa soon," he told me, shaking
his head.

"And did you think that Nkrumah could happen so soon?" I
countered.

"It's a matter of time—This is too *fast!*"

"How do you know how *fast* people can develop? Has it ever
really been tried? Tested? All right, make Africa a test and see. No
matter what you do here in your fight for freedom, as long as it's
for freedom, you can't lose. . . ."

We were going at it so hot and heavy that I didn't notice that it
was almost one o'clock. During lunch there was a lull. I'd at last
talked freely to my first intellectual African; he didn't agree with
me, but at least he knew what I was talking about. My position in
the Gold Coast was indeed strange; the Convention People's Party
was afraid to talk freely and frankly to me, yet I was for them in a
more fundamental sense than they could accept. And it was only
with the opposition that I could talk freely, and they disagreed
with me!

Must it always be that the middle class must go down to defeat
complaining and rejecting reality . . .? I'd seen the same thing in
Buenos Aires. . . . There I'd had to consort with the decadent
nobility who sat huddled and afraid in their huge houses, cursing,

swearing that peons could not operate telephones, could not run railroads. . . . Industrialization had made the world simple, yet those who opposed the masses operating that world dared not oppose industrialization. Why, their profits came out of it. . . . One's respect for man sank as one watched this same stupid drama re-enact itself from country to country, almost without variation.

Was Dr. Ampofo's attitude the only contribution that English education and missions had given to the upper-class Africans of the Gold Coast? The doctor knew, of course, what Britain had done to his people, how it had shattered their culture; he knew, deep in his heart, that Nkrumah's overthrowing the chiefs came only after Britain had long undermined the very basis of tribal life, that Nkrumah had only deliberately and self-consciously dealt that system its last blow. . . .

What bitter pathos churned in the hearts of the African middle class! How they felt that Britain, their idol, had let them down! Yet, what could Britain do? She had no roots among the masses of African people and yet she had heavy investments in gold, timber, diamonds, bauxite, manganese. . . . She had denounced Nkrumah as dangerous, but, when faced with losing her material interests, she, like Jesus, conferred upon the black rebel an "act of grace" . . . Britain had acted to save not right, not hope, not honesty; she acted to defend her interests. And that is as it should have been. One's real quarrel is that the British could never say so frankly. Maybe they didn't know how to. . . .

XXVI...

If I was to continue my taxi excursions into the "bush," it was now clear that I would have to rent a car for a long period. I finally approached a Swiss car-rental agency whose officials told me that a car that could withstand a "bush" trek would cost me twenty pounds a month, plus the driver's salary, plus the cost of gas and oil; and, beyond a twenty-five mile radius of Accra, I'd have to pay a premium of a shilling a mile because of bad roads; further, while on trek, I'd have to maintain the driver's food and lodging. . . . I resolved to rent the car and keep rolling until my money melted, and then I'd go home.

While in the offices of the car-rental agency I noticed that the Europeans dressed much more simply and comfortably than the Africans. The whites were striving to keep cool in the torrid heat, but the petty bourgeois black clerks and secretaries, etc., wore heaps of woolen clothes to draw a highly visible line of social distinction between themselves and the naked, illiterate masses. An educated African could not afford to be seen dressed comfortably, that is, in sandals and a toga; he had to dress like the British dressed in Britain! And the Britisher wore shorts and T-shirts!

Having rented a car, I began to plan a tour of the triangle enclosed in the lines drawn between Takoradi, Accra, and Kumasi, an area that held three-fourths of the nation's wealth and population; and, what was more, it comprised a big slice of the high rain forest, the real jungle.

But, if I went on trek, where would I sleep, what could I eat? The Americans I questioned had no suggestions. I approached the Prime Minister's office and was urged to talk to the British. I balked. I'd come to be with Africans and I was being shunted into the hands of the British! I brooded for a couple of days and, in the end, I knew that I either had to depend upon the British to see the interior or go home. . . .

I presented my request to the Gold Coast Information Service and was told that they would draw up an itinerary for me in a few days' time. Meanwhile, I hired a chauffeur, an ex-middleweight champion of the Gold Coast, Battling Kojo, black, quick, and loyal. I was advised that I needed someone of his pugnacity if I was to be on my own in the jungle.

I waited, fighting against a never-ending sense of enervation. I was eating a normal amount, but the food seemed to give me no strength. I was told that vegetables grew so swiftly in this hot and red earth that they were not really nourishing! Lettuce refused to form a head here. Corn shot up so quickly that the ears became full-sized before the grain matured on the cobs. Other vegetables turned into soft, pulpy masses. Among the Europeans, tropical ulcers were common and they were forever dosing themselves with vitamins. Fresh milk and butter were unknown, being shipped from Europe in tins. The threat of sleeping sickness from the tsetse fly was so acute to both cattle and humans that no large herds of cattle were kept. From the Northern Territories cattle were marched five hundred miles down to the coastal area and when they arrived they were gaunt, tough, and weak-eyed from the long trek in the awful heat. . . . In the hotel restaurant I've never been able to tell from the taste the kind of meat I'm eating.

The heat makes insect life breed prolifically: mosquitoes, ants, lizards, and myriads of other creatures swarm in the air and under-foot. A lump of sugar left in a saucer will draw ants in an hour even to the second floor of a stone building in which stewards are con-stantly cleaning. Everything seems to develop faster here; life gushes up in a careless profusion; the universe seems in a state of biological hurry, as though nature were prodding and driving all living organ-isms beyond their normal rate of reaction.

The cheapness of labor clutters the landscape with odd sights. One sees gangs of black workmen cutting grass with long cutlasses. Couldn't it be done with machines? Sure; but labor is cheaper than machines, and machines get rusty and wear out. The problem of the repair and upkeep of the laterite roads has also been solved in a fashion that indicates that men are cheaper than materials. The torrential rains wash out the roads periodically and, instead of anchoring the roads in beds of rock or cement, which is expensive, large gangs of workers are kept constantly busy shoveling the soil back into place.

I've not seen a single wood carving or art object since I've landed in the Gold Coast. The advent of the missionary has driven under-ground much of the religious expression of the tribal people; they no longer allow it to be known that they fashion those odd, elongated ebony figures that Europeans seek so ardently. In the eyes of the new black Christians those figures hold no value; they are obtain-able, I'm told, but you will have to convince a chief or a fetish priest that your interest is favorable to tribal life. Instead of many gods, the Gold Coast African now has one Who is nailed to a cross and Whose image is stamped out by mass production.

Just as he has been shamed into hiding his religion, so has the Gold Coast African attitude toward political symbols become more Western than the West's. One day I was asked to comment upon the unofficial (of course!) designs for the new flag which the Gold Coast will adopt when freedom comes. After examining all kinds of newfangled geometric patterns, I said that I could not conceive of a Gold Coast flag without a "stool" upon it. What? My African listeners were speechless with rage and indignation. The "stool"? Never! They were sick and tired of "stools"! But, I argued, look at America. The thirteen original colonies had hated their colonial status, but, when they designed their flag, they were confident that they would eventually be free and they included in their flag a symbolic representation of their original colonial status. . . . You too, I argued, will some day be so far removed psychologically from this struggle that you will look back and want to acknowledge your early religious and national symbols. . . . But, no, *never* . . . !

I was invited to a party and did not want to go, but somebody whispered that I'd meet some of the local CID men and the head of the Accra police, a Mr. X. That decided me. I've long been interested in the psychology of policemen; of all the functionaries in a country, they share the outlook, the fears, the aims, and the attitudes of the group holding power. Enforcers of the law generally partake of the impulses both of the lawmakers and the lawbreakers, and they are mostly men devoid of illusions.

Mr. X was about my height, nervous, talkative; in fact, he resembled a foreman in a factory; he looked anything but a policeman. We were immediately drawn to each other: he wanted to know what I was doing and I wanted to know what he was doing, and we spent most of the evening talking together.

"Just what do you do here?" I asked him.

"My job is to keep law and order in this city," he asserted with pride.

"Is it difficult?"

"No more difficult here than it is anywhere else," he told me.

"But I thought that Africans were so *different* that you'd have to use special methods to catch them. . . ."

"Not a bit of it," he argued. "The same thing that makes an Englishman steal makes an African steal. There's but one slight difference: the African is more prone to be prouder of his theft than the Englishman—"

"How do you account for that?"

"I don't know," he said. "But he just is."

"Maybe the black criminal thinks he's right. . . ."

He blinked, then asked:

"In what way?"

"Well, it's *his* country, you know. Maybe he thinks he's evening up scores."

"Maybe," he said thoughtfully. "But, for my part, it *is* his country. I'm here just to do a job—"

"Does that include training Africans to take over the enforcement of law and order?"

"Absolutely. We've got them right now studying in Scotland Yard."

"Do they have much chance to get experience in London?"

"No; they're sent back here for that."

"Do you find any emotional differences between an African murderer and an English one?"

"Well, what I told you about stealing goes also for killing. The African feels that he has done right, most of the time," Mr. X explained. "If an African kills his woman, it's because he feels that she deserves it. He'd scorn running off and hiding. He even takes a kind of pride in telling why he did it. You don't get much of a sense of guilt out of them."

"Does that stem from tribal influence?"

"Maybe. He kills her because what she did was not right—"

"Under what law would he be tried? Tribal or English?"

"Under our laws."

"I don't want you to divulge any of your confidential matters, but tell me: suppose a crime has been committed and you are called in. What do you do?"

He thought a moment.

"I'll tell you about one. . . . A few weeks ago a safe was robbed here. The safe belonged to a European auto firm. They had a repair shop. The metal of the safe was cut through—"

"With an acetylene torch?"

"Exactly."

"That smacks of New York or Chicago."

"Of course it does. Now, my job was to catch the criminal. Who did it? I can't be bothered with fancy theories. I have a practical job to do. Who cut into that safe and took the money? Now—"

"Maybe a European or an American safe-cracker came ashore. . . . Truly, no black boy could do that, unless he has had experience. It's a daring feat—"

"That's where you are wrong. First of all, we know pretty well who comes into this colony. There are no American or European safe-crackers within reach. So, I must concentrate upon the Africans.

"Now, finally everybody is cleared but one boy. He's average; he's never been out of the colony. He has only recently been hired. He works on the bodies of the autos; he has just recently learned to use the acetylene torch. . . . We take fingerprints. It was *his* job. . . . We confront him. He confesses—"

"No coercion used?"

"None whatsoever."

"But did he put two and two together so *quickly?*"

"You'd be surprised how bright these boys really are," he assured me.

"Do you think that brightness is confined to crime?"

"God, no!"

This policeman was, ironically, the most liberal-minded Englishman I'd met so far in Africa! As a law-enforcement officer, he had to admit that it didn't take years or months, but only days, for that young boy to see that if he could cut through the steel of auto bodies, he could also cut through the steel of the boss's safe and take the money. It was strange that this man who had served for years in Scotland Yard should turn out to be so frank and intensely perceptive! His mind was not encumbered with bulky theories of

sociology or anthropology that insisted that certain spans of time
had to elapse before people could absorb knowledge. He didn't
complain that Africans were progressing too fast. If he'd allowed
his attention to become cluttered up with such nonsense, he'd have
lost his job pronto. A policeman has to assume the equality of man;
hence, he sees the possibilities of Africa, especially on the level of
crime, much more clearly than the Colonial Office or the professors
in English universities.

Now that I'd rented my car, I decided to find out how rapidly the
pounds would mount up at the rate of a shilling a mile. Prampram
had been pointed out as a typical ancient village and I directed Kojo
to drive there. It was raining and the roads were under water most
of the way. As we heaved in sight of the village, I saw the usual
mud huts with thatched roofs and a few cement houses built up out
of blocks. I heard drums beating and I looked out and saw a group
of men clad in togas and dancing in the cloudy light of the rainy
morning. It was a funeral; an elder had just died. Not far from the
men was a group of women, some sitting, some standing, some
dancing. I waved and smiled at the men and they waved and smiled
in return. There seemed to be no grief; they were all relaxed. Now
and then a man would leap out in front of the drums and do a
frenzied dance, signaling the gods to look down with favor upon his
tribe. Then I started violently, for a musket had gone off right behind
my back. . . . I spun to see what was happening; a man was kneeling,
holding a gun from which wisps of blue smoke curled. The gun
was pointing toward the sky. . . .

A black young man came up; he spoke English.

"Why do they fire those guns?" I asked him.

"It's custom," he said.

"But there must be some *reason* for it," I insisted.

"Why do you send flowers to a funeral in America?" he asked me,
laughing.

I stared, unable to answer.

"It must be custom," I said and laughed too.

The young man seemed intelligent and willing to answer questions, and so I waded right in.

"Why are they beating the drums?"

"The drums 'talk,'" he explained. "Not everybody now can interpret drum language. But those drums are announcing to the spirit world that the elder is on his way."

"Don't the women sing?"

"Yes; they sang this morning. They wailed too," he said.

The funeral ritual flowed on; they danced war dances, the muskets fired, and the drums beat on and on.

"Where is the dead elder?"

"He's on his bed. Do you want to see him?"

"Yes."

I followed the young man to a paneless window through which I saw a long, black man wrapped in a brightly colored shroud; he was stretched out upon a bed and a white strip of cloth was bound over his mouth.

"What's that cloth for?"

The young man said that he didn't know.

"Who handles the dead, that is, prepares them for burial?"

"The women handle the dead, wash them, dress them, and make them ready for the grave," he explained. "The women bring us into the world and they see us go out of it."

I saw women going to the foot of the dead man's bed and whispering a few words into his ears. I could not hear or understand what was being said.

"Are they praying?" I asked.

"Well, not exactly," he told me. "They are telling him good-bye. They are giving him messages for their relatives in the spirit world, you see."

It was not death as we know it; in fact, it was not death at all. It was a departure.

The "talking" drums recounted the man's life, celebrating the trouble he had seen, and they also sought to pacify the "dead" man for the perils he had to encounter in the world of spirits. For there was a transition period from the world of the living to the world of the dead. For a certain number of days the "dead" man's spirit was supposed to hover in the vicinity of the living as it climbed a steep hill toward the land of his ancestors, and that climb was long and hard. Hence, as the "dead" man had been breathing his last, his soul had already begun, in terms of native imagination, to pant and heave with effort. The death rattle was interpreted as physical exertion; therefore, as the old man was "dying," his relatives poured water down his throat to help him quench his thirst. (Maybe it actually hastened the poor man's end. . . .)

In Africa the "dead" live side by side with the living; they eat, breathe, laugh, hate, love, and continue doing in the world of ghostly shadows exactly what they had been doing in the world of flesh and blood. The Akan feel that the "dead" get lonely in that world and are anxious for the living to come and keep them company. Thus, the pacification of the "dead" constitutes one of their biggest problems of life.

The drums of state beat on, encouraging the "dead" man to mount the steep hill of the other world. Naked black children stood about, their mouths agape in awe. Already the other world was as real to them as this one. . . . Instinct ruled here; fear and guilt and doubt and hope held sway in the dismal morning air.

How did this come to be? It looked simple, but it had its origins in a complicated and subtle balancing of many emotional factors. On my way back to the hotel, I visited a bookstore and bought a stack of literature; I wanted to see what the "authorities" had to say about this. And was there a better way to spend a rainy afternoon in Africa than in reading what they say about their "dead"?

Thumbing through old pages, one learns that the African does not believe idly in another world; for him, there *is* another world. Every object in existence has a twin, itself and its ghostly shadow. (Plato seems to have been somewhat primitive too!) The origin of this notion came from his dreams. Did he not move about and see people and objects many miles away when he slept? Just as he is convinced that spirits dwell in trees, rivers, in fact, in all inanimate objects, so a spirit, he is persuaded, dwells in man.

From this point on, matters become a little complicated. The spirit, known as *kra*, that dwells in man is distinct from him. In death, when *kra* leaves a man, it has two possibilities: it can, if the man was old, go straight to the world of spirits. If, however, the man died before his time, if he was unaccountably ill or accidentally killed, his *kra* would linger on in the world of the living for an indeterminate length of time.

With the normal "death," all goes well; the family places food, water, tobacco, alcohol, clothing, etc., at the side of the grave. (Weapons are expressly excluded, for fear that the "dead" would use them harmfully against the living.) But with the *kra* that lingers, for whatever reason, trouble starts. This *kra* can "embrace" children and induce illness in them. Indeed, *kra* have been known to enter into newborn babes, thereby reincarnating themselves. It is, therefore, a matter of conjecture when someone has just died in a family and when someone has just been born in that family if that "dead" man's *kra* has returned in the form of the new baby. . . .

Life in the ghost world is an exact duplicate of life in this world. A farmer in this world is a farmer there; a chief here is a chief there. It is, therefore, of decisive importance when one enters that world of ghostly shades to enter it in the right manner. For you can be snubbed there just as effectively and humiliatingly as you were snubbed here.

From this belief that the "dead" live as we live, the following deduction is simple: to the degree that we love, honor, and revere our "dead," we must help them to establish themselves in the world of shadows. So, in the end, the extreme sacrifice will be made. If a chief had slaves in this world, his slaves would be sent to serve him in the beyond; and so would his several wives be dispatched to comfort him. Fortunately, most Africans are poor and their duties in the next world will be as modest as they were in this world and they will have no need of many slaves or wives to keep them happy. . . .

All of these seemingly gruesome duties are performed with awe and tenderness. Make no mistake about that. . . . Even human sacrifice is solemnly ritualized. What strikes us as being monstrous is done by them with a sense of exaltation. Yet, suppose it's not done? Ah. . . . The "dead" do not like neglect, and they are quick to revenge such by returning to the world of the living and snatching you into their dreaded domain. Why the "dead" insist upon acting in this vengeful manner is a question to which the Akan has no clear-cut answer.

How did these strange notions come about? Yes; it was about time that I dipped into the muddy metaphysical waters of those African intellectuals who had tried to explain these spiritual riddles. And I selected as my guide a learned African who was still living, a man to whom I could talk after I had read his ideas. That man was none other than the leading political opponent of the Convention People's Party, Nkrumah's Nemesis, Dr. J. B. Danquah; and forthwith I plunged at last into his *The Akan Doctrine of God.*

I hastened to confess that I'm far from being the most suitable person in the world to report on metaphysical doctrines. A fair report on such subtleties requires a man who, through empathy, can follow the curling and dipping of such notions with anxious love. I possess no such love. . . . In relating the following, I am, no doubt, doing a degree of violence to the astute learning of Dr. Danquah; but, since I'm of another culture, another time sense even, and since I cannot express myself other than directly, this is how it must be.

The first fact that impresses one in Dr. Danquah's exposition is his unjustified feeling that he must demonstrate that the African has a religion whose concepts are on par with that of the religion of the Western world. In a manner that smacks of an unconscious apology, he assumes that Christianity is believed superior and that the devotees of that religion are too filled with racial prejudice to acknowledge that the religion of the African is just as good, in fact, according to Dr. Danquah, it is, in some respects, better. I'd agree with the good doctor about this; the African religion has no hell and no sin, and hell and sin have always struck me as boresome and static conceptions. Africans manage to fuse hell and sin in an organic and concrete manner, and their lives thereby become as charged and exciting as the moving tables and floating trumpets in a séance in a dreary London flat.

Each race, says Dr. Danquah, apprehends God through a "seed"-quality of ideas; thus:

"... When the family is the chief idea, things that are dishonorable and undignified, actions that in disgracing you disgrace the family, are held to be vices, and the highest virtue is found in honor and dignity. Tradition is the determinant of what is right and just, what is good and done."

The Akan regard the sky and the earth as great gods. The sky-god is the Saturday Sky-God, *Nyame*. The earth-god is the Thursday Earth-Goddess, *Asaase Yaa*. But the most important gods to which the people appeal daily are the spirits of the departed ancestors of the clan. Over and above this there are hundreds of minor gods, who, when appealed to, act as intercessors to the higher gods; these higher gods, in their vast concern with other worlds and other matters, do not have the time to give full attention to the prayers of millions of ordinary men. . . .

The Akan believe that the spirits of his ancestors find a repository in the Golden Stool, which represents the soul of the nation. The head of a Stool is called Nana, and this meaning, rising from the Nana who is chief of the family, goes right on up to the Nana of the Universe, this final Nana occupying the great Stool of all existence. There is, then, a direct line of relation from the head of the family, rising by degrees, to the great god who rules all things. And the bridge between the head of the family and the head of the universe is to be found in the friendly or baleful spirits of ancestors who hover about the families in which they once lived.

To show how the Akan concept of God operates in a real social sense, Dr. Danquah addresses himself to the baffling problem of the "omnipotence" of God, for, if each head of a family, clan, tribe, or state partakes of God, are they too "omnipotent"? Dr. Danquah says: ". . . The Akan idea is of a community, continuous with the past, present, and future of his relations of blood. The 'omnipotence' of the high-father cannot be greater than the reality of this community. A father, of necessity, is what all his children are."

On page 82 of *The Akan Doctrine of God*, Dr. Danquah clearly, in the name of the West African, rejects some of the most central concepts of Christian religion. Sin and remission of sin are tossed out of the window. Original sin is flatly rejected. The notion that, because two remote ancestors had sexual relations and bore a child, there was imposed upon all mankind a threat of suffering, is, to the African mind, simply ridiculous. And that one can only be saved through God's grace from this "sin" is something that the African cannot conceive. (He may pay lip service to such in the face of white Christians, but in his heart he knows that it is not true.) That the world is "worldly," sinful, a place to abhor, is a joke to the African mentality. And that one must belong to a certain church in order to be saved merits a smile from black lips.

The Akan believe that one comes into the world to try to perfect his soul, and, failing one try, he returns again and again until his soul is ready to join that of the universal. Closer and closer does Dr. Danquah approach the linking of man and God until finally, through incarnation, he sees a blending. On page 95 of *The Akan Doctrine of God*, he states: ". . . we have a superman born, but not born as a superman by his parents, but because, and in virtue, of his own previous achievement in a previous incarnation . . . he may have lived in that same community in his previous life, or he may have chosen or been assigned that community for his present essay in life, believing that a new country, a new environment, lacking in some of the opportunities, and some, possibly, of the resistances of his previous life or community, may afford him just that beneficial advantage and accommodation for actualizing his soul for an accelerated progress towards the good . . ." And when a man overcomes great odds, distinguishes himself, "that superior nature shines through the superman, as if a god had revealed himself in him . . ."

The religion of the Akan is not primitive; it is simply terrifying. And even Dr. Danquah seems to feel that what he claims for the African is a little too tall, for he modestly asserts (page 116): "I do not, of course, recommend to modern European thought to follow the Akan and worship this mystery that explains why any man, at his choice, has it in him to become a god or a beast."

Death does not round off life; it is not the end; it complements life. Dr. Danquah's theories of death are expanded (page 156): "To the Akan, therefore, death is less than a negation of life . . . It is but an instrument of the higher consummation, a planting or fruition of it." And then Dr. Danquah gives philosophical dignity to the

African mood about death (page 160): "Death, therefore, is not a natural thing. Basically, there is no reason why any man, any being, should die. . . ."

The door is now wide open for any man to become suspicious when death strikes a loved one; the cause of death seems inexplicable, due either to witchcraft or poison. Dr. Danquah spells it out clearly: "Deep down in the natural being of man there appears to be an instinct that man is not a dying animal, that he was not made to die, and that he has that in him which ought to keep permanently his vital function working interminably."

I come up for air, to take a deep breath. . . .

These are the broad religious propositions underlying the beliefs of the Akan people of the Gold Coast.

XXVII...

I at once, of course, bent my efforts to meet this man. I had the good luck to see him a few days later at a great formal gathering, and, alas, it was to an Englishman that I had to appeal for an introduction to him. And, uninhibited, I told him:

"I want to talk to you."

"What about?" he asked me.

"About your ideas about the people of the Gold Coast."

"What do you want to ask me?" He was equally direct.

"I'd like to know why you hold such views," I said. "Why are you with the opposition? What are you really trying to do? What is this business of the African being so different?"

"How long have you been in Africa?" he asked me.

"About two months," I said.

"Stay longer and you'll *feel* your race," he told me.

"*What?*"

"You'll *feel* it," he assured me. "It'll all come *back* to you."

"What'll come back?"

"The knowledge of your race." He was explicit.

I liked the man, but not as a Negro or African; I liked his directness, his willingness to be open. Yet, I knew that I'd never feel an
identification with Africans on a "racial" basis.

"I doubt that," I said softly.

"What specifically do you want to ask me?"

"What's going to happen here? I'm trying to figure it out. You
have lived here; you are African. Can this last? Why are the masses
following Nkrumah? He talks a language that they have no background to understand, except his campaign for national liberation.
Now, you talk about their religion, the religion they live each day.
Why do the masses follow Nkrumah and not you?"

That got him; he stared off above the heads of the crowds of
people dancing over a glassy floor. Then he said:

"All right. Come to see me Thursday. At four."

I was there on the dot of four. I met a trained lawyer, gracious,
affable, generous-hearted, a man who was deeply baffled and tried
to hide it, a man whose mind was desperately trying to grapple with
a new and alien reality which he hated. He had the bearing of an
aristocrat, relaxed, poised; he was on his mental toes each moment
I spent with him. No honest Englishman could ever really quarrel
with this man; he personified, alas, exactly what England wanted to
make every African into. . . . And yet they had unceremoniously
ditched him! And he felt it; he never said one word about it; but it
was deep and bitter in him. He had been betrayed by England, the
land that had given him his ideals and his sense of honor.

"What are the differences between you and Nkrumah?"

"We really have no differences," he said blandly.

"Oh, really, now. You are at each other's throats!"

"We are one in our aim for self-government for the Gold Coast,"
he said.

"But you are not together," I said.

He took a deep breath, looked off, then glanced at me and said:

"Nkrumah is selfish. With wiles and tricks he stole power. We
sent for that man to come and help us. Then, while pretending to
work for us, he secretly built up his own following within our ranks.

Ruthlessly, he split the national front, then made a filthy deal with the British. . . . One day he said that he wanted national freedom, and the next day he compromised with the British."

"Do you think he'll keep power for long?" I asked.

"Yes; until the illiterate masses wake up," he said.

"Why don't *you* try to win the masses to your side?"

I watched a grimace come over his face; he looked at me and smiled ruefully.

"Masses?" he echoed the word. "I don't like this thing of masses. There are only individuals for me—"

"But masses form the basis of political power in the modern world today," I told him.

"You believe that?" he asked me. "I know you fellows dote on this thing of masses. . . . I've read that you claim that this mass unrest comes from the industrialization of the Western world—"

"Where else could it come from?" I asked him. "Look, how did Nkrumah learn his techniques of organization? In New York, in Chicago, in Detroit, and in London he saw men organizing and he studied their methods. Then he came to Africa and applied them. . . . You're facing the twentieth century, Dr. Danquah."

He shook his head. Every word that I had uttered clashed with deep-set convictions. And it suddenly flashed through me that this man was not a politician and would never be one.

"Why is it that you cannot appeal to the masses on the basis of their daily needs?" I asked him. "You're a lawyer; you're used to *representing*. . . . Well, *represent* them. As we say in America: Be a mouthpiece for them—"

"I can't do things like that—"

"It's the only road to power in modern society," I said. "No matter how deeply you reject it, it's true."

"It's emotion," he protested.

It was the lawyer speaking. He was used to those facts which the tradition of law said were admissible; all other facts had to be excluded.

"I heard your speech," I told him. "I'd like to make a suggestion—"

"Go ahead," he said.

"Had I been you," I began, "I'd have stood up there and told those people: 'I'm Her Majesty's Opposition. I do not agree with the methods of Nkrumah. But, today, gentlemen, we have heard a motion for self-government. I'm an African. I want, above all things, to see my country free. So, for what it's worth, I hereby vote for this measure. And, in so doing, I challenge Nkrumah to keep his word and drive for self-government. I'm here to see that he does not lag, does not tarry. . . .' Dr. Danquah, had you said that, you would have become the hero of that hour. Those masses outside of that Assembly would have been galvanized. Nkrumah himself would have been speechless. And the British would have been thunderstruck; it would have put them on the spot. . . . Don't you see?"

He stared at me and shook his head slowly.

"I can't say things like that," he protested.

"Why not?"

"I don't believe in it," he said.

"It's not a matter of believing; it's politics! You would have voiced the demands of your country's masses, and you would have, with one stroke, pushed the British to a point where they would have had to act. . . ."

He was shaking his head. . . . It was no use. He was of the old school. One did not speak *for* the masses; one *told* them what to do. . . .

"You are a Christian?" I asked him, switching the subject.

"Yes," he said.

I was dumfounded.

"But I've read your book, *The Akan Doctrine of God.* You are a pagan too?"

"Yes," he said.

"Don't you find a conflict in the two religions?"

"No. Not at all. I go to church and serve God, and then I go to the Stool House and worship my ancestors," he explained. He was on familiar ground now and he grew expansive. "You see, the Christian worships the Son. We worship the Father. It's the same thing."

I wanted to ask him why he felt the need to worship both the

Father and the Son in that manner, but I shied off digging into delicate areas. It was evident that he knew nothing of the impact of the industrial West; the destiny of the disinherited would never be his; he was anchored for always in the calm waters of belief. . . . Our apprehensions of reality were too profoundly different to permit of much talk along religious lines. With a promise to meet and talk again, I took my leave.

It bothered me that I couldn't find among educated Africans any presentiment of what the future of their continent was to be. The more highly educated they had been, the more unfit they seemed to weigh and know the forces that were shaping the modern world.

It must not be thought that I did not give a full measure of respect to the ideas of Dr. Danquah. It's rare in our world today to feel that the sky has a value over and above that of space to be conquered, and that the earth means something more than an object out of which to dig minerals, or that human personality is something beyond a mere consumptive-productive unit. . . . The good doctor's grasp of life was essentially poetic; it was close to that which our fantasies and daydreams would have reality be; its essence was woven out of what we call human traits. Yet, if he would pit himself against his political adversaries, if he would win a struggle for the liberation of his country, he would have to lay aside such poetic preoccupations and adopt more realistic measures. He could, of course, declare that he would have no truck with such methods, that they were beneath him; but, if he did that, he would go down to defeat as so many others had gone before him.

What amazed me was that men like Dr. Danquah saw and knew each day what the British wanted from the Gold Coast; they knew that the hunger for raw materials and the opportunity to sell merchandise at high prices constituted the crux of British imperialism. An educated African might well curse those mysterious forces of geography that had made his country so fabulously rich in those raw materials that served as the fulcrum of world power politics. . . .

XXVIII...

I had long wanted to come to grips with the chiefs of the Gold Coast and finally one evening one was served up to me at the dinner table of the American Consul. This chief was a tall, gentle black man with a delicate face, sensitive fingers; it was obvious that he was burning to have his say, but he inhibited himself, declaring that he was not a political man. He was a Christian from the town of Odumase, the state of Manya Krobo. Gently, I steered the conversation toward native religious practices.

"Really," he told me, waving his hands a little impatiently, "our religion is basically the same as that of all other people. You mustn't get the idea that there's anything fantastic in ancestor worship."

"I agree with you," I said, anxious that he should talk freely. "All people have in them the germs of ancestor worship. The Russians are always talking of Marx, Lenin, and Stalin as being the *fathers* of the Russian Revolution. In America, we speak of our *Founding Fathers*. What they did in establishing the foundations of our country has assumed almost a magical sanctity." I could see the chief relaxing, and that was just my aim.

"There is nothing that we do in a Stool House that is strange," he explained. "There are stools there. To us they are sacred. Just as other churches have holy things, so do we. And you must realize that even in the illiterate masses there is a certain wisdom. By trial and error, they have learned a lot. For example, there is a certain leaf of a certain tree. If you hold it in one of your hands, you can catch a scorpion in the other, and the scorpion cannot sting you—"

"How was that discovered?" I asked.

"I don't know how these fetish men found it out, but they did," he said.

It was strange how his mind seemed to prefer to deal with such magical manifestations. The African places mystery between cause and effect and there is a deep predilection toward omnipotence of

223

thought, of spirit acting on spirit. The more I listened to Africans describe their achievements in the realms of the magical, the more I felt that it was how one related fact to fact that constituted the real difference between the Western and non-Western mind. When the chief had saturated my understanding with mystery, I launched into a discussion of politics where, I was certain, he could give me no facts tinged with mysticism.

"What do you think of the Convention People's Party?" I asked him.

"I'm not a political man," he began, "but, of course, politics influence my life. I'm a chief. Nkrumah has reduced the power of the chiefs, but he could not have done it unless the British had consented to it. You must understand that. I'm not bothered about all this talk about the wicked British imperialists. It's against their code of action that I inveigh. They betrayed a sacred trust that we chiefs had given them—"

"Tell me more about that," I urged him.

"It's simple," he explained. "Most of us chiefs gave the British our power. They didn't conquer all of us. Our tribes had been fighting one another. Now, for decades we'd watched the British and we liked the way that they did things. . . . Then, orally and in writing, we made agreements; we surrendered our power to them; we told them to establish peace. . . . Now, I contend that that power was *not* theirs to give away. . . . They should have handed it back to the men from whom they had got it. But they went and gave it away; they didn't even consult us; we knew nothing about it; they just did it and told us that we had to like it. Our ancestors had no notion that some day the power that they had tendered the British would one day be given away to people who are our enemies. . . . The British could not have ruled this country for the past hundred years without the consent of the chiefs. . . ."

"I see your point," I said. "But listen to another side of the story. What did the British give your people? In the light of the gold and diamonds and manganese and timber that they took out of the country, and all for a pittance, could they not have built roads for

you other than in those areas where they had to bring their raw
materials down to the ports? Could they not have built more
schools? Could they not have improved the health standards of the
people?"

He didn't answer. He knew that the real responsibility for those
matters had rested, in the last analysis, with the chiefs. . . . And
those chiefs had not been anxious to bring reforms into the lives of
the masses of the people. They knew that widespread literacy
marked the termination of chieftaincy. Under the British the chiefs
had had it soft and they'd wanted to keep it soft. Now, in looking
back, they were wishing that they had acted a little differently; but
that time had gone. . . . A new political party had condemned them
on the very grounds which they had claimed were their own: moral
grounds.

In the old days the chiefs had, through the hereditary rights of
royal families, formed the sacred instruments of rule and had ordered the lives of the people; now Nkrumah had insisted that the
instruments of rule be made secular, elective, that the entire legislative body of a given community could not be completely hereditary.
And the young men of the nation had marched in agreement with
that democratic aim.

"Don't you think," I asked him, "that the new schools that will be
built, the new health measures now in operation, will outweigh the
claims of those who lost power?"

"Our ancestors, to help us," the chief said, "made a gentleman's
agreement with the British, then the British broke their promise and
leveled their guns at us. They let us down. That was not *right!*"

The concept of honor was being evoked against the right of men
to live and breathe without fear and poverty. The black elite was
asserting its claims against the younger men who yearned to toss off
the yoke of imperialism and banish the blindness of centuries of
illiteracy. Blacks against blacks!

"We are not used to political parties, central governments," he
lamented.

"Look," I argued gently, "all nations have central governments.
A central government is an absolute necessity if man is to live at all

rationally. How can you trade with nations of the world, how can you educate your children, how can you wipe out disease, how can you defend yourself against aggression unless you have a strong central government?"

"But we are not educated; we don't know how—"

"Then learn," I said. "Make your mistakes. A central government is simply national housekeeping. Why let another government do this for you? Your people are passionately anxious to try. Then let them try. Common people rule elsewhere; why not here?"

The chief sighed. What pathos! He was a "decent" man, but it seemed that all "decent" people were being driven out of power in the world today.

In the old days a chief's children had, by hereditary and pre-scriptive right, first choice to enter what limited schools existed. Now, all students, regardless of background or social origin, had to pass an entrance examination to be admitted to the universities of the nation. . . . And the chiefs, the old and great families, did not like it. Their blood was the best blood in the land, hallowed by the stools containing the souls of their ancestors—stools that had grad-ually turned black by the constant dripping of sheep's blood upon them. Now that the magical authority of those blackened stools over the minds of their subjects had gone, they didn't like it; they wanted a chance to turn the clock back; they didn't want history to catch up with Africa. . . . But the past had gone; the magic wouldn't work any more; the sheep, goats, chickens, and even human beings, when slain as sacrifices, were of no avail. . . .

The Gold Coast was being strait-jacketed into the future; events were moving fast to overcome the inertia of the chiefs. But was the pace so swift that the native genius of the people was not being taken into account? In olden times the undertakings of the people had been communal; they had labored to the sound of drums and music. Today prefabricated houses were being thrown up over-night. . . . Was enough thought being given to what had happened in other industrial countries?

The pathos of Africa would be doubled if, out of her dark past, her people were plunged into a dark future, a future that smacked of Chicago or Detroit. . . . But how can these harassed politicians, working in such a heated and partisan atmosphere, battling both the British and the black elite, have time to think and plan? What would be the gain if these benighted fetish-worshipers were snatched from their mud huts and their ancestor idolatry, and catapulted into the vast steel and stone jungles of cities, tied to monotonous jobs, condemned to cheap movies, made dependent upon alcohol? Would an African, a hundred years from now, after he has been trapped in the labyrinths of industrialization, be able to say when he is dying, when he is on the verge of going to meet his long dead ancestors, those traditional, mysterious words:

> *I'm dying*
> *I'm dying*
> *Something big is happening to me . . . ?*

XXIX...

To find opinions on these questions, I sought to talk to Dr. K. A. Busia, one of Africa's foremost social scientists. He was with the opposition, but he had indisputable facts in his grasp.

I called at his office in the Department of Social Sciences at Achimota University. Dr. Busia turned out to be a short, medium-sized, affable man who had about him a slightly worried and puzzled air. He was the author of *The Position of the Chief in the Modern Political System of Ashanti* and *Social Survey Sekondi-Takoradi*. I could tell at once that he was orientated and could express himself with ease.

"Dr. Busia, to just what degree are the traditional rituals and ceremonies of the Akan people still intact?" I asked him.

"They are completely intact," he told me. "The people hide them from the West, and they make peripheral concessions to Western opinion. But the central body of our beliefs and practices still functions and is a working frame of reference from day to day."

"You are with the opposition, are you not?"

"I am."

"Do tribal rituals play a part in the Convention People's Party?"

"They most certainly do," he snapped.

"Why has not this been pointed out before? Why has no one shown the vital link between modern politics in Africa and the religious nature of tribal life?"

"Westerners who approach tribal life always pick out those manifestations which most resemble their own culture and ignore the rest," he said. "That which they recognize as Western, they call progress."

"What is the significance of the oath-taking and libation pouring at Convention People's Party's rallies?"

"It's to bind the masses to the party," he said. "Tribal life is religious through and through. An oath is a great thing to an African. An oath links him with the past, allies him with his ancestors. That's the deepest form of loyalty that the tribal man knows. The libation pouring means the same thing. Now, these things, when employed at a political meeting, insure, with rough authority, that the masses will follow and accept the leadership. That is what so-called mass parties need. . . . The leaders of the Convention People's Party use tribal methods to enforce their ends."

"I take it that *you* wouldn't use such methods?"

"I'm a Westerner," he said, sucking in his breath. "I was educated in the West."

I had the feeling that he was speaking sincerely, that he could not conceivably touch such methods, that he regarded them with loathing, and that he did not even relish thinking that anybody else would. My personal impression was that Dr. Busia was not and could never be a politician, that he lacked that innate brutality of force and drive that makes a mass leader. He was too analytical, too reflective to even want to get down into the muck of life and organize men. I sensed, too, that maybe certain moral scruples would inhibit him in acting. . . .

"What has been the influence of Christianity?"

"Despite all the efforts of the missionaries, the Akan people have not changed their center of cultural gravity. Where you do find changes, they are mainly due to the church and the factor of urbanization. But even there you find a curious overlapping, a mixture. You have literate chiefs, for example, who practice an unwritten religion; you have lawyers trained in England who feel a tie to the tribal legal conceptions of their people. Such mixtures go right through the whole of our society. It's not simple."

"Have any psychological examinations been done to determine how this mixture is reflected in the minds of the people?"

"Nothing has been done in that direction," he said.

I next inquired of Dr. Busia the reasons for the low population level of the Gold Coast. I pointed out to him that the geographical area of the Gold Coast was more or less the same as that of England, but the Gold Coast had less than one-tenth of England's population. . . .

"Two things have kept the population level low," he said. "The lack of water and the tsetse fly. Seventy-five per cent of our population live in the forest area. If we could banish the tsetse fly from that area, we'd have horses to draw our carts and cows for meat and dairy products. Now, in the Northern Territories there is no water; it's filled with scrubland that can barely support its meager population."

"Dr. Busia, if you don't want to commit yourself on the question I'm going to ask, you can just tell me," I told him. "How do you, a British-trained social scientist, feel about the British recognizing the Convention People's Party . . . ?"

"Sure; I'll tell you," he said readily. "I'll tell you exactly what I told Sir Arden-Clarke, the Governor of this Colony. . . . The British here care nothing for our people; they are concerned with their political power which enables them to defend their financial interests. They sided with the Convention People's Party in order to protect those interests. It's that simple. We educated Africans looked to the British for but one thing: the maintenance of standards. Now that they have let that drop, what are they good for?"

Again I heard that echo of pathos. . . . A scientist had been trained by Britain to expect certain kinds of behavior from Britishers; now British behavior had turned out to be something that even their best pupils found somewhat nauseating. . . .

"The British call such abrupt changes 'flexibility,' do they not, Dr. Busia?"

Dr. Busia laughed ruefully.

"But tell me . . . In your book, *Social Survey Sekondi-Takoradi*, you show pretty clearly the disintegrating forces of urbanization at work in the cities of the Gold Coast. Now, is there any widespread awareness of this?"

"No," he said.

"Is there any plan to see that the growth of your cities can take a new direction?"

"There is no plan," he said.

"I feel, from reading your book, that when tribal life and rituals break down under the impact of urbanization, and when no new sense of direction takes the place of what tribal culture gave, you will find a new kind of pagan among you: a pagan who feels no need to worship. . . ."

"The germs of that are making their appearance in our country," he admitted. "It's not widespread as yet; but it's evident."

"Do you think that Nkrumah can easily wipe out the old habits of the people—?"

"The African will react in that matter just as all people react," he said. "In the crucial moments of life, people fall back upon the deepest teachings of their lives; hence, in matters like politics, death, childbirth, etc., it's the teachings and beliefs of the tribe that all people—even those who are literate—turn to, give support to and trust. . . ."

There were other questions that I wanted to ask Dr. Busia, but I felt that they were too delicate. Had I not been afraid of wounding his feelings, I'd have asked him how was it that he, a social scientist, who saw so clearly the forces that were breaking down tribal life, could oppose those forces? If those forces had given way under the impact of industrialization in other countries, would they not do so in the Gold Coast? And, knowing that, why did he take his stand with the opposition? But I'd been told that Dr. Busia came of royal stock, that his brother was a chief, that he too might possibly some day be a chief. . . .

I'd now talked to enough educated Africans of the Gold Coast for there to emerge in my mind a dim portrait of an African character that the world knew little or nothing about. . . . I could imagine a young boy being born in a tribe, taking his mother's name, belonging to the blood-clan of his mother, but coming under the daily authority of his father, starting life by following his father's trade. I could well imagine this boy's father's coming in contact with missionaries who would tell him that his religion was crude, primitive, that he ought to bring his family into the church of the One and Living God. . . .

I could imagine that family's trying to change its ways; I could sense conflicts between husband and wife, between the father's family and the mother's family over the issue of Christianity; and I could readily picture the father, in the end, winning his argument on the basis of his superior earning power gained from working for Christian Europeans.

Let us assume, then, that the boy is the first child that the family has consented to send to the mission school. . . . There, he learns how "bad" is the life of his tribe; he's taught to know what power the outside world has, how weak and fragile is his country in comparison to the might of England, America, or France. Slowly he begins to feel that the communal life under the various stools is a childlike and primitive thing, and that the past of his tribe reeks of human sacrifice.

He now begins to identify himself with his mentors; they teach him to eat a balanced diet; he becomes ashamed to go about half nude; he feels that painting the body with lurid colors signifies nothing; he grows to loathe the mumbo-jumbo of the chiefs and the incessant beating of those infernal drums of state; and, above all, he squirms in the grip of the sticky compound life where every man is his brother and every woman is his sister or mother and can lay claims upon him which, if he refuses to honor them, can make him an outlaw. . . .

He develops a sense of his own individuality as being different and unique and he comes to believe that he has a destiny, a personality that must not be violated by others. He cringes in his heart at the memory that he once had to obey orders but confusedly heard and dimly understood from the shades where his ancestors dwelt.

Christ is offered and he accepts the way of the Cross. He now has a stake in the divine; he has a soul to save, and there seeps into his young and yearning heart that awful question: Where will I spend Eternity? The future looms before him in terms of a romantic agony: he can either live forever or be consigned to a lake of fire that never ceases to burn those whose sins have found them out. . . .

Yes, he must redeem himself; he must change; he must have a career. He reads of the exploits of the English and the Americans and the French, and he is told that they are strong and powerful because they believe in God. Therefore, finishing his mission studies, he elects to go to England or France or America to study. . . . He is baptized and his name is changed from Kojo or Kwame or Kobina or Kofi or Akufo or Ako or Kwesi, to Luke or Peter or Matthew or Paul or Mark or John. . . . He adopts a Western style of dress, even if it does not fit his needs or the climate. He no longer eats with his brothers, squatting on the floor about a common dish and lifting the food with his fingers; he insists upon sitting at a table and using a knife and fork.

If he goes to America to continue his studies, he is elated upon arrival. What a country! What a people! The seeming openness, the lavish kindness, the freedom of the individual, and the sense that one can change one's lot in life, the lightheartedness, the almost seeming indifference with which religion is taken, the urban manner of Negro living and what the Negroes have achieved against great odds—all of this contrasts with the bleak mud huts and the harsh life of the African compounds. For the first time in his life he sees black men building and operating their own institutions in a Western manner, and a sense of social romance is disclosed to him, and he yearns to emulate it. . . . All of this makes him apply himself to the study of his chosen subjects with a zeal that is second only to the religion that he'd been taught back in his African mission school. But . . .

He begins, as the years pass, to detect that the Americans are not a happy or contented people. He learns how to be afraid, how to decipher the looks of desperation on the American faces about him. He learns how it feels to be related to nobody. What at first had seemed a great romance now seems like a panting after money with a hotness of emotion that leaves no time to relax. And he begins to wonder what would happen to him in such a life. . . .

And he learns the meaning of the word "race." What he had failed to notice before now strikes home: he is free, but there are certain things he cannot do, certain places where he cannot go, all because he's black. A chronic apprehension sets up in him; the "person" in him that the missionaries had told him to develop is reduced, constricted. He'd never thought of being rich, and now he knows that if he is not rich in this land, he's lost, a shameful thing. . . .

That sense of poetry in him that even religion had not dulled makes him ask himself if he wants to be defined in terms of production and consumption. The feeling of security he had first felt is gone; the more he comes to know America, the more he, stammeringly at first and more forthrightly later on, begins to ask himself: "Where's it all going? What's it all for?"

And the only answers that make sense to him are heard in Union Square or Washington Park. Yes; he'd go back home and try to change things, to fight for freedom. . . .

And if he went to England for his education, his sense of alienation would be the same, but differently arrived at. Indeed, his blackness is swallowed up in the vast grayness of London. Perhaps he might have difficulty getting a room in which to live because of his blackness, but he soon meets another Englishman who feels free to do what he likes with his own home. But what puzzles him is the English assumption that everything that is done in England is right, that the English way is the only way to do it. He sees that no black man could ever sit in the House of Commons, that he is not expected to participate in English life on any level except that of a doctor. It seems that the English entertain a quaint notion that all Africans have sensitive hands that can heal the sick!

At Oxford or Cambridge he is far from the world of "race." He is a black gentleman in a graded hierarchy of codes of conduct in which, if he learns them, he can rise. He can, even though black, become a Sir. . . . The more he learns, the more Africa fades from his mind and the more shameful and bizarre it seems. But, finally, he begins to gag. The concepts that are being fed to him insult him. Though he will have a place of honor, that place will be with the lower and subject races. . . . Every book he reads reveals how England won her empire and this begins to clash in his mind with the codes of honor that he's learning so skillfully to practice. Soon he knows that he has to avoid saying certain things; for example, if it's known that he's a nationalist, he will surely not pass his bar examinations. Inhibition sets in and he has to choose whether he's to be among the favored or the scorned.

He learns that his blackness can be redeemed by service, but this service is not in the interests of his people; it's against them. . . . He begins to wonder why his missionary teachers never hinted at all about this. Were they parties to this deception? At the bottom of English society he sees servility and suffering and he senses that what has ensnared the people of his country has also ensnared these poor whites, and the first blow to his confidence is received. He could have been like those drab and colorless millions of London's slums; indeed, his mother and father are like that in far-off Africa. . . . He becomes afraid of his choice, and slowly he begins to sympathize with the fear and insecurity of the poor whites around him and, in the end, he begins to identify himself with them. It's not in the schoolrooms or the churches that he can hear moral preachments denouncing what is being done to his country; he hears it only in Hyde Park. But he's too afraid as yet to agree with what he hears; it sounds too violent, too drastic; it offends those delicate feelings that the missionaries instilled in him.

His first clumsy criticisms are addressed to religious people and he's disturbed that they defend the system as it is. He's secretly enraged that the English do not feel that he is being dishonored. Just as the missionaries taught him just so much and no more, he finds that the English accept him just so much and no more. He's praised when he's like the English, but he sees that the English are careful to make sure that he's kept at arm's length and he begins to

feel that he's a fish out of water—he's not English and he's not
African. . . .

If he chooses to go to France, he will encounter the same theme,
but with even subtler variations. Indeed, in France he'll need all of
his will power to keep from being completely seduced by the blan-
dishments of French culture. None of the blatant American racism or
that vague social aloofness which so often prevails in England will
meet him in Paris. Instead, he'd be eagerly received everywhere,
but . . .

He senses that the Frenchmen he meets are sounding him out
about the national liberation movement in his country. If he makes
the mistake of being forthright about his country's demand for
freedom, he'll encounter no overt racial discrimination; he'll simply
find everything suddenly becoming extremely difficult. He'll learn, as
he talks to animated and polite Frenchmen, that they feel that they
have worked out, in the last two thousand years, just about the most
civilized attitude on earth; he'll be obliquely but constantly dis-
couraged to think in any terms save those of extreme individualism.

Suppose he discovers that the French know nothing of his country
and its culture, and, to remedy this lack, suppose he tells his French
friends that he plans to launch a magazine in which young Africans
can express themselves to the people of the Western world . . .? A
good idea! But, *mon ami*, you don't need to create a new magazine!
You have the freedom to contribute to any magazine published in
Paris! In fact, *mon vieux*, we'd welcome any contribution you might
make. By the way, we'd like to make you a co-editor of our review!

The more intelligent the French think he is, the more he'll be
watched; but this surveillance is not done in terms of crude spying,
not yet—but in terms of social cultivation. He'll hear his professors
in the classrooms constantly asking him: "What do you intend to do
when you get your degree?" And if he says he's seriously thinking
of settling down in France and pursuing his profession, marrying, no
matter what woman of what race, his professors nod and smile their
encouragement. But if he says that he wishes to return to his homeland and fight to lift up the standards of living, to free his country

from foreign rule, from French domination, he feels a coolness of attitude that, in time, will change to freezing. . . .

He sees that many of his fellow blacks are obtaining university degrees and that almost all of them are at once put into civil service where they can be effectively controlled!

The black colonial Frenchman in Paris, like his counterpart in London or New York, will encounter the men on soapboxes preaching revolution, but, to his surprise, he'll find that the French are fairly indulgent toward his budding interest in Marxism! It's only upon nationalism that they frown. . . . He'll find, in Paris as in the colonies proper, that the French will prefer his becoming a Communist rather than his embracing the cause of his homeland. In time he sees that the French have a great deal of experience in dealing with Communists, but that they shy off in a state of terror when confronted with nationalists.

He learns that in French eyes nationalism implies a rejection of French culture, whereas they regard Communism as a temporary aberration of youth. Let him yell for revolution all he can; he might find a few French millionaires at his side, helping to spur him on . . . !

Alone in Paris, he'll take up with some French girl and she'll sympathize with him, but will tactfully point out how hard and long will be his fight, that there are so many pleasures to be savored, and he'll be lucky if he does not yield. He sees that many of his black brothers who came to France are sophisticated, successful black *Frenchmen!*

Still thirsting for self-redemption, thwarted in pride, he dreams of showing the French that he too can build a nation. He realizes now that his resolution to do this must be ten times as strong as that of an African in New York or London; also he begins to realize that the culture of France is so profound that it can absorb even Communism and pat its stomach. . . .

It's a desperate young black French colonial who resolves to return to his homeland and face the wrath of white Frenchmen who'll kill him for his longing for the freedom of his own nation, but who'll give him the *Legion d'honneur* for being French. . . . Through books he finds that other men have forged weapons to defend themselves from the domination of the West; he learns that the Russians, the Chinese, the Indians, and the Burmese saved themselves and he begins to master the theories of how they did it.

Strangely, he now yearns to build a land like France or England or America. Only such a deed will assuage his feelings of shame and betrayal. He too can be like they are. That's the way to square the moral outrage done to his feelings. Whether America or France or England have built societies to the liking of his heart no longer concerns him; he must prove his worth in terms that they have taught him.

But when he arrives in his tropical homeland, he is dismayed to find that he's almost alone. The only people who are solidly against the imperialists are precisely those whose words and manner of living had evoked in him that sense of shame that made him want to disown his native customs. They want national freedom, but, unlike him, they do not want to "prove" anything. Moreover, they don't know how to organize. They are willing to join him in attempting to drive out the invaders; they are willing, nay, anxious, on the oaths of their ancestors, to die and liberate their homeland. But they don't want to hear any talk of ideas beyond that. . . .

So, the young man who spurned the fetish religion of his people returns and finds that that religion is the only thing that he has to work with; it's muck, but he must *use* it. . . . So, not believing in the customs of his people, he rolls up his sleeves and begins to organize that which he loathes. . . . Feeling himself an outsider in his native land, watching the whites take the gold and the diamonds and the timber and the bauxite and the manganese, seeing his fellow blacks who were educated abroad siding with the whites, seeing his culture shattered and rendered abhorrent, seeing the tribes turned into pawns that float about the harbor towns, stealing, begging, killing —seeing that the black life is detribalized and left to rot, he finally lifts his voice in an agonized cry of nationalism, *black* nationalism!

He's the same man whom the missionaries educated; he's acting on the impulses that they evoked in him; his motives are really deeply moral, but pitched on a plane and in a guise that the missionaries would not recognize. . . . And almost the only ones who answer his cry of nationalism-at-any-price, nationalism as a religion, are the tribes who are sick of the corrupt chiefs, the few who share his emotional state, the flotsam and jetsam of the social order! But, things being as they are, there's no other road for him; and he resolves: "So be it. . . ."

The strange soil of the Western world, composed as it is of individualism, hunger for a personal destiny, a romantic sense of self redemption, gives birth to fantastic human plants that it is ashamed of!

PART THREE

THE BROODING ASHANTI

Not only might human development have never over-stepped the pre-scientific stage and been doomed never to overstep it so that the physical world might indeed retain its truth whilst we should know nothing about it; the physical world might have been other than it is with systems of law other than those actually prevailing. It is also conceivable that our intuitable world should be the last, and "beyond" it no physical world at all . . .

Ideas, by EDMUND HUSSERL

XXX...

At last I've got from the Gold Coast Information Service an itinerary that will take me up into the high rain forest, to Kumasi, Kumawu, Bibiani, etc. The British were, in the end, kind enough to allow me the use of the few government resthouses which were dotted here and there in the jungle area. I had a long list of personalities to see: doctors, lawyers, chiefs, and politicians. . . . The Britisher who gave me the itinerary cleared his throat and said casually:

"I say, old chap, it'd be better to stick to the itinerary, you know."

I assured him that I would, that I had no desire to wander at random in the jungle.

I bought a half-gallon thermos jug for water, about £30 of tinned food, a bottle of germicide to put into the water before using it for washing, a big box of DDT, cigarettes, and a five-yard length of colored cloth to use as a sheet at night when I'd be bunking in out-of-the-way places. I examined my budget and decided that I'd go as far as a shilling a mile would take me. I'd no notion that I was to find the jungle the most expensive place on earth!

On the morning of August 4, with Battling Kojo behind the wheel, I took off. Ahead of me, across the flat plains of Accra, I could see the bluish-green escarpment rising towards a misty sky. Half an hour later we began to climb the escarpment itself on a red laterite road that mounted and wound amidst palm and coconut trees. Gradually the sky began to darken a little and the vegetation became a deeper and more prolific green. Suddenly the sky seemed to lower itself to the tops of the tall trees and the air became clogged with humidity. As we lifted still higher, I could feel the temperature dropping sharply. I turned my head and stared out of the rear window of the car and saw the coastal plain drenched in sunlight, with here and there, gleaming balefully, a mud village or two—and I knew it was sizzling hot down there. . . .

The vegetation turned a still darker green and I could sense the jungle beginning, becoming dense. The car churned up steep hills and to either side of the road loomed walls of dark green from which, now and then, appeared black faces of men, women, and children, half nude, carrying vast burdens of plantains, bananas, or wood upon their heads. Their faces were stolid, set, humorless; once or twice I saw a startled expression leap into someone's eyes as he glimpsed my face staring at him. Some waved at me and I waved back, wriggling the palm of my hand in that salute which is so native and which, by now, I had come to feel was normal.

As we crawled still higher, the trees became taller: the wawa, mahogany, palm, and cocoa trees flanked both sides of the road with leafy curtains of brooding green. Jutting skyward were a few gigantic white cottonwood trees. Thick creeping vines, three and four inches in diameter, entwined themselves amid the branches and leaves of the trees, giving the impression of some hovering mystery, some lurking and nameless danger. What was down those narrow paths leading into the jungle—paths so shaded and black and wild . . . ?

Past Mampong we still mounted; the road was good, the earth was red, and the vegetation denser still. The people had a quieter look than those of the Accra plains. We sped past villages of mud huts; men and women were sitting and staring calmly into space. Yams were piled before doorways. Africa was a dark place, not black but somber, not depressing but slightly haunting—moody, with a kind of dreaminess floating over it. We were in the thick jungle now and moisture clung to the car windows.

This is, it is said, the home of the true Negro—whatever that means. Speaking a poetic language which, ironically, they feel describes reality, the Negroes themselves claim that they came out of holes in the ground; the white anthropologists contend that they came from farther north, Timbuktu or above the Sahara. Who knows? So much prejudice has entered into these calculations that perhaps nobody will ever know what the truth is. One thing, however, is true: an astounding religion, complicated and abounding in taboos, came to birth here and no one has ever really fully traced its growth or origin. It is not definitely known if the Akan religion influenced the Egyptian religion or if the Egyptian religion influenced the Akan religion. Briffault feels that the Egyptians got the moon-worshiping phase of their religion from the Negroes; some authorities feel that the Negroes never produced anything original but borrowed everything they've got. Other authorities contend that they can find traces of Ethiopian religious practices among the Ashanti. Yet the manner in which the Akan wears his native toga is exactly the way in which the ancient Romans wore theirs. How is that possible? Did the Romans penetrate this far before the days of Christ? Or did Negroes get as far as Rome? Or did the two peoples evolve the same kind of dress independently, without coming in contact with each other? No one really knows. It might well be that people in ancient times had much more social intercourse than we now suspect, that they were much less conscious of "race" than we are. . . .

At last we came into Koforidua, a small, clean-looking town of about 25,000 people. It has paved streets and the inevitable open sewer drains at each side of the road. Trees are everywhere and a relaxed atmosphere pervades the town. Koforidua is the center of a once rich cocoa-producing region and, under the auspices of the United Africa Company, many agents from many European countries are stationed here to buy cocoa from the African farmers. The Gold Coast produces more cocoa than any other country in the world and its sale abroad makes the Gold Coast the single largest dollar-earning area in all of Africa.

I put up in the modern home of Mr. R. A. O. Eccles, the district manager of the United Africa Company. Mr. Eccles was not at home, but word had been left to feed me. . . . While at lunch the sound of bells and drums came from the green and hazy distance. I asked the inevitably barefooted, white-jacketed steward boy what was happening and he told me:

"Somebody dead, Massa. So drums beat."

A young Englishman, a friend of Mr. Eccles, called; he was a buyer of cocoa in an area about sixty miles square.

"How do you go about buying this cocoa?" I asked him.

"Well, we have subagents. They get the stuff from other agents who, in turn, buy directly from the farmers."

"What local business group gets the cocoa in the end?" I asked.

"It works like this," he explained. "The Gold Coast Government has created a Cocoa Marketing Board to buy up the cocoa crops from the agents and then this Cocoa Marketing Board sells the cocoa on the world markets at prices advantageous to the farmers, always keeping a pool of money in reserve, so that if there is a break in the cocoa market, the farmers will have some money to fall back upon."

"How, in a concrete way, does one of these agents buy cocoa?"

"At the beginning of the cocoa season—and we're getting into it right now—an agent looks over a crop of cocoa, estimates the yield and by that the value the crop will have when it ripens. He then advances cash against the crop. Generally, when the time comes to harvest the crop, the farmer's money has been spent. Hence, most of the cocoa farmers are about a year in debt, even though the Cocoa Marketing Board helps them in many ways. This is an area rich in money, though the appearance of the streets and houses and stores would not indicate that such is true," the young man went on.

"But what do they do with all the money they get from selling the cocoa?"

"Well, it's funny, you know," the young man said, twisting his mouth into a wry smile. "What happens to the money earned by an enterprising African cocoa farmer is something that economists have never been able to grasp. In this town you'll see no huge, rich-looking houses, no green lawns, little attempt at conspicuous consumption, etc. In fact, the town is, as you can see, rather shabby. Well, this is the way it works. . . . When an African earns a pile of money, it is not his alone. He belongs to a tribe and a family. That money, under tribal law, is as much his sister's children's as it is his own. In fact, his first duty is toward his sister's children. Now, let's suppose such a man got a thousand pounds. At once, before he can derive any personal benefit from it, his relatives descend upon him, making demands which, under the family system in Africa, he cannot refuse. They cling to him like leeches, demanding bicycles, sewing machines, radios, clothes, phonographs, etc. The man is soon broke. But he does not worry. The system of native African communism saves him from want, for all he has to do is go to another relative and sponge on him. Individual initiative is not very popular in Africa. Why amass a lot of money? You'll have to give it away anyhow. . . ."

"Has there been any attempt to change this right of the relative to take a share of the wealth of another relative?" I asked.

"It's hard," he explained. "Religion is law in Africa. How can you change religious beliefs?"

"And what do you think of those beliefs?"

He looked at me, then raised his forefinger and shook it in my face.

"There's more to it than meets the eye," he said solemnly. "I've heard things that cannot be sneered at."

"Like what, for example?" I asked him. "Really, all of this *juju* stuff has a simple, psychological explanation. Now, tell me something that has no such explanation."

"Well," he began gently, cocking his head. "I've an educated young African working for me. He speaks English as well as I do; he speaks French too. Now, he told me the following story . . ."

I sat hunched, trying to suppress a smile. It was impossible for the English to live side by side with the Africans without becoming infected with the African's religious beliefs. The African had pro-jected an invisible world out of himself and he was living in and reacting to that world, and the English found themselves, in the end, obliged to give a certain kind of assent to that nonexistent world. . . .

"One day this young African and his wife went to a nearby town to do some shopping. Now, the husband had to return home before the wife and he waited for her. The wife was supposed to return around six o'clock and when she didn't put in her appearance, the husband began to worry.

"Well, late that night the wife came in, looking deeply disturbed. The husband upbraided her and demanded to be told what had happened. Now, the wife told the following story . . .

"It seems that while on the bus en route home, the wife had been in the center of a violent argument. A woman's purse had been stolen on the bus and there had been a hue and cry about it. Finally, the driver of the bus declared that every passenger on the bus had to go to the police station. This was done and the police questioned everybody and could arrive at no solution.

"The people were dissatisfied with the work of the police and then somebody suggested that only a fetish priest could find out who the culprit was. They argued pro and con and, in the end, the whole crowd went to the house of the local fetish priest. This priest made the entire crowd sit in a circle on the ground and he placed a bowl of water in the center. He then placed a reed in the water, making it stand up—"

"No!" I exclaimed.

"That's what my friend told me and I believe it," the young Englishman swore. "Now, I don't know how that priest managed to make that reed stand up; but he did. . . . My African friend wouldn't lie to me. Now, the fetish priest had an old knife that had been owned by an ancestor. He told the crowd that each person must hold the knife over the standing reed and when the guilty man's turn came, the reed would fall. . . .

"That knife was passed from hand to hand and it was held over the standing reed. The reed still stood. Finally, when one man took hold of the knife, the reed promptly fell. . . . The man got excited and declared that it was all a mistake, that he had not stolen the woman's purse. . . .

"Three times the knife was passed around, and each time the guilty man took the knife and held it over the standing reed, the reed fell. The crowd was so angry that it wanted to lynch that man. But the fetish priest calmed them down, took the trembling young man into a room and asked him to give up the woman's purse or he'd turn him over to the police. The man produced the purse—"

"Where had he been hiding the purse all the time?" I asked. "Why didn't the police find it in the first place?"

"I don't know," the suave, clean-shaven, intelligent, well-dressed young Englishman told me. Then he concluded: "This is a true story. What do you say to that?"

"Did you ever personally see anything like that?"

"No."

"You're telling me, no doubt, exactly what the young African told

you," I said. "But I doubt the whole thing. The only trouble with
these wonderful tales is that you can never check them. I'm convinced that the story has a psychological explanation. The guilty
man believed in the power of the priest. By the way, where is this
young African? I'd like to talk to him."

"Unfortunately, he's on leave," he said.

"And the man's wife?"

"She's gone too," he said. "But there's something to this *juju*."

Yes; this nonsense had caught him too. I decided to haul the conversation down to a practical level.

"Look, if these Africans have some powerful, wonderful, deep
secrets, why in hell did they wait so long to kick the British out?
Why didn't they use their knowledge to defend themselves? They
had to wait until a man trained in Western thought came to lead
them before they could even dream of fighting for their freedom.
Is that not so?"

He grinned at me, shook his head, then stared at the floor.

"That's true," he admitted.

That afternoon I had Kojo drive me about the town; the sky was
gray and a fine drizzle of rain was falling. Ringing the town was a
chain of green hills and the clouds were so low that their edges were
entangled in the treetops. I could feel a somber mood of mystery
lurking up there in those high, dim hills.

"Massa wanna see the chief?" Kojo asked me.

"Exactly," I told him. "Drive me there. Do you know where it is?"

"Yasa. Chief's house biggest house in town; it passes 'em all, sar,"
Kojo said.

The house of the chief was a huge yellow structure built in a
strange style of architecture, half Western and half Oriental.
Timidly, I walked up the long, wooden steps, hoping that Kojo
would follow me, but he did not. And I did not want to betray my
nervousness by asking him to. . . . I had heard those funeral drums
beating and I hoped that no African of importance had died. I'd
been told that the sacrifice of a stranger to accompany the dead was
looked upon with particular favor by the ancestors. . . . I walked
into a vast rotunda that reminded me of the pictures I'd seen of early

Roman buildings. Under a high dome to the left was a dais upon which—I was later informed—witnesses stood when the chief was conducting court with the aid of his elders.

"Hello! Hello!" I called.

A young boy, dirty and badly dressed, came up to me.

"Is the chief in?"

"Yes, sar."

"May I see him?"

"You American, sar?"

"Yes."

"Wait, sar."

He left. Five minutes later I heard footsteps behind me; I turned. A slight, brown man of about forty came forward. He had on an old dark-colored cloth and he wore sandals.

"Good afternoon, Nana," I said, addressing him according to custom.

"Welcome," he said.

I took his right hand in both of my hands, which, I'd been told, was the proper way to greet a "father of the people." He spoke English with a tribal accent and was most polite, gracious. He bade me sit and we talked casually. A group of toga-clad young men drifted in and seated themselves on the floor around us, listening, smiling. Meanwhile, the chief was observing me closely. A boy brought in two bottles of beer. The chief poured out several glasses. As he handed me a glass, he said:

"Pour a libation for us."

"*Me?*"

"Yes," the chief said. "*You.* You are African."

"But I've never done it before."

"Then try."

"But what am I to say?"

"Anything that's in your heart."

I tilted my glass and let a few drops of beer fall into a huge wooden vat in which cigarette stubs and trash were collected. As the beer dribbled downward, I declaimed in a tolling voice, calling upon our common ancestors to witness that I had come from

America, that I wished health and happiness to everybody, that I
yearned to see Africa free, that I was a stranger who bore no ill-will
toward anyone; I beseeched the ancestors to watch with care and
love over those who were present; I begged them to bless the fields,
to make the women fertile, and to protect the children. . . . My glass
was empty.

"You did fine," he said, filling my glass again.

We drank and when our glasses were empty, the chief took me
gently by the hand and said:

"Come with me."

"Yes, Nana," I said, following him obediently.

As we walked down the long veranda, he whispered to me:

"I want to show you a mystery."

We came to a corner of the veranda that overlooked a dismal
courtyard. He caught my arm, stopping me. I wondered what he was
about to reveal. Then he pointed off into some shadows.

"Do you see that box?" he asked me.

I squinted and saw a dark, oblong metal box about eight inches
thick, about two feet long, and about a foot wide.

"Yes."

"What's in that box?" he asked me.

"I don't know," I said.

"Look at it. . . . Go closer and look at it," he urged me.

Maybe it contained some foolish, but, to his mind, powerful fetish?
I wanted to burst out laughing, but I inhibited myself. I bent forward and examined the box and saw that it seemed to be covered
with flies or some other insects. Then I knew; they were bees,
crawling. . . .

"What's in the box?" he asked me.

"Honey's in the box," I said brightly.

"You think that those are bees?" he asked me.

"Yes," I said, puzzled at his insistence.

"They are *not* bees," he said.

"Well, maybe you've got some insects in Africa that I don't know
about," I ventured. "What are they?"

"That's a mystery," he said.

I stood looking at him and he stood smiling at me, watching me. He led me back to the group of young men. I was trying to think hard, but the material I had to think with was slippery. Maybe a joke was being played on me?

"Say," the chief asked me suddenly, "do you like riddles?"

I felt that I was playing a game with little boys and I said:

"Well, yes. But I'm not too good at them. . . ."

"I'd like to ask you one," the chief said.

"Well, try me."

"What's smaller than an ant's mouth?"

I thought a moment and said:

"The ant's finger."

There was a moment's silence. The young men began asking, I gathered, what I'd said and, when the chief translated my answer for them, they burst into wild laughter, clapping their hands. The chief poured me another glass of beer.

"You are clever," he said.

"Was that the right answer?" I asked.

"It *could* be," the chief conceded. "The right answer is the food that goes into the ant's mouth. But if the ant had a finger, his finger would have to be smaller than his mouth."

A furious discussion took place between the young men and the chief; they spoke in their tribal tongue and finally the chief rose, pushed his forefinger into his mouth to demonstrate that what I had said was true. Evidently the chief won the argument, for the young men lapsed into silence. The chief sat and looked at me with admiration. I felt enclosed by a dream.

"You are *too* clever," the chief said.

"Oh, I'm not," I said. "But what's the mystery in that box?"

There was silence. Beyond a paneless window I saw a dark green mountain rising and melting into a gray and lowering sky. Was this the normal, day-to-day reality of a chief's entourage?

"Say," the chief asked me suddenly, "did you ever see a dwarf?"

"A what?"

"A dwarf. A little man. . . . You know what I mean?"

"No," I said.

"But you have heard of them?"

"Yes."

He rose and crossed to the paneless window, then called to me.

"Come here."

I rose, crossed, and stood beside him.

"You see that mountain?"

"Yes."

"Well, there are dwarfs on that mountain."

I held very still. Was he pulling my leg? I studied him; his face was intensely solemn.

"Really?" I asked, letting my voice spill over with curiosity.

"Yes."

I decided to pretend to believe it all.

"How big are they?"

"Well, they are so tall," the chief said, holding up his hand to show the height. "They have feet that are turned around—"

"Backward?"

"Yes."

"Do they talk?"

"No: they whistle."

"Are they friendly?"

"Yes; very friendly."

"You've seen them?"

"Yes; I've seen them," the chief said.

"But this is wonderful," I said, wondering what the meaning of it all was. Did he think that I would believe this? "What do they look like?"

"They have long, silky hair."

"Do they wear clothes?"

"Yes; of course."

"If I went up there, would I see them?"

"No. You're a stranger," he said, shaking his head. "You mustn't go up there."

"Why?"

"The dwarfs would beat you up—"

"But you said that they were friendly—"

"They are. But to *us*—"

"But suppose I took a gun to protect myself?"

"But *you* can't see them," he told me.

"They're invisible to strangers, is that it?"

"Yes. And they'd beat you up. And when you came down, you'd be covered with sores and bruises."

Well, that was that. But that mystery box . . .

"Now, tell me about the mystery in the box?" I asked him.

"That box is my protection," he told me.

"What's in it? Guns?"

"No. Bees—"

"But I *said* that they were bees—"

"No; no. . . . You don't understand," he said. "My army's in that box."

"*What?*"

"I have an *army* of *bees* in that box. The bees protect me," he said with deep conviction.

Silence. Was the man mad or pretending?

"Say, Nana, how many people are in your town?"

He looked surprised and spread his hands in a wide, helpless gesture.

"We are many, many, *many*," he intoned.

"But you don't know *how* many?"

"No."

"All right. Now, why do you say that those bees are your army?"

He thought a moment, then told me the following story:

"Two years ago I had a hard fight with some of the chiefs in this town. It was a long fight, but I won it. The night after I'd won that fight, I went into my room and saw that box. I'd never seen it before and I didn't know who put it there. . . . I saw those bees on it and it puzzled me. I asked the fetish priest why a box with bees on it had been put in my room. . . . You see, I knew that there was some reason for it. The fetish priest told me that the bees had been sent by God to take care of me. They were my army.

"Now, that was why I took you to see that box. . . . If you had
been an enemy of mine, those bees would have buzzed you out of
here. . . . They sting and drive out all of my enemies. Only last
week a man came here with evil intentions against me. Those bees
drove him out; he ran away, screaming. . . ."

"What did the man say to you?"

"Nothing. He didn't have a chance—"

"Then how do you know that he had evil intentions?"

"Because the bees attacked him!"

Yes; the bees had attacked the man. That was proof. . . . What
could I say? He was sincere. I sat confronting men who were
dreaming with their eyes wide open. Beyond the paneless window I
could see the upthrusting cross of a Christian church. Yes; Christianity was here in Africa. For centuries the missionaries of the
Western world had tried to alter the mental habits of these people,
and they had failed. But had they really tried? There were missionaries in Koforidua, isolated, apart, white. . . . These people
were black. . . . Only a fool could not see the simple lesson of
that. But why had the missionaries tried at all? It may be that the
motives that made them try could explain why they had failed.

And it was more than clear now why Nkrumah had to get rid
of these old chiefs. Here was a man who was the head of a town
of 25,000 people and he didn't know that there were 25,000 people
in the town! No modern political organization could possibly
have need of a man like that; only the British could use him. . . . It
was chiefs like this who had, for more than a century, bartered
away the mineral and timber resources of the nation for a few paltry
pounds and a few cases of gin. . . . Indeed, I felt, after having
talked with this chief for an hour, that the Convention People's
Party had been rather kind. The party was offering men like him
"honorary" positions.

I learned later—in Kumasi—that the chiefs had been demanding
a second house, a sort of senate, in short, a bicameral system of
government in which their "voices" could be heard. But when they
were informed that they would, in that setup, be in a position to

veto the legislation passed by the lower house, and that, if they did veto the wishes of the people, they would find themselves no longer "fathers" of the people, but just plain, ordinary politicians and that they would be treated as such, attacked in public, criticized, and opposed at the polls, the chiefs had thought it over and had finally said:

"No, thank you."

They were wise. They knew in their hearts that their authority came from mumbo-jumbo and not from rational thought; that it came from spells, mystery, and magic which could not possibly succeed at the polls. . . .

I stood at the front door and the chief identified himself to me proudly: he was Barima Osei Kwesi, Omanhene of New Jauben. He asked me if I had a place to stay, if I was being properly fed, if there was anything that he could do for me. I realized then why the old tribal setup in the Gold Coast had had no need of hotels. The chief was generously offering me the hospitality bred of the long traditions of his people, but he didn't know how many people were in his town. . . .

Before taking leave, I asked him:

"Those dwarfs . . . How can they walk like you and me if their feet are turned backward?"

"That?" he said. "It's easy. Watch me. . . ."

He walked rapidly backward several feet.

"See?"

"Yes."

"It's simple," he said.

"Yes; I see it is. Good night, Nana."

"Good night," he said. "And keep well."

I held his right hand between my two hands.

"Good luck to you."

"The same to you."

"Good night."

"Good night."

XXXI...

It has been raining steadily now for several hours; there is so much moisture in the air that a piece of paper grows quickly limp. Outside the colors are white and green: white mist and rain and dark green of the foliage of the trees.

It's about six o'clock and all's quiet. The green hills, haloed by clouds, bend broodingly over the town. No wonder the mind of "primitive" man felt that there were spirits in this jungle, for it does seem that some presence, some living but invisible being is hovering here. It is, of course, the weather, a weather that dominates everything, seeping into the senses, creating a mood. One feels that one is not living in the world; one feels—Yes; I've got it. . . . I feel more or less the way I felt long ago when I first made a visit to witness a Catholic mass. . . . Imagine living in a world whose dramatic setting evoked in you a continuous mood of wonder and awe and dread! And imagine being unable, because of a lack of the capacity of reflection, to step outside of that mood and question it . . . ! One would be trapped. I'm not saying that the weather accounts for everything here; but I swear that it helps. . . . The mist and rain of these jungle hills complement and stimulate those feelings in one which one always tries to ignore: that sense of something untoward about to erupt, that feeling that one's un-wanted moods are about to intrude upon one's waking, rational thoughts. At any moment a big, shiny-eyed cat might leap out of the rainy black jungle, just as an impulse toward impiety might leap compulsively out of the unconscious of a deeply devout Christian. . . .

It's only natural that a man, misapprehending the nature of cause and effect, should think that his dead father was somewhere out there in the depths of that unpredictable jungle, that that father was still watching over him, ready to encourage or censor his thoughts and actions, to bring down upon his head praise or blame. Especially would this be so if he'd both loved and hated

255

that father, wanted his guidance and rejected it when it came as being too severe. No wonder he feels that he must pour libations continuously, offer gifts, make sacrifices. He views his ancestors as being huddled together in loneliness in that other world, seeking the most unheard-of ways and means of re-entering life, ready at any moment to find an excuse for snatching one of the living into their dreadful world of shades, of nonbeing. . . .

Is this not merely a turning upside down, a reversal of what the African lives and feels each day? To put it plainly: are not these living men projecting their hostile impulses upon the dead and converting those dead into a dead that can never die? For every tree in the jungle forest there is a taboo in the tribal home; there are a hundred thousand don'ts which they long to violate.

But they cannot violate them: the menstrual taboo must be observed; one must turn one's stool over when leaving it, for fear an evil spirit might possess it; one must never give another something with the left hand, for the left hand is used in cleaning one's self after answering calls of nature; a portion of each meal must be set aside for the dead, or else the dead will be displeased; men must never plant seeds, for the planting of seeds is the task of women: seeds are more likely to grow if women put them in the ground; boys of a certain age must not be with their mothers; girls of a certain age must not be with their fathers; and so on. . . . Wild savages? No! Just too afraid, overburdened, too civilized. . . .

Yesterday, amidst a green and towering nature, the distinction between the objective and the subjective was wiped out; one lived, nervous and afraid, in two worlds and one could not tell them apart. The urge to kill the beast stalking in the green and wet jungle, the urge to kill the enemy who was trying to kill you and take your wife, the urge to kill the chief who was sending you to death in war or captivity—the urge to kill must have been ever-present. And how the heart must have fought against killing, felt that killing was wrong, loathed and dreaded killing; and, finally, the heart found a way to stop killing and at the same time to kill with justification, that is, kill with ritual. . . . The heart then killed to satisfy the demands of the heart, but it deluded itself into feeling that it was killing to satisfy the demands of the angry and dead father, to appease and keep him quiet. And killing like that made the heart feel better, safe once more, for the heart was really killing for its own sake, for itself—killing for itself but in the name of another. . . .

What a contagious quality of emotion must be in the lives of men who live like that. There is no way to check one's perceptions or feelings against any objective standard. What one feels, one's neighbor also feels instantaneously by the mere fact of communication, for, in that state, to feel something is to make it true. What one imagines instantly exists. What one fears comes immediately into being. Thought and feeling become omnipotent.

Hour after hour it rains and I hear the water dripping from the roof of the house. . . .

XXXII...

Next morning at breakfast my host, Mr. Eccles, put in his appearance. He was a tall, affable young man with English public school mannerisms. He immediately told me that he'd arranged a cocktail party at which would be all the "important" people of the area. I protested, but he said that they would be disappointed if he did not give a party.

At nine o'clock about twenty guests, English and African, stood around with glasses filled with scotch and soda and talked. British CID men, businessmen, and government men tried to get me to commit myself on the question of colonialism; I talked for three hours and said absolutely nothing. It was exhausting. . . .

After the party we drove a long way in a heavy rain to a bar where Mr. Eccles introduced me to an African businessman. He was a dour, huge, black fellow; he was in his shirt sleeves and his collar was open. He was drunk; his breath smelled like a brewery.

"You know," the black money-maker began, "after you leave the Gold Coast, you mustn't say anything that'll hurt these people."

"What do you mean?"

"We're getting along all right," he assured me. "Many people don't understand Africa. And we'll be so hurt if people laugh at us—"

"What do you want me to say about Africa?"

"Tell 'em we're getting along," he said. "You can make money. These English boys here—they're my friends—"

"What kind of business are you in?"

"Timber."

"What's your attitude toward self-government?"

"It's all right, but—" He belched. "Look, what's the use of making trouble always? We're progressing fast. . . ."

"What do you call *fast*?"

"Now, don't take that attitude—!"

"What attitude? I've only asked you a simple question."

He grew nettled, hostile. He rose and walked a few feet off and returned and sat again.

"You want a drink?" he asked me.

"All right."

"I asked you do you *want* a drink?" He was belligerent.

"Sure. Okay. I'll drink one with you."

The waiter brought over two scotch and sodas.

"You don't always know what you're looking at," he told me. His tiny red eyes glittered malevolently.

"That's true," I said. I felt that he could have slit my throat without a single qualm.

"Do you realize that these Englishmen wouldn't be here in this town if it was not for *me*?"

"I didn't know that," I said.

"My family owns timber and cocoa farms here," he said.

"I see."

"Just because you meet me in a bar, drinking, don't think that I don't know what I'm doing," he argued.

"I've no doubt about your capacities," I said.

"Now, look," he said. "Take these chiefs . . . I don't give a damn about 'em. They say that they are masters of men. All right. How do they prove that they are masters? By letting men carry them

on their shoulders. You ever see a palanquin? Four men carrying
one man? Well, when four men are carrying you on their shoulders,
that's a visible sign that you are a master of men. . . . The world
sees and knows that a man being carried like that is a master.
Now, I'm no chief. I'm a businessman. How do I let the world
know that I'm a master? I have a hundred men working for me.
But they don't carry me on their shoulders. Now, come here and
let me show you something. . . ."

He rose and went to the door; I followed him. He drew aside
a dirty, tattered curtain and pointed out into the rainy night.

"See that car?" he asked me.

At the edge of an open sewer ditch was a long black sleek car
whose soft white and red lights gleamed in the wet darkness.

"Yes."

"That's my car. It's a Jaguar."

"It's beautiful," I said. It was.

"That's *my* palanquin," he told me. "Understand? I've got a
hundred and fifty horsepower to carry me around. And these people
round here, black and white, know I'm a master of men when they
see me in that car. . . . I'm *modern*. I'm no chief with half-naked
men sweating and carrying me on their shoulders. . . ."

"I get the point," I said. I clapped him upon his back. "You
know your way around."

We sat again; he sipped his drink and glared at me from under
his eyelids.

"You don't always know who you're talking to," he said.

"That's right," I agreed.

"Have another drink."

"All right." I didn't want to offend him.

Halfway through emptying his glass, he dozed, tilting the drink
in his hand. I took the glass from his numbed fingers and set it
softly on the table. He sagged against a wall, mumbling. Mr.
Eccles passed and I signaled to let him know that I had had
enough.

"You don't know who you're looking at," the black businessman
mumbled.

Well, he had made it. It was the first time I'd heard an African express his sense of how to make the transition from tribal life to the twentieth century, from tribalism to capitalism, from man-power to horsepower!

With Kojo behind the wheel, I started out next morning in a downpour of rain for Kumasi. Leaving Koforidua, we plunged into deep jungle. Steadily we mounted the curving road with red earth and dark green vegetation flanking both sides of the car. The road slanted, dipped, lifted; at times, when I stared out of the rear win-dow of the car, the undulating highway seemed like a bridge strung between high green poles. Mile after mile rain splashed against the car windows. Suddenly there were spots of sunshine and the jungle glittered evilly. The rain came again, then stopped. The metal inside the car breathed sweat. The backs of my hands were damp. When the rain stopped, moisture still formed on the car windows and Kojo had to turn on the windshield wipers in order to see the roadway. There was not much difference between rain and sun; moisture hung in the air in any case.

The jungle reared thickly sixty feet into the air. Out of the virgin green, cottonwood trees jutted up like white sentinels. Drenched villages of mud huts, each with its rusty tin roof, flashed by. Along both sides of the road were droves of Africans walking in the rain, wearing those somber-colored cloths, black shoulders wet and bare, black breasts wet, uncovered, heads supporting huge piles of wood or charcoal or yams or cassava or vast calabashes of steaming *kenke*—walking barefooted with short, jerky, almost dainty steps. It was odd how they would stop suddenly in their tracks at the sound of the approaching car, leap nimbly into the muddy ditches at the side of the road, and stand immobile until the car had passed, their eyes staring bleakly. . . . Had they been conditioned to leap out of the way like that? Or were they simply afraid? And it was strange how the women always walked with the women, the girls with the girls, the men with the men, and the children with the children; they did not mix. African society seemed to divide, like unto like. They walked in single file, their naked feet

barely lifting from the wet ground, their insteps flat, their necks
straight, their shoulders square, their heads erect. . . .

Ahead the horizon was a stretch of blue mist and the rearing hills
were half lost in the brooding clouds. Near Nkawkaw, some sixty-
six miles from Kumasi, the jungle reached smack to the top of a
tall mountain. The air was wet, sticky, yeasty. This earth and
climate could grow anything; indeed, here man must wage an
incessant battle against this vegetation in order not to be smothered
by it. For two minutes the sun breaks through a rent in the sagging
clouds, lighting up the drops of water on the palm leaves and
jungle grass, and then, without warning, the world is plunged
again into green gloom.

I tried to imagine the state of life that existed here before the
coming of the white man. According to R. S. Rattray, who inter-
viewed aged Ashanti men and women during the 1920's, there was
little or no war among the widely scattered tribes. With the coming
of the Europeans, the Ashanti began to dream of selling their slaves
directly to the white men in the coastal forts, thereby avoiding the
middlemen and augmenting their profits. They launched a series
of crushing attacks upon neighboring tribes and conquered them
and were on their way to building up a formidable kingdom when
the combined forces of the coastal tribes and the British, in war
after war, bled them white and laid them low. . . .

Before that, what . . . ? Life was family life. When the head of
the family died, he passed his authority on either to his younger
brother or to his sister's son, and his dying words of caution, advice,
admonition were remembered and followed with a tenacity which
today we can scarcely conceive of. The dead ancestor was buried
under the floor of the hut and when the members of the family
slept at night, he visited them in their dreams, reprimanding,
cajoling, demanding, complaining. The belief that the other world
was thronged with spirits was the order of the day.

Yet, there was something inherently modest about these jungle
children; theirs was a chastened and sober mood. The pre-Christian
African was impressed with the littleness of himself and he walked
the earth warily, lest he disturb the presence of invisible gods. When

he wanted to disrupt the terrible majesty of the ocean in order to
fish, he first made sacrifices to its crashing and rolling waves; he
dared not cut down a tree without first propitiating its spirit so
that it would not haunt him; he loved his fragile life and he was
convinced that the tree loved its life also.

So violent and fickle was nature that he could not delude himself
into feeling that he, a mere man, was at the center of the universe.
It was not until the meek and gentle Jesus came that he waxed that
vain!

Above all, the sight of blood exercised a magical compulsion upon
the emotions of the Akan and does so to an inordinate extent even
to this day. The monthly menstrual flow of women made them feel
terror and dread, made them think that a child was struggling
futilely to be born. The woman was believed to be the nexus of a
battle between the visible and invisible worlds, and what man, in
his right mind, would have sexual truck with a woman so involved
with the dark and abysmal forces of a deified and polytheistic
nature. And no doubt in those early days they lived a life of sexual
communism, like so many other tribal people, and did not connect
coitus with conception, and when a woman was menstruating or
pregnant, she was a deadly creature whom one had better avoid—
a tabooed being coming directly under the influence of the unseen. . . . Far, far back there must have been cults of moon worship-
ers among the women, for there are traces of moon images in their
decorations and ornamentations even today. Silver is for women;
silver symbolizes the moon; and does not the moon make the
women bleed and pull the tides of the sea? On one of the trucks on
a highway I saw a painted sign which proclaimed: FEAR WOMAN AND
LIVE LONG. . . .

What symbols did they have in those bygone days, symbols of
wood and iron which have long ago rotted in this hot and humid
earth?—symbols whose forms and meanings flowed from an order
of emotional logic forever lost to our minds and feelings? The ego
felt continuously threatened by ghosts and goblins against which
resistance had to be offered night and day. Food, and children to
help to grow more food, were the crux of existence. Pray the an-

cestors to let us have more children so that there will be more
hands to grow more food. . . .

People were valuable *per se* as people; indeed, they were a kind
of currency; one could pawn one's children, one's nieces or nephews.
You gave people in exchange for goods, in exchange for land; you
gave people in exchange for other people; and, to own another
person to help you with your daily chores was, of course, natural.
When the West saw these pawns in the African households, they
called them slaves and felt that these people would be fit to labor
on the plantations in the New World.

Arriving at Nkawkaw at midday, I ate, rested, went out upon the
narrow veranda of the resthouse. . . . Emotionally detached, I feel
the spell of this land. Those still, stagnant clouds snared in the
tops of those tree-clad mountains—must not that have been an
ominous sign in the old days? And that blood-red sun at sunset, what
did it mean? That crawling line of ants, was it not pointing the
way to a guilty man? Was not the veering flight of that bird the
gesture of an unseen ancestor trying to communicate something?
Why did the wind blow down that tree and make it point north-
ward? That huge rock tilting at so strange an angle, what did it
mean? And that child dying so young? Who did that . . . ? What
punishment was being visited and for whose sins?

Night comes suddenly, like wet black velvet. The air, charged
with too much oxygen, drugs the blood. The scream of some wild
birds cuts through the dark and stops abruptly, leaving a suspenseful
void. A foul smell rises from somewhere. A distant drumming is
heard and dies, as though ashamed of itself. An inexplicable gust of
wind flutters the window curtain, making it billow and then fall
limp. A bird chirps sleepily in the listless night. Fragments of
African voices sound in the darkness and fade. The flame of my
candle burns straight up, burns minutes on end without a single
flicker or tremor. The sound of a lorry whose motor is whining as it
strains to climb the steep hill brings back to me the world I know.

XXXIII...

These shy people of the mud villages seem to live lives extending more into space than into time. They are static; they move and have their being, but it's a kind of being that bends back upon itself, rests poised there, settled. . . . For housing, they do not build a house; they erect a shelter. For food, they do not eat for taste, but from hunger, habit, from what they recall of what their fathers ate.

There is not enough foundation to this jungle life to develop a hard and durable ego; more than ever do I know that that sudden burst of laughter which they give forth when my eyes meet theirs is acute embarrassment, a yearning to vanish, to have done with their personalities while someone is looking at them—a shyness that would fain give up and have no more dealings with strangers—a laughter that is so sweet of sound and yet so bitter in meaning. I look at a black child and it sinks right down upon the floor and hides its face, giggling. I look at a boy and he looks at me as though hypnotized, startled, awed, then he breaks into a wide, still, scared grin which he holds as he keeps staring at me, as though I'd put some kind of spell upon him. A black girl comes into a liquor store and when I glance at her, she pauses, smiles, gathers her cloth tightly about her, tucking and twisting it across her chest, bends in her knees, laughs, ducks her head, and moves forward in a shuffling and stumbling manner which keeps up until she vanishes around a corner; and her laughter is caught up and contagiously echoed by others who guffaw loud and long. . . .

The tribal mind is sensuous: loving images, not concepts; personalities, not abstractions; movement, not form; dreams, not reality. . . . Hence, institutions based upon royalty of blood are natural to that mind. Endow a thing or a person with a rolling, sonorous name, and the tribal African must needs feel that there is something noble about it. "Fine!"; "A big, big man!"; "I want a wonderful life!"; "I like your emotion!"; "I'd like to serve you.": "I like you too much!"—all of these are phrases of full-bodied emotion, passion, joy as they roll from black lips. From a strictly tribal point of view, they cannot really conceive of a political party except in the form of a glamorous leader. When they honor, adore, obey it's toward a person and it is absolute in its intensity. The tribal African does not really love, he worships; he does not hate, he curses; he does not rest, he sleeps; and when he works, his work becomes a kind of dance. . . . He transforms that which he touches into something else which is his and his alone; he dreams naturally, spontaneously, without even being aware that he does so. To live, with the tribal African, is to create.

System is the enemy of the tribal mind; action proceeds on a basis of association of images; if feeling is absent, the tribal African mind is in doubt. There is something which is lord over him and there are things over which he would be a lord. . . . A chief whom I met casually could give me but a few moments of his time; as he shook my hand warmly, he told me:

"I must go now. I must preside over a ceremony and I must make myself gorgeous for my people. . . ."

He meant that he was going to deck himself out in silk and gold. . . . The tribal African feels caught between greater and lesser powers, feeling that some are harmful and some are helpful. Hence, he evolves the notion of propitiation to aid him in controlling those powers. Since he likes to receive splendid gifts, he reasons that the spirits of rivers and trees and rocks and wind would also like to have gifts; and especially do the dead love gifts. . . . Imagine four hundred gods! Every possible combination of impulse and desire are projected and symbolized; the subjective and the objective melt; through ritual, man and nature fuse. . . . Jesus Christ? God number 401. . . .

But maybe the Africans are so biologically different that no matter what they are taught or what influences they are subjected to, their attitudes will remain unaltered. Is the African less adaptable than other races to change?

In America anthropologists have long debated what is in academic circles referred to as "African survivals." But when one sits in Africa and observes African people, the problem of "African survivals" takes on a new dimension and becomes possible of statement in terms that admit of a solution. The truth is that the question of how much of Africa has survived in the New World is misnamed when termed "African survivals." The African attitude toward life springs from a natural and poetic grasp of existence and all the emotional implications that such an attitude carries; it is clear, then, that what the anthropologists have been trying to explain are not "African survivals" at all—they are but the retention of basic and primal attitudes toward life.

The question of how much African culture an African retains when transplanted to a new environment is not a racial, but a cultural problem, cutting across such tricks as measuring of skulls and intelligence tests. Barring a racial prejudice which keeps the African at bay, he, when transplanted, identifies himself with the rational, urban, industrial (for whatever it's worth!) order of things, and, to the extent that his basic apprehension of the universe is coincident with that of the Western environment in which he finds himself, he changes as would other human beings. In short, he remains black and becomes American, English, or French. . . . But, to the degree that he fails to adjust, to absorb the new environment (and this will be mainly for racial and economic reasons!), he, to that degree, and of necessity, will retain much of his primal outlook upon life, his basically poetic apprehension of existence.

There is no reason why an African or a person of African descent —in America, England, or France—should abandon his primal outlook upon life if he finds that no other way of life is available, or if he is intimidated in his attempt to grasp the new way. (It must be said, however, that the African, in his effort to assimilate the Western attitude, starts from a point of reference that is not completely shared by the Irish, the Italians, the Poles, or other immigrants. The tribal African's culture *is* primally human; that which *all* men once had as their warm, indigenous way of living, is his. . . .) There is nothing mystical or biological about it. When one realizes that one is dealing with two distinct and separate worlds of psychological being, two conceptions of time even, the problem becomes clear; it is a clash between two systems of culture.

If the American Negro retained, in part and for a time, remnants of his background of traditional African attitudes, it was because he couldn't see or feel or trust (at that moment in history) any other system of value or belief that could interpret the world and make it meaningful enough for him to act and rely upon it. What the social scientist should seek for are not "African survivals" at all, but the persistence and vitality of primal attitudes and the social causes thereof. And he would discover that the same primal attitudes exist among other people; after all, what are the basic promptings of artists, poets, and actors but primal attitudes consciously held?

XXXIV...

I left Nkawkaw in rain pouring from a sky that was at the level of the treetops, and the dark green vegetation filled the universe. Rice fields, rubber and coffee plantations, men, women, and children heaved into sight and vanished. I asked Kojo the meaning of those oblong smoking packages held high above the heads of the people and he told me that there were many farmers who, living far back of the highway, had no matches and came down to seek homes having fires; and, when they found one, they lighted their dry sticks or charcoal, wrapped them carefully in palm leaves as protection against the rain, and walked, holding them aloft, going home to make a fire. . . .

The area through which I was passing was thickly populated and was about forty miles from Kumasi, the capital of Ashanti, the home of the most stubborn and warlike of all the Akan people. But, if they were belligerent, they revealed none of it in their facial expressions which, if anything, seemed detached. The hard red clay road was dangerously slippery during rain and the car lurched and skidded. The Africans trudging in the rain had no covering for their heads except those lucky enough to be carrying ballooning burdens of yams or calabashes which, of course, they balanced upon their skulls. . . .

At about eleven o'clock in the morning I came to Ejisu, a village some ten miles from Kumasi. This quiet, drowsy cluster of houses was known in the old days as the "fetish capital" of Ashanti. It was from this village, in 1900, that Queen Ashantuah, the Queen Mother of Ejisu, emerged to lead a vast army against the British in what was to be the fifth and last British-Ashanti war.

In 1896 the British had entered Kumasi with a strong military force whose object was, to quote Wynyard Montagu Hall, a British officer who participated in that campaign, to "put an end to human sacrifice, slave trading, and raiding, to secure peace and security for the neighboring tribes, and to exact payment of the balance of the war indemnity of 1874." The real aim, of course, was to bring Ashanti into the British Empire by force and to forestall the imperialistic aims of France and Germany. But such intentions could not be publicly stated.

Sir Francis Scott, the leader of the expedition, informed the King of Ashanti, King Prempeh, that he was to submit himself and his people in accordance with "native forms and customs" to the Governor of the Colony, who was then en route to Kumasi.

The Ashanti knew that this meant the end of the sovereignty of their kingdom, but, the British military forces pitted against them being formidable, they complied. King Prempeh bared his body to the waist, the Ashanti sign of humility, and embraced the Governor's feet, an act of abject surrender which the Ashanti had never suffered before. The British then read a long list of demands which the Ashanti, though conquered, claimed that they could not fulfil.

The King, the Queen Mother, the King's father, his two uncles, his brother, the war chiefs of Mampong, Ejisu, and Ofinsu were at once seized by the British and shipped to the coast. The Ashanti population was numb with amazement. With King Prempeh in captivity, the British now proceeded to break up the African kingdom, making separate treaties with the tribal states.

The population seethed at what they felt to be a gross betrayal and proceeded forthwith to prepare for war. On March 28, 1900, Sir Frederic Hodgson—with Lady Hodgson, a party of Europeans, and a few native soldiers—entered Kumasi and made his famous demand for the Golden Stool, a demand which the assembled chiefs listened to in silence. The Governor sent a military expedition to hunt for the Stool and, on the 24th of April, the Ashanti signaled their determination to resist with force by cutting the telegraph line between Kumasi and Cape Coast. . . . The Governor and his party fled to the fort which was quickly surrounded by enraged Ashanti. Natives seized the Ashanti Goldfields Corporation, one of the richest in the world.

Many of the Ashanti states remained neutral or actually helped the British, but the tribes around Kumasi answered the call of black Queen Ashantuah of Ejisu and made an unsuccessful attack upon the fort. Meanwhile, the British sent out a frantic call to Central and West Africa for troops. In London the press played up the rescue of the Governor and the "besieged white ladies and missionaries," but the journalists omitted to mention that the freeing of the Ashanti Goldfields Corporation was the most immediate objective of the British military forces. . . .

With an army of 20,000 men fanned out and blocking the approaches to Kumasi, Queen Ashantuah's aim was to stall and harass the British troops pending the arrival of the rainy season. If, however, the British tried to force their way to Kumasi to free the Governor and his party, she would trap them. . . . In fact, the holding of the Governor was a deliberate attempt to entice the British to attack the Queen's army. . . . The Queen, with her drums of state, her loyal chiefs, and her soldiers, lay athwart the road to Kumasi at a point about a mile from Esumeja.

From the fort the Governor sent native runners with frantic appeals for help. Food and water were dwindling daily. Would those desperate appeals lure the British into the old sly Queen's trap? She waited in sun and rain, praying for time, offering counsel to her chiefs and soldiers. But the British were wary; they knew that a trap had been laid for them and they camped and waited for reinforcements.

The jungle and the rain, the allies of the Ashanti, created in the British a sense of dread, making them feel that the enemy was everywhere. Illness too took its toll of the white men who looked upon West Africa as "the white man's grave." Against the Dane guns of the Ashanti, the British had carbines, incendiary shells, and 75-mm. guns. The only advantages of the Ashtanti were their numbers and a fanatical love of their country.

As the British troops huddled in the jungle rain at night, they could hear the war drums of the Ashanti and they could not sleep. Continuously threatening attack, with her war drums vibrating twenty-four hours a day, the black Queen launched a war of nerves against the enemy. It was rumored that she was sacrificing human beings to her ancestors, propitiating them for victory. (I checked this in Kumasi and highly placed Africans told me that it was true!) And the British soldiers knew that if they were captured, they would be decapitated and their blood would be smeared on the sacred skeletons of the long-dead Ashanti kings that lay in the dreaded mausoleum at Bantama . . . !

Throughout the rainy jungle nights the Death Drum of Queen Ashantuah would sound three times:

"BOOM! BOOM! BOOM!"

That meant that a victim had been selected, his cheeks thrust through with knives to keep him from hurling a curse at his executioners or the Queen.

An interval of time would elapse, and then the Death Drum would sound:

"BOOM! BOOM!"

And that would mean that the victim was prepared.

"BOOM!"

This single dreadful sound would indicate that the head had rolled from the victim's body. Most of these victims were captured enemies, slaves, and convicts saved for the express purpose of sacrifice. But this did not lessen the terror struck in the hearts of British troops who shivered and wished that they were home in London or Leeds. . . . Night after night they listened to those drums and they knew what was happening. And the Governor's letters appealing for aid, smuggled out by native runners, continued to pour in upon the British troops and commanders.

April and May passed. June came. From Southern Nigeria, Northern Nigeria, Sierra Leone, from England, and from Central

Africa British troops were rushing. Above all, the British yearned
for the arrival of white troops, for it had long been proved that black
troops fared badly against the ferocious Ashanti warriors. But how
long could the Governor and his party of missionaries and white
ladies hold out?

At daybreak on June 23, the Governor, feeling that he could wait
no longer, took his soldiers and his party and stole out of the fort,
plunging into the jungle, heading for the coast. The Governor felt
that any jungle fate was better than falling into the hands of the
determined Ashanti.

It was on the 22nd of July that the British threw their fully
assembled forces against the Ashanti and finally routed the old
Queen and her army, though fighting continued in different parts
of the country until the end of the year. It was no accident that a
black Queen was the last Ashanti to stand against the forces of
Europe in the Gold Coast, for, in the hands of Ashanti women the
religion of the nation rested. It was they who instilled in the young
the meaning of their rituals, their festivals, and their sacrifices. . . .

Though the Ashanti were defeated, it is doubtful if the British
aim of modifying the tribal religion was actually achieved; indeed,
one could ask if the British attack did not have as its final result the
driving of the tribal religion deeper into the people? Just how many
human sacrifices Queen Ashantuah made to propitiate her ancestors
to come to her aid are not known; but, if she was offering these
hapless victims as atonement to her ancestors, might she not have
been led to do so because the British were attacking? It might well
be that British policy stimulated precisely what it sought to defeat.

Had the Akan people been able to look objectively upon British
achievements, had they been in a position to weigh and judge the
value of British institutions without fear of British aggression, they
might have voluntarily altered many of their religious practices
without outside threat or persuasion. I'm inclined to believe that
Nkrumah will achieve in months what the British failed to achieve
in many long decades with their smoking guns and "indirect rule."

XXXV...

How different Kumasi is from Accra! A brooding African city, hilly, sprawling, vital . . . You get the feeling that the white man is far away. The population is about 70,000 and there is a mood of quiet confidence in the air. This is the heart of historic Negrodom; it was from here that hundreds of thousands, perhaps millions of slaves were marched down to the coast and sold to white traders; it was here that the Negroes stood stalwart against the British in war after war; it was here that the idea of a black empire once agitated the minds of Negroes; it was from here that raids, fierce and unmerciful, were visited upon neighboring tribes—raids that left no hut standing, no men free, no children living, no women unchatteled, no crops growing. It was from here that tribute was levied upon the outlying tribal states—states that were subjected so long and steadily that in time they felt that their loyalty to the Asantehene was being given of their own free will.

It was here that the great fetish men of the kingdom lived, each with his special array of gods, his strange powers; it was here that the bones of the dead kings reposed in brass coffins, each coffin having a "ghost wife," that is, a woman whose life was dedicated to cooking and serving food to the bones of the dead king. . . . It was here that the sacrificial victims were brought, their heads lopped off, their blood caught in huge brass pans and laved lovingly over those dead kings' bones, presumably to give them life, to propitiate their care and love for the stability and prosperity of the Ashanti kingdom. It was from here that calls went out for war—and woe to the chief who refused to furnish his quota of troops, slaves, carriers, gold, and sacrificial victims. . . .

The Ashanti, short, black, reddish of eye and quick of tongue, is a hard man to deal with. He stands rooted in the world of his strange culture and looks out at you, waiting, judging. He kowtows to no standard but that of his own pride. Christian church steeples rise through the white mist from the hills of the city, but the mood of the people is pagan. The symbol of the Golden Stool—upon which no man sits but which itself lies upon its side upon a special throne of its own—is the magic that makes more than a million people one. Ashanti is vaguely Oriental; there is something hidden here, a soul that shrinks from revealing itself. The Ashanti are polite, but aloof, willing to do business with you, but when business is over, they turn from you. They will learn the codes of the Western world and will practice them; but when day is done they go back to their own.

Kumasi is the core of what young Africans love to term "Divine Communism"; it is here that the matrilineal conception of the family rules in matters pertaining to inheritance and descent, where the nephew or brother inherits the stool, where, even if you don't work, you can eat, that is, if you're black and belong to the clan. It's here that even until today society is basically religious, military, and political—all one organic whole under a fierce patriarchal leadership sanctioned by the "mystic" powers of woman. The law that obtains in the family is the religion and the constitution of the state. In that society all men are soldiers and are sworn from infancy to die for the state; all women are destined by the magic of the moon and the stars to bear many children, to rear them and transmit to them the religion of the state. No man is free unless he accepts society's grim mandates; and no man would dream of violating the taboos, which are many and varied; if he did violate them, he'd be put beyond the pale. . . .

With the exception of a mission society here and there, the main streets are lined with European stores: The United Africa Company, the United Trading Company, Barclays Bank, the British Bank of West Africa, Kingsway Stores, etc. As in Accra, there are many Indian and Syrian establishments. African business firms are conspicuous by their shabby triviality. Less vibrant than Takoradi, moodier than Accra, dreamier than Koforidua, Kumasi has huge black vultures wheeling in its cloudy sky all day long.

I stopped at a dank and musty African hotel. Night fell and a clamor rose from the street below my window. Children screeched and played games. Downstairs a band played Western dance music. From far off came the dull throb of a beating drum. Tired, I closed my eyes and, it seemed, a moment later I was awake and staring at a dull, daylight sky.

It's six o'clock, but the streets are alive. Out of my hotel window I see an African family beginning the day in their front yard, which is a combination of bathroom, kitchen, dining room, and living room. The mother, nude to the waist, is bent over washing dishes in a tin pan that rests upon the red clay ground. An old woman sits on her stool and is combing her hair. Another woman kneels and is fanning a charcoal fire. A man is chopping kindling. Three children are squatting on the red earth, playing. A tall black girl is pounding corn in a vast wooden vat.

Enervated from the heat and dampness, I had to urge myself against my will to visit the offices of the leading opposition paper, the *Ashanti Pioneer*. The editor turned out to be fluent, putting himself at my disposal.

"How are things looking to you?" I asked him. "How do you feel about these impending changes?"

He drew a deep breath, shot me a glance, then laughed an African laugh; but at once he was solemn.

"What progress we make ought to be built upon our own institutions," he said. "We have our own traditions. It's a bad policy to impose the West upon us. Leave us alone to work out our destiny, to develop as our inward bent directs us."

Mr. John Tsiboe is in his early forties; he is the owner and publisher of his paper which has been appearing for fourteen years.

"What do you think of political parties as instruments of the popular will?"

"For us, the introduction of the party system was much too soon," he declared. "And that's the consensus of opinion in Ashanti. Now, it's not widely known, but the British offered us the party system before Nkrumah came along. We refused it. It clashes with our deepest traditions. We rejected it because it divides us. Our outlook upon life is based upon social cohesion.

"The Convention People's Party won, but the British are now using that party in the same manner that they once used the chiefs.

The present government is for British interests; it's the same situation with the chiefs in reverse. . . .

"Until recently, I didn't know what politics was. We Africans still don't know. In its election campaign, the Convention People's Party painted everybody black and white; all who were for the Convention People's Party were white, those who were against it were black bribe-takers, agents of imperialism. . . . Our simple tribal people believed it all.

"Do you realize that, for six weeks during the positive action period, my home and office had to be protected by the police? The Convention People's Party so incited the population that I lived in fear of my life. . . . "

The more I talked with the Ashanti, the more I sensed tension. These people had once ruled themselves for centuries and now they were embroiled in something which they did not understand, something which they had no preparation to accept. Bewildered and disillusioned, they thought one moment of out-Nkrumahing Nkrumah, of going to the masses and organizing against him; but the next moment they remembered their hallowed traditions of unity and they shrank and felt guilty. They knew that the victory of the Convention People's Party had multiplied their enemies: they now had the modern, streamlined Convention People's Party against them *and* the armed might of the British.

Next morning I visited the British District Commissioner's office to pay my respects, a formality with which foreigners were supposed to comply. I found a stoutish, brisk, pleasant enough man. Our chat was interrupted when his telephone rang.

"Excuse me a moment, will you?" he asked me.

"Go right ahead," I said.

He listened at some length on the phone, then sighed and said into the transmitter:

"I say, let me call you back, eh? Good-bye."

He hung up and turned to me.

"Here's a typical problem," he told me. "That was a call from a Fanti delegation. Now, they want to send a petition to the Prime Minister. But, in the Fanti language, there's no concept for Prime

Minister and they've addressed him as: Otumfuo. . . . That means
The All Powerful One. Well, to say the least, that's not an accurate
designation for a Prime Minister. They realize that, but they don't
know what other expression to use. They're asking me to help
them. . . . "

"In other words," I said, "when the Fanti language evolved, there
was no concept for Prime Minister, and the Fanti people want to
call the Prime Minister the name they used for their king. . . ."

"Exactly," the Commissioner told me.

It was a problem, all right, and it was not the first time in the
history of the Gold Coast that these cultural differences had manifested themselves. Happily, this was a rather innocent misunder-
standing.

I recalled reading that, in 1863, a subject of the King of Ashanti,
the Asantehene, found a big nugget of gold and, instead of surrendering it, as was required by Ashanti law and constitution, to
the Asantehene, he kept it for himself. The Asantehene, upon hearing of this, summoned the culprit to Kumasi to stand trial. The
man hid his gold nugget and fled to Cape Coast and begged the
protection of the white Governor.

The Asantehene sent a delegation to the Governor, and this delegation took with them a famous Ashanti symbol: a Golden Ax.
Now, in Ashanti, a Golden Ax is a symbol of peace; it signifies: Let
us cut down trees and clear the land and make farms in common. . . .

But the British Governor, a Mr. Pine, grew frightened at the sight
of the Golden Ax. The only associations that that ax evoked in his
mind was that he, Mr. Pine (maybe he was reacting to the magical
relationship between the words *tree* and *ax?* After all, his name was
Pine . . .) would be cut down from his place of power; to him the
Golden Ax was a symbol of war. Accordingly, he invented on the
spot a tall tale of a nonexistent treaty between him and the Asantehene; this treaty, he declared, stated that he did not have to return
an Ashanti criminal to the jurisdiction of the Asantehene.

As a result, the Ashanti declared war and invaded the colony in
three columns and, after a costly and protracted campaign, won

the war. So serious did the British position grow that the House of Commons debated withdrawing from the Gold Coast *in toto*. . . .

Two worlds did not understand each other's symbols and they tore at each other's throats, each convinced that the other was a devil and had to be killed!

That afternoon I told Kojo to drive me to one of Ashanti's most sacred bodies of water, Lake Bosomtwe, a lake which is second only to the River Tano in the degree to which it inspires ritual, dread, devotion, and sacrifice from those who live near it. Viewed from the surrounding hilltops, it is a beautiful lake, calm, majestic, gleaming like a jewel amidst the dark green forest hemming it in. Tiny mud villages lay humbly about its almost perfectly circular rim. I was told that those villages were filled with leprosy. . . .

Clinging to Lake Bosomtwe is that same halo of legend that clusters about so many rivers and brooks and ponds among the Akan Africans. Though local legend holds that the lake has no bottom, British scientists have measured its greatest depth, which is about 233 feet. . . . It is a fresh-water lake and was no doubt formed by a meteor. The lake's most astonishing manifestation of "spiritual" action is that every three or four years there is an "explosion" deep in the depths of the water and dead fish, floating to the surface, can be caught by the thousands. . . . This so-called "explosion" is referred to by the natives as "Bosomtwe's firing his gun."

The scientific explanation of the "explosion" is quite simple. The organic matter at the bottom of the lake—rotting leaves, etc.— would form from time to time masses of gas which would, because of mud and slime, be gathered and held down. When a sufficient volume of such gas was collected, it would force its way upward rather violently to the surface of the water, creating the "explosion" that the natives so much feared and loved. The reeking odor of the gas was what made them believe that some mystic gun had been fired.

The dead fish that could be so easily gathered would be the lake's "gift" to the people. (Psychoanalysts would clap their hands in joy over this one!) So, when the lake failed to "explode," it was said that the lake's taboos had been violated. These taboos included:

no metals, no oars, no paddles, no strings, and no poles could be used on the lake.

Despite the mass of written material that exists on the lake's natural idiosyncrasies, even literate Europeans as well as Africans love to dote on the lake's "mysteries." Everybody likes to dream.

I intercepted a fisherman coming up the steep slope of the lake and examined his catch. The string of fish he held in his hand looked and smelled like ordinary fish from an ordinary lake.

XXXVI...

I was a guest at a dinner attended by the King of Ashanti, the Asantehene, officially known as Otumfuo Sir Osei Agyeman Prempeh II. He was of medium height, slender, about sixty years of age, not quite black in color but definitely Negroid of features, quick of expression, and flat of nose. His skin was pitted with smallpox scars; his lips were clean-cut, his head slightly bald. He was poised, at ease; yet, like other men of the Akan race, he smiled *too* quickly; at times I felt that his smile was artificial, that he smiled because it was required of him. During the meal he had an occasional air of preoccupation and there was something definitely cold deep down in him. He was the kind of man about whom I'd say that, if there was to be a fight, I'd wish that he was on my side and not against me. . . .

He was installed by the British in 1931 as Omanhene of Kumasi, and, in 1935, upon the restoration of the Ashanti Confederacy, as Asantehene. He struck me as a man who had suffered much in silence, as one who could really talk frankly only to his trusted and intimate friends. Though a king, a British Commissioner really ruled over him. I asked him to grant me an audience and he was kind enough to consent at once.

From a young, intelligent African I heard a queer story. When I asked him why so many of the women who were scantily clad had markings of various sorts cut into the flesh of their stomachs, he told me that there is a legend that when women die and go to heaven, God carefully examines all the skins of women's stomachs to see if they are good enough for Him to use in His making of drums. Only women whose stomach skins are smooth, taut, and strong can be used. Hence, when God looks for a skin and sees that the skin of a given woman's stomach has been deformed, marked, cut into, He will pass it by. . . . I was so intrigued with this story that I forgot to ask my friend just why God had need of drums. . . .

Mornings dawn gray and damp. There is little or no sun. Somber is the word for the sky over Kumasi during the season of rain. Weather broods over the city; always it feels like rain, looks like rain, smells like rain; and then, suddenly, a fine drizzle falls. I'm sure that a few hundred feet in the air this city and its surrounding vegetation are invisible. Outside of my hotel window the ranging hills recede and fade in mist; now and again a slight wind agitates the tops of the stately palm trees.

To my hotel this morning came a young photographer whom I'd met in London; he is a grandson of the Asantehene and has agreed to accompany me to Mampong, a village about thirty-six miles from Kumasi. I was delighted to have him along because he, being of royal blood, could help to make the dour and brooding Ashanti open up.

Upon our arrival in Mampong, a typical mud village, we went to the local council over which the chief was presiding. We were admitted and sat while the council members conducted their business in their native tongue. The meeting adjourned and we followed the chief, Nana Asofo Kamtantea II, Mamponghene, to his office. The entourage surrounding the chief was amazing. One little boy held the big state umbrella, another carried the stool, and still another carried a bushy fan of some kind.

"Who are these boys who follow the chief?" I asked the Asantehene's grandson.

"They just follow him," he told me with a shrug of his shoulders.

But I knew better. I'd inquired to check his answer against what I'd read about entourages of this sort; I was convinced that he knew the answer. Then why was he lying? He was Catholic and was evidently ashamed to tell me that one boy was an umbrella carrier, another was a stool carrier, and that the third boy was a "soul" carrier, that is, the chief had selected this last boy for his innocence and had asked him to serve him so that he could be constantly reminded to keep his own soul in a state of innocence. . . . I looked at the Asantehene's grandson and he grew uncomfortable, then he smiled and said:

"I must show you where Okomfo-Anotchi, the great fetish man, drove a sword into the ground and no one can pull it out."

"Why can't anyone pull it out?" I asked.

"They just can't," he said. "Okomfo-Anotchi is the man to whom God sent down the Golden Stool from heaven on golden chains."

"The Golden Stool originated in that way?"

"Absolutely. And it must never touch the ground," he explained.

"And what else did Okomfo-Anotchi do?"

"Well, there's a sacred tree on which his footprints are still visible. You see, he climbed that tree and wherever his feet touched, they left impressions. You can see them."

But why had he not told me the truth about the roles played by the little boys? And he was willingly telling me about the supernatural origin of the Golden Stool!

"What has the Catholic Church to say about the Golden Stool?" I asked him.

"Oh, they say it's all right," he explained. "It has been Christianized."

I began to understand. Some things he was ashamed of because the church forbade them; other things he could accept because the church had endorsed them. I learned later that the strength of the Catholics was five times that of other Christian sects in the Gold Coast.

In the chief's office I met the Queen Mother; she was a daughter of the Asantehene and was accompanied by a tall, black woman who, I was told, was Head Woman of the Queen Mother's household. I noticed that when the Queen Mother rose to speak to me, she turned over her silver stool to make sure that no evil spirit would take possession of it.

"Why did she turn over her stool like that?" I asked the Asantehene's grandson in a whisper.

"Oh, that . . . ? It just fell over; that's all," he said lamely.

He had again evaded telling me the truth, and yet I held under
my arm a volume by a British anthropologist which explained the
turning over of the stool! I was to encounter this shame and shyness
many times in Ashanti; they believed in and practiced their customs,
but they were ashamed of them before the eyes of the world. . . .

The chief sat silent, waiting for his elders; he could not talk
to me until they were present as witnesses—a universal practice
among the chiefs of the Akan. I met many chiefs who refused to say
more than "good morning" or "good evening" for fear that their
elders would accuse them of misinterpreting the customs and traditions of the people to strangers. The Mamponghene's elders never
came and we took our leave without talking to him. The Queen
Mother, ever gracious, saved the hour by inviting me to her "castle"
for a drink. I accepted. Her "castle" looked like a tenement on
Chicago's South Side.

Seated in the Queen Mother's living room, I was struck by the
number of men and women wandering in and out without being
introduced. They sat and looked at me out of the corners of their
eyes, then would rise and hurriedly perform some order of the
Queen Mother. While the Queen Mother and the others were
chatting among themselves, I whispered to the Asantehene's grandson:

"Who are these people? Are they guests of the Queen Mother?"

"Oh, no."

"Are they friends?"

"No."

"Are they servants?"

"Well, no."

"They all live in the same household?"

"Yes."

"Are they paid?"

"Well, no; we don't pay them."

"But they work for her?"

"Yes."

"Can they leave when they want to?"

"They'd never want to leave."

"Are they slaves?" I asked him finally and bluntly.

He was irritated. He bit his lips and looked off.

"You don't understand," he said. "They wouldn't want to leave us. They live with us all of their lives. If they left, they wouldn't have anywhere to go. We feed them, clothe them; they live with us till they die. They are like members of the family; you see?"

"But other people would call them slaves, wouldn't they?"

"Yes; but that's not right; it's not the right word. It's not right to call them that."

It was slavery, all right; but it was not quite the Mississippi kind; it fitted in with their customs, their beliefs. There was no lynching. . . . I stared at the slaves. I tried to swallow and I could not. The Asantehene's grandson seemed to be worried at the impression I was getting and he said:

"We live differently; you see? We take care of these people. We give them all they need. You see?"

"Yes; I see," I said.

After a lunch of hard-boiled eggs, beer, bread, and tinned butter, we drove out along the roadside to look at the stool-makers. Entire families were engaged in this ritual-like profession, for the making of a stool was a complicated affair. They were carved whole out of tree trunks, with long knives attached to tree limbs for handles. There were no nails, screws; no measurements were taken. The black boys hacked at the wood and their aim and precision were amazingly accurate. Families selected a certain type of stool and commissioned the stool-makers to carve them for each member of the family. No one was supposed to sit upon your stool; it was yours, personally, and it was believed that, since you sat on it all of your life, some of your spirit adhered to it. When you died, your stool was placed in the Stool House along with other stools of the dead members of the family. If you were a chief or a king, sheep's blood would be dripped on your stool to revivify it; in the old days the blood of human beings was dripped or smeared on the stools. Such stools, in time, were referred to as "blackened stools."

I returned to my hotel in a heavy downpour. My room was as
damp as an underground cave. Water pounded on the roof like
somebody beating a big drum. Now and then a European car sped
through the wet streets, making a swishing noise. I glanced out
of the window and there was no sky. For hours the rain tumbled.
Weather dominated everything, created the mood of living, framed
the passing hours, tinted the feelings with somberness, with an
unappeasable melancholy. . . .

Most of the Akan people, I've noticed, have a peculiar way of
making odd mouth and head noises when engaged in conversation.
For example, when we would say, "Unh hunh," an Akan would
say, "Haaaan," to let you know that he was following or agreeing
with what you were saying. Hence, when listening to a roomful of
Ashanti talk, your ears are startled by a succession of "Haaaans"
uttered sometimes with the mouth open and sometimes with the lips
closed.

And why do most of the people spit all the time? Young and
old, men and women, people of high and low stations in life, spit.
I observed a young girl of about twelve years of age for about five
minutes and she spat six times; And this spitting is not just ordinary
spitting; it's done in a special manner. First, taut lips are drawn back
over clenched teeth and from out through the clenched teeth comes
a jet of saliva, straight, clean, strong, like a bullet from a gun, never
touching the lips. The people do not seem to be ill; I've seen no one
chewing tobacco or dipping snuff. Is this spitting at all times and
in all places a kind of reflex? Or does the climate here engender a
universal catarrhal condition . . . ? I tried, before my mirror in my
hotel room with the door locked, to spit like that and I succeeded
only in soiling the front of my shirt. . . .

XXXVII...

I spent the next few days visiting chiefs and there formed in my
mind an image of a vast purgatorial kingdom of suppliant and
petitioning multitudes ruled by men wielding power by virtue of

their being mediators between the guilty living and the vengeful dead. What a fabulous power structure these chiefs have built up through the ages, a structure whose essence consisted of a kind of involuntary emotional slavery! Only in an illiterate society could these "fathers" of the people have derived so much absolute authority from their exploitation of the loyalty, of the love and fear that men feel for their mothers and fathers. How these poor, half-naked beings rushed compulsively to obey their chiefs' interpretations of a menacing and vindictive shadow world whose emotional claims they could not conceive of questioning or denying . . . !

One chief's house was like another. One part of a vast, sprawling rectangle was given over to the living compound, another to the women and children. (Each chief, according to his wealth, had a houseful of wives; he also had wives who did not live with him.) Then there was the inevitable meeting hall, and, lastly, a police station. . . . And, somewhere usually more or less out of sight, was the Stool House holding the precious ancestral trinkets about which the spirits of the long dead were supposed to hover or could be persuaded to do so. In full view were the huge state drums used to summon the populace in tonal rhythms of joy, anger, or alarm. . . . No one was supposed to play upon those drums unless authorized to do so; to tamper with them irreverently merited a penalty of imprisonment. (In the old days the penalty was death.)

Some of the chiefs were literate; most of them were not. Inside of his rectangular building was a courtyard in which, at most all hours, large or small crowds of natives gathered, arguing, or waiting for an audience with the chief. The so-called "enstooling" and "destooling" of chiefs provided one of the most popular, passionate, and chronic activities of the colony. Hardly a day passed but what some chief somewhere, on a cloudy pretext whose density would be difficult to grasp by an outsider, was tossed out of his august spiritual position and some other aspirant placed on the stool in his stead. Though the chief, in theory, partook of the divine while he was in a position to mediate between the living and the dead, the moment he was off the stool he was no longer considered divine; indeed, he was someone to fear, for he might begin scheming at once to regain possession of the stool. "Destooled" chiefs, therefore, were urged to get as far as possible from the scene of their former divine activities. . . .

It struck me that the attitude toward these "destooled" chiefs was remarkably like that of their attitude toward the dead itself: nothing but harm could be expected from them, it seemed. And, being alive, they were not nearly as easily propitiated as the dead. It often occurred to me, while in the Gold Coast mulling over these mystic matters, that a dear dead friend, or brother, or father would be of much more benefit to the living than a living, sentient dear friend, or brother, or father. The dead had access to spirits that, for a reason no one could really satisfactorily explain, insisted on hanging around and haunting the living. I was certain that there was some gross misinterpretation here, for I could not conceive of a dead Ashanti, if he had any real intelligence at all, wanting to hover spiritually amidst these mud huts and rain and poverty and disease when he had entry to all the vast and interesting worlds far from the sodden high rain forest of British West Africa. . . .

There is, however, one great stroke of luck which the Akan dead have performed for the living. Since it is supposed that the dead and not the living own the land upon which the living dwell, the living are not at liberty to dispose of that land. If there is any issue about which an Ashanti will fight, it is about the disposition of the land upon which he lives, for he does not feel that it belongs to him. He is merely holding it in trust, cultivating it, and, when he dies, it is to be passed on to his or the tribe's children. This fact, plus that of the climate, has kept the white settler out of the high rain forest and has spared the inhabitants of the Gold Coast the agony of Kenya's Mau Mau making a war to recapture stolen ancestral lands. . . .

The dubious nature of land ownership has, however, mitigated against social and economic development in other directions. Since nobody in particular owns the land, no bank will advance money upon it. Land can be leased only, except in certain sections of the Colony area where Christianity has taken shallow root. Hence, though the British have gobbled up most of the rich gold and diamond mines, their right to those properties is limited to designated stretches of time.

The tracing of boundaries between plots of land was always a matter of sharp conflict. Land litigation is, therefore, one of the most widespread sources of legal activity in the Gold Coast. Lawsuits over narrow and almost profitless bits of land have been known to drag on year after year and the legal expenses would rise far beyond the value of the land in dispute.

The African attitude in legal matters is strange, one might almost say, idealistic. When he goes to law it is not only to obtain what he thinks is his right, but he wants that right done in a certain and particular manner. There was a story of an American who gave his "t'ief" man, that is, the man who slept on the porch of the American's house at night and watched for thieves, a Sears, Roebuck catalogue. A friend of the "t'ief" man borrowed the catalogue and, after many warnings, refused to return it. The "t'ief" man approached his American employer and told him that he was forthwith starting legal proceedings against his friend for the recovery of the catalogue. The American, feeling that such massive legal machinery was not needed to recover so trifling an object, offered to replace the catalogue, but the "t'ief" man would have none of it. He insisted upon going through with his legal action and did eventually repossess his valued catalogue, much to his pride and joy. He felt that he had vindicated himself, had proved his "right," which, to him, was a precious thing indeed.

Typical of a broader outlook and a more intelligent order of chiefs is one called the Efiduasihene, Nana Kwame Dua Awere II. Efiduasi is a little village (population indeterminate) of swish huts and is the center of trade and agriculture for an area which has a radius of ten miles. Sitting in his stuffy little office surrounded by his illiterate elders, the chief complained bitterly that his people were leaving the land in droves to go to the cities where life was more interesting. He frankly admitted that life in the villages was hard, that there were no modern amenities to lighten the burden, no conveniences for transportation, communication, etc. Yet, he pointed out, the government was crying out for the villages to grow more food.

The chief is president of the local council which has a membership of twenty-one, all of whom are members of the Convention People's Party. He has achieved a rare sort of psychological detachment about his position and spoke about it without lamenting.

"It's hard for people to understand that what has happened to us in the past was done by the chiefs. The rise of our way of life was inspired by the chiefs. All crafts were under their leadership; the goldsmiths, the silversmiths, the blacksmiths—all trades were at the behest of the chief, and the people were loyal to him." He paused and pointed openly to the half-clad men who sat around him, smiling and not understanding a word of what was being said. "Now, take these men . . . All of them are older than I am. Yet I'm their chief. They serve me willingly. I don't ask them to; their serving me is the meaning of their lives. They want me to dress up in these bright garments. It's their sense of what's good; they yearn for something to serve, to fight for, to maintain. . . . You see? Their loyalty to the Stool is deep and genuine. They cannot grasp politics. Yet, history is making severe demands upon us and we are not prepared. How will this illiteracy fit into the machine age?

"Yet, I don't see the end of the chief. He's closer to the people than anyone else. I'm convinced that it will take a long time for the social habits of the people to die out. The clan spirit is strong. We must find a way to bridge that gap. . . ."

As the chief propounded the problem, there were in full view his huge state drums which he used to call his people together. And he knew that telephones and wireless and newspapers were taking the place of those drums. But could the new means of communication equal in emotional value the things that the drums said, drums which could, at a moment's notice, throw a people into anger, joy, sorrow, or the stance to fight and die? That was the problem. The base upon which the new order had to build was so slight. . . . How could these people be taken from these ancestral moorings and be made to live contented lives in a rational industrial order?

"You are an American," the chief said to me. "You fellows are,

in a sense, our brothers. You've made the leap. What do you think of
our chances?"

He was an intelligent man, an ex-schoolteacher, and I didn't want
to misguide him. He had me stumped. The problems involved were
stupendous. Above all, I had to disabuse him of the illusion that
American Negroes had attained a kind of paradise, had solved all
of their problems.

"Nana," I said, "you don't have a race problem as severe as ours.
Your problem is much simpler and yet much harder, and much more
important. . . . The American Negro has done no reflective thinking
about the value of the world into which he fought so hard to enter.
He just panted to get into that world and be an American, that's all.
The average American Negro is perhaps the least qualified person
on earth to guide you in matters of this sort.

"I'm black, Nana, but I'm Western; and you must never forget
that we of the West brought you to this pass. We invaded your
country and shattered your culture in the name of conquest and
progress. And we didn't quite know what we were doing when we
did it. If the West dared have its way with you now, they'd harness
your people again to solve their problems. . . . It's not of me, Nana,
that you must ask advice. You men of Africa must be able to tell
the West something about how to live. Get it out of your head that
we are all happy and have no problems. That's propaganda. . . .

"If you go into the industrial world, Nana, go in with your eyes
open. Machines are wonderful things; love them for what they can
do for you; but remember that they cannot tell you how to live or
what aims you should hold in life. If you have no sense of direction
before you embrace the world of machines, machines will not give
you one. . . . "

I was convinced that the meaning of the industrial world was
beyond that chief. He could grasp it with his mind, but he could not
feel or as yet know the emotional meaning of the lives of wage
workers in Chicago or Detroit. The question facing him was a
bigger one than merely becoming modern. Must he leave behind
him his humanity, such as it was, as he moved into that industrial
world, as he built his Volta Projects? Or could he take it with him?

Must his culture, though condemned by the West—a culture evolved under unique conditions and over long centuries—be cast unthinkingly aside as he embraced plumbing, printing, and politics?

And what would the Akan religion be if grafted, in its present state, onto the techniques of atomic energy? The West had taken hold of the world of modern techniques with its old humanity intact, and now, in Paris where I lived, men were huddled together in indecision, numbed with despair, facing a myriad of possibilities, none of which they wanted, all of which sickened them. . . .

The pathos that rose from my talking to Africans about their problems was that their minds were uninformed—thanks to the contribution of a British education—about the bodies of knowledge relevant to their situation, bodies of knowledge which other peoples had erected at a great cost of suffering, toil, and sacrifice. Hence, I felt that almost any decision that the Africans would make, perhaps for some time to come, would be a hit-or-miss proposition, that they would have to tread ground already laboriously trampled by others. But there was no turning back; historic events had committed the Africans to change. . . . For good or ill, the die was cast. The game was up. What had been done, could not now be undone. Africa was moving. . . .

XXXVIII...

Most of the Africans I've met have been, despite their ready laughter, highly reserved and suspicious men. It would be easy to say that this chronic distrust arose from their centuries-long exploitation by Europeans, but that explanation would not elucidate the total African attitude. They never seem to feel that they have judged a man rightly unless they project some ulterior motive behind his most straightforward conduct. I'm willing to admit that, through the centuries, the Africans have had to bear the brunt of coping with the cream of Europe's confidence men; but I'm persuaded that Europe's smooth chicanery served but to augment elements that were already lodged deep in the heart of African culture. I submit

that the African's doubt of strangers, his panic in the face of reality
has but peripheral relations to objective reality. Behind the most
ordinary happenings the African is inclined to suspect the mirac-
ulous; to him casual signs point away from present facts.

Unless you exhibit strong, almost passionate emotion, the African
is never quite sure that you are honest. Consequently, he possesses
an inordinate faith in the force of mere words to dispel or hide facts.
With many Africans words assume an omnipotent power. . . . Knowing that the outside world is curious and perhaps scornful of their
magical beliefs, being devoid of a written history, they have devised,
out of psychological necessity, methods of verbal jockeying to cast
doubt into the minds of those who would try to know them. For
example, in questioning one of the chiefs about the rituals of his
people, I was told with a superior smile that:

"You don't know all of our secrets. You can't know them all."

"But," I told him, "Rattray and others have written pretty clearly
about your religious practices."

"Oh, Rattray. . . . We didn't tell him *everything*. We told him
some things. But we *never* tell *anybody everything* . . ." he said.

I was convinced that the many anthropologists who had studied
Ashanti had put down, by and large, the basic truth of their
religious customs, and I think that the chief knew this. He was
trying to make me believe that the Ashanti had secrets *behind*
secrets; and if I pried out *those* so-called secrets, he could at once
allude to still other and more dreadful secrets behind *those* secrets,
and so on. But what value have these secrets? Obviously, to his
mind, a "secret" possessed the psychological value of intimidating
others, of making them think that any move they might make
against him would be met with some countermove of a surprising
nature. . . . In short, in his eyes, you were an enemy until, by his
own standards, he had decided that you were not.

At times this denial of plain facts on the part of chiefs became
laughable. One chief would tell me a story that was flatly and
passionately contradicted on the same day by another chief in a
neighboring state. These effacings of reality went so far as to include
objective evidence. For instance, with an anthropological volume

under my arm showing clear photographs of "blackened stools,"
one chief defiantly informed me:

"There are *no* such things as blackened stools! There are no such
things and there *never* were any! That's a fiction invented by the
British to smear us!"

All of this dodging and denying is, of course, aided by the fact
that there is no written history. If the Ashanti had a concrete manner
of ascertaining what went on yesteryear, they might have escaped
the more bizarre aspects of their religion, its more bloodthirsty
phases. With a vivid account of what they had done, uncolored by
the emotionally charged recital of a "linguist," they might have been
able, perhaps, to remember their bare, objective actions and, in
remembering them, they would have been made to pause and
wonder, would have been able to get beyond the circling coils of
abject fear. . . .

Dr. R. E. Armattoe of Kumasi, an African doctor educated in
England and Germany, and who has lived in the United States
for a time, told me:

"You have to open your mind to believe that these people believe
some of the things that they do believe."

"Does human sacrifice still exist?"

"It does."

"It's hidden, then?"

"Yes; they don't want the British or outsiders to see or know
about it."

"What do the British do about it?"

"Nothing, as long as it's kept out of sight."

"What reasons do the Ashanti offer for doing it now, this killing
of innocent people?"

"It's to appease the dead ancestors. They fear that their ancestors
will return."

"That sounds like a psychological compulsion."

"Could be."

"What method do they use in this killing, that is, sacrificing?"

"You see, they have a way of seizing you quickly, running your
cheeks and tongue through with a long knife so that you cannot

speak. They cut off your head and take your blood in a brass pan and bathe the bones of their ancestors with that blood, mumbling and praying the while:

" 'Dear father, here is some blood for you, to strengthen you. . . .' "

"Do they seem calmer after such deeds?"

"My friend, I've never got that close to it. . . . I can only tell you what they have told me about *that* part of it. But when they speak of it, they're exultant, adamant. They get some kind of conviction out of it."

"Does the mood vanish after the deed, or can you detect traces of it in their everyday life hereabouts?" I asked.

"Well, when you talk to some of these people, you might notice that often they have a calm, abstracted air. That means that even while they are talking to you, they are listening, waiting to hear the advice of their ancestors. . . . Now, if you should telephone anybody here in Kumasi at night, late—and if that person is an oldtime African—no one will answer your ring until after you've rung at least *three* times."

"Why is that?"

"It's said that the dead ring twice. Only a living person will ring three times," Dr. Armattoe told me.

"Is that, then, why they don't want to talk about this thing?"

"Yes, and as long as they don't and can't talk openly about it, it means that they are still under the spell of it," he said.

Later, in talking to a British doctor who asked to remain anonymous, I learned that Dr. Armattoe's words were true.

"We don't publicly acknowledge it," the British doctor said. "But we try to interfere as little as possible with the religious habits of these people. Of course, all kinds of persuasion are brought to bear upon the local Africans to stop this business of human sacrifice; but it happens. When a big chief dies, the local police collect a barrel of human heads and haul them, like carting furniture, to the police stations. What can we do?"

If you fear your ancestor, it's because, psychologically, you feel guilty of something. But of what? That guilt, no matter how confused or unconscious, stems from one's having wanted to kill that dead ancestor when he was alive. In the life of the Akan people the thought that is too horrible to think finds its way into reality by identifying itself with the dead ancestors. Killing for that dead ancestor is a way of begging forgiveness of that ancestor; their own murderous conscience assumes the guise of their ancestor's haunting them. . . .

If the human sacrifice—and that of animals: bulls, sheep, goats, and chickens—does not represent displaced hate of the living, why then is blood the gift that will appease the dead ancestor? The staunch conviction that the dead ancestor wants blood is their inverted confession of their own lust for blood. So they feel that by killing a stranger and bathing the bones of an ancestor in the blood of that stranger, the ancestor will, for the time being, hold off haunting them, will leave them in peace. Through such collective compulsive murders their emotional tensions are resolved.

Their homicidal attitude toward the stranger is evidence of their present but deflected lust to kill the not-yet-quite-dead but prospective ancestor whose edicts they hate deep in their hearts. The tight vise of taboo-ridden tribal life, holding the hearts of simple, non-reflective men in a strait-jacket, finds its apogee of protest, its psychological balance in venting its hate and lustful rebellion upon the stranger, but that stranger is symbolically the living dead which that heart hates and fears. So crime and forgiveness for crime are magically combined in a single act of ritualized violence. . . . Men whose hearts are swamped by such compounded emotional problems must needs be always at war with reality. Distrust is the essence of such a life.

There is too an element of vicarious suicide in this psychologically complicated business of human sacrifice. The millions who support this bloody ritual know in their hearts that they too might be killed, know that they have no control over the selection of victims. Terror reigns when a king or a queen mother dies, for anyone might be seized and dispatched for service in the shadowy world of ghosts. So the sense of guilt lingers on, becoming a palpable and public thing that spreads and grows and enshrines itself in ritual and ceremony. . . . The wild and dark poetry of the human heart!

I'm in my hotel room. There is still no sun. A faint, humid wind blows in, bringing the smell of rain. Then it begins to drizzle; soon the fuzzy water thickens and slanting strings of rain are drenching the red clay. The city is hushed. The rain slackens, then stops; people emerge and cook and wash and talk. At this moment, in a space twenty yards square, I see: carpentering, nursing of babies, pounding of *fufu*, a game of checkers, children leaping and jumping *ampe*, a barber shaving a man, a man repairing a pair of shoes, a public letter writer scribbling a missive for a customer, etc.

Until now I'd not seen the central market of Kumasi at close range; today I decided to descend into the maelstrom. But, before going, I mounted four floors into a European commercial establishment to get a full view of it. It was a vast masterpiece of disorder sprawling over several acres; it lay in a valley in the center of the city with giant sheds covering most of it; and it was filled with men and women and children and vultures and mud and stagnant water and flies and filth and foul odors. Le Marché aux Puces and Les Halles would be lost here. . . . Everything is on sale: chickens, sheep, cows, and goats; cheap European goods—razor blades, beds, black iron pots three feet in diameter—nestle side by side with kola nuts, ginger roots, yams, and silk *kente* cloths for chiefs and kings. . . . In these teeming warrens shops are social clubs, offices are meeting halls, kitchens are debating leagues, and bedrooms are political headquarters. . . . This is the Wall Street of the Gold Coast.

Coming on foot, you are aware of a babble of voices that sounds like torrents of water. Then you pause, assailed by a medley of odors. There is that indescribable African confusion: trucks going to and fro, cooking, bathing, selling, hammering, sewing. . . . Men and women and children, in all types of dress and degrees of nudity, sat, lay, leaned, sagged, and rested amidst packing boxes, metal barrels, wooden stalls, and on pieces of straw matting. As far as my eye can reach is the African landscape of humanity where everybody did everything at once.

I paused at a place where native medicines are sold in the form of various gnarled and blackened roots. Kojo, who accompanied me, swore solemnly that these roots could cure almost any ailment; you boiled a root—a special root for each illness—in water and you drank it.

"Did your family ever give you any medicine like that?" I asked him.

"Nasa, Massa. Not yet."

"Well, if your relatives ever give you anything like that, they'll be making sacrifices to you, asking you to forgive them."

Kojo was startled for a moment, then he burst into a loud and long laugh.

The market's most amazing stall contained about two hundred black men, women, and children squatting upon many mounds of charcoal. At first I could not make out what was happening, so generally black did the scene seem; only after a few moments' gazing did I see that the color of the charcoal was blending so evenly with the black skins as to create an over-all impression of pall. Slowly I distinguished whites of eyes staring at me as I stood gaping. . . .

One part of the market is set aside for the manufacture of the African toothpick, known locally as chewingstick; it's about four inches long and is kept in the mouth for hours. Men or women walk, talk, work, or just stare off into space, slowly and carefully worrying the end of the stick with tongue about teeth and gums. It's publicly done, no shame being attached to cleaning the teeth in this manner. Africans regard it about as we regard chewing gum.

It rained and cleared; then rained and cleared again; now it looks as though it would rain once more. . . . It rained.

The rain stops. Gray clouds hang behind the stately palm trees—clouds that glow with a touch of red and gold and silver, turning dark purple as the light fades. . . .

The evening arrived for my audience with the King. He received me in his palace, dressed in a native costume, a dark blue silk *kente* cloth draped gracefully about him. He was accompanied by his secretary and he spoke slowly, in a low voice, and again I had an impression of melancholy from him. He was a sensitive man and knew that his day had gone. I wondered how much of a *prisoner* he was of the rituals and ceremonies of his people. He was well

informed: we talked about England, Russia, France, America, the
atom bomb, and American Negroes. I asked him about the chance
of the institutions of his people weathering the political storm, and
he told me emphatically:

"I warned my people—I told them that they had to learn!"

While sitting and talking with him, sipping a glass of orange juice,
feeling the essential pathos of his position, I remembered that if
this old man, seemingly kind, fatherly, should suddenly have a heart
attack and die in my presence, I'd be killed, no doubt, by his
executioners and dispatched forthwith into the world beyond. . . .
I'd be commissioned, perhaps, to write his biography for the ancestral ghosts of Ashanti!

Could that happen? Yes; I'd been assured by prominent Ashanti
men that if the King died, every paramount chief of Ashanti would
be called upon to send his quota of victims and that those victims
would be furnished. . . . Lawyers, doctors, serious politicians, men
of sober judgment told me that they would not venture out upon
the streets of Kumasi if the Asantehene or any of his relatives died,
or if any of the paramount chiefs died; they were convinced that
such foolhardiness on their part would be worth a first-class ticket
to the other world.

"What about the Golden Stool?" I asked him.

He spoke in a low tone to his secretary who rose and got a
mimeographed sheet of paper which he handed to me. I glanced
at it and it stated clearly that the stool system was a "political
fiction" . . . He made no attempt whatsoever to cling to the old
symbols in terms of their supernatural potency.

"I've told my people to *change*," the Asantehene said solemnly.
"I've told them that they've got to *change!*"

I was more or less convinced now that he was an unwilling
prisoner of the religious traditions of his people! He was a Methodist;
he had been a clerk in a mercantile establishment before he'd been
elevated to his position. He was no doubt struggling to find ways
and means to let his people know that he was not akin to any mystic
powers; but *could* he . . . ?

He showed me his portrait painted in oil by a European artist;

it depicted him dressed in his most formal regalia and the canvas gleamed as it reflected the huge masses of gold about his arms, his head, and his legs. I was told later that, on festive occasions, he was so burdened with gold that he could not move, that he had to have help when he stood or walked.

"It's our culture," he told me softly.

Yes; that was the way the transition was made; religion turned into culture; holy days turned into holidays. . . .

After an hour I shook hands with him and left, heading in the car for Berekum, which lay about a hundred miles to the north and west. I was accompanied by a local member of the Gold Coast Information Service who, while we lurched over the laterite road, regaled me with information about the royal family. We were entering the tsetse fly region and the forest jungle was not as thick as it had been about Kumasi; the air was less heavy and I felt almost normal for the first time in many days. The heat was there, all right, making you feel that it would push you down, but a horizon opened out to all sides, relieving me of that hemmed-in feeling that the jungle gives.

We passed a funeral procession in a tiny village and we stopped to observe. A young man had died and he lay upon a litter wrapped in a brightly colored shroud. The women were chanting a funeral dirge and the men who carried the litter all had unlighted cigarettes in their mouths, the significance of which I was unable to determine. The procession marched slowly over the bare red earth and the colors of the cloths seemed to blend with the bloody red soil and the green vegetation. A brass band blared out a jazz tune and I was startled to see that some of the chanting girls were shuffling their feet in time to the beat of the music. I mingled with the procession for a while and I could smell palm wine on the breaths of the young men. The sun beat down pitilessly, lighting up the somber procession, outlining it against the sky as it moved off with dragging feet, threading its way past sheep, goats, and chickens. The mourners descended into an eroded gully and began to go downhill. I watched them until the vegetation screened them from view. . . .

"Tell me," I asked of the young gentleman of the Gold Coast

Information Service, "is there a committee or somebody who decides who is to be sacrificed when a member of the royal family dies?"

"Oh, no," he told me. "It's all arranged in terms of ritual. You see, the executioners go about their work at the silent bidding of the Queen Mother. When death strikes one of the members of the royal family, the theory is that the bones of the sacred dead are not satisfied, that they are restless, that they are hungering for life. Now, the ritual goes something like this. The Queen Mother paints her mouth red, which is the Akan sign of acute sorrow. She then enters the room where the executioners are stationed. She does not speak. She sinks slowly to the floor and weeps. That is all. She does not open her mouth; the rest is understood. She is telling them by her silent sorrow that death has claimed one of royal blood. . . . Death is hungry and must not be allowed to devour another member of her family. Death must be fed the blood he wants, and quickly, or he would take yet another one. . . . The weeping of the Queen Mother is the signal for the dreaded executioners to go into action. . . ."

"Just how many deaths are needed?" I asked.

"That depends upon who dies," he told me. "And the exact number is a secret. I've heard some say that twelve deaths are needed for a paramount chief. Undoubtedly more are needed for the King himself."

The car lurched on. I remembered those Bible verses that my grandmother used to quote (Exodus, 29: 20):

Then thou shalt kill the ram, and take of his blood, and put it upon the tip of the right ear of Aaron, and upon the tip of the right ear of his sons, and upon the thumb of their right hand, and upon the great toe of their right foot, and sprinkle the blood upon the altar around about.

And (Leviticus, 17: 11):

For the life of the flesh is in the blood; and I have given it to you upon the altar to make an atonement for your souls; for it is the blood that maketh an atonement for the soul.

The voice of the Ashanti joins that of the human race in testifying that the human heart has need of blood. And, in the matter of this peculiar need, there is no difference between the agony of the Ashanti and the Christian. With Christ the human sacrifice is offered up symbolically; you merely have to feel it and not do it. Yet, the compulsion derives from the same burden of fear and guilt, a longing to go down and placate the dark powers of one's heart. The Ashanti sacrifice human beings; Christians offer up Christ maybe 300,000,000 times a day in the form of the mass. . . . But the blood that flows from the Cross is imaginary blood, magic blood, make-believe blood, and the blood that flows from the knife of the Ashanti is no less magical, but all too real. . . . The advantage of the white Westerner is that he found a way of killing and dodging the consequences of it; he found a way of stifling that awful need in a socially acceptable way. The African believes straightforwardly; his heart lacks the artful sophistication of the white man who shrank from the direct demands of the heart and found a substitute. Who is right here: the Ashanti or the Christian? I think that both are lamentably right, terribly childlike, and tragically human. Neither has the inner strength to stand aloof from himself and wonder at his dread; neither distrusts his irrational feelings, feelings as wild as the heaving ocean, as demanding as the sweeping and tearing wind. Neither can resolve not to spill blood to still that churning in him which he does not want. . . .

XXXIX...

Another sultry morning. The sun cannot be seen, but its heat can be felt through the white mist that overhangs the sky. Scores of black vultures wheel silently over the city, moving their revolving circles from spot to spot on the horizon. Sometimes they are high up and far away, sometimes they are very low, so low that you can see their scaly heads and long, sharp beaks.

I entered Barclays Bank and took my place in a queue before a teller's window. Before and behind me were cloth-draped Africans. One man had a bundle wrapped in newspaper; it was filled with pound notes; there must have been hundreds of them and they made a gigantic heap. I looked at him; he was unshaven, barefooted, and wore a tattered cloth. I was never able to tell the wealth or social position of an African by his dress. Had he entered a New York bank, dressed as he was and with such a pile of notes, I'm sure that he would have incited the suspicion of the officials of the establishment.

I started, hearing a noise behind me. I turned and saw a young African leap into the bank through an opened window. I tensed, thinking that maybe a holdup was about to take place. But he walked smilingly forward and took his place in line. Then another African leaped through the window. . . . I relaxed. It was no holdup; it was simply some Africans' way of entering a bank. The door was too far and so they just jumped calmly through the window and went about their business.

At lunch today I was told that the Gold Coast Government was importing prefabricated wooden houses from Sweden. I said that I didn't believe that, not with all the huge forests that I'd seen in Ashanti. But a young African volunteered to take me to see the houses.

We drove to the edge of the city and, amidst a plot overgrown with tall weeds, I saw rows of neat, new wooden houses.

"Is Swedish wood better than Gold Coast wood?" I asked the young man who had accompanied me.

"No. Our wood is the best in the world," he said. "We export it everywhere."

I approached the houses and examined them; they seemed well put together, solid, but they were uninhabited.

"With such an acute housing shortage, why are these houses standing empty?"

"They cost too much; Africans can't buy or rent them."

"Haven't you got wood like this in the Gold Coast?"

"Yes; we have plenty of it."

"Then it's possible that this very wood could have come from the Gold Coast?"

"That's right."

"So, other than cut it in lengths, etc., what did the Swedes do to this wood?"

"I think that they spat on it," the young man said, laughing. "All we know is that the government awarded contracts to some Swedes to build these houses for us."

"Why wasn't this work done here in the Gold Coast?"

"I don't know. There's a lot of whispering about graft," he said, pulling down the corners of his lips. "Look, I want to show you something else. . . ."

We drove to the heart of the city, upon a hill, overlooking a race track.

"See that big white house over there?" he asked me, pointing.

I saw a vast structure that looked like a hospital surrounded by a high cement wall.

"Yes. What is it?"

"That's a home of one of the new members of the black government."

"He must be rich," I said.

"Well, he wasn't rich four years ago."

"Then how did he get that house? Did he inherit it? And what's a house like that worth?"

"Nobody knows how he got that house," the young man said. "But there's plenty of speculation. . . . He didn't inherit any money. A few years ago he was making two pounds a week as a newspaper reporter. The house cost fifteen thousand pounds. . . ."

"You seem to be hinting at widespread corruption in politics here."

"I'm doing just that."

"How does it work?"

"It's done mostly through the awarding of contracts for the building of roads, schools, hospitals, etc."

"Good God! And who awards these contracts?"

"A special board created by the government."

"How many members are on that board?"

"Eight."

"How many Africans?"

"Three."

"Ah, then the Africans cannot really be guilty of all this corruption. At least, not alone. Do the Africans and the English work together?"

"No; the Africans manage to do it alone."

"But how's that possible? They're outvoted five to three."

"It's complicated and when I explain it to you," he said, "you'll have to admit that the African boys are smart. Now, there's a lot of undercover tension on that board between the Africans and the English. On the surface, you'd think that everything was all right, but it's not. Each side distrusts the other. Now, let's say that a hospital is going to be built. This board lets it be known that it will accept bids from firms all over the world to do the job. The bids flow in. Meanwhile, the African boys approach the firms submitting bids and tell each firm that it can have the job for, say, three thousand pounds. Of course, the firm wants the job. It pays."

"But the Africans can't *guarantee* that a firm will get the job," I protested. "The white members of the board will outvote them—"

"That's all been figured out," he said. "When the board votes the contract (the African boys don't care *which* firm!) to a certain firm, they keep the three thousand pounds from *that* firm and to the unlucky firms they return all the other batches of three thousand pounds!"

"Is this widely known?"

"It's talked about here and abroad."

"But how could they risk their drive toward self-government with such petty thieving?"

"Well, for one thing, they're cynical," he explained. "They've watched the British grab and conquer, so they've grown to think that anything that you can get away with is right. And, strangely, tribal customs encourage such attitudes. If one wants a favor, one gives someone something. They deal that way even with their dead. . . ."

"But the African thief is not nearly as clever as his European counterpart. The African is still dealing in pennies. What is really bad about it is that the African can't be made to feel that his stealing is wrong; you can make him cautious, but not repentant. His being conquered and plundered are the two central facts of his life. He feels that he's an amateur in these matters; after all, he's never grabbed a country of four million people and milked them for his benefit for over a century. . . ."

Wherever I probed in the Gold Coast I found this sense of having been violated by a stronger power, and that the actions of that stronger power proved that might made right. . . . And too there was always this question: Can we trust that stronger power to teach us? Since so many of the moves of Europeans have been tricky, must not *all* of their moves be tricky . . . ?

This distrust manifested itself in a novel manner in Elmina, in 1953, when the local authorities told the people that they were going to "give" them "free" education, good roads, etc. The people agreed quite readily to accept these gifts. But when they learned that they had to pay an increase in taxes for them, they felt that they had been tricked! They were being asked to pay for what had been promised as "free," as a gift.

Outraged, they massed and moved on Elmina Castle to protest. The British official in charge, serving under a black cabinet, ordered them to disperse. They refused and answered with a shot that killed the white official. The police returned the fire and several natives lay dead. . . . The rest of the mob was driven off with rifle butts.

A rather peculiar economic structure has served to blunt the sense of the Gold Coast population to the realities of modern industrial life. Out of a population of 4,500,000 (1952 census), there are roughly about 1,500,000 able-bodied males of working age. Yet, the total number of actual wage earners number but 250,000. There are about 1,000,000 petty traders and farmers. Out of the 250,000 wage earners, 93,000 work for the central government, which makes government the most thriving industry in the nation. There are about 40,000 employed in mining gold, diamonds, manganese, bauxite, etc. The strength of the army is roughly 10,000. The United Africa Company employs nearly 6,000.

Most of the menial labor is done by non-Gold Coast Africans. The Krus from Liberia move the night soil; the Nigerians work in personal services. In Accra, Cape Coast, and Kumasi there is a fairly large middle class composed of teachers, preachers, doctors, lawyers,

etc. It's estimated that about 200,000 migrants from French territories come each year to work in the mines, to help harvest the huge
cocoa crop, and, once they have earned the amount of money that
they have their hearts set on—enough to buy a wife or a cow—they
return to their native haunts. Next year another and almost entirely
new flood of migrants come to take the place of the old wave. . . .
This almost 100 per cent turnover does not, of course, make for
efficiency in modern industry. The lessons learned last year are
washed down the drain of tribal life. . . .

Capitalism has to buck a strange set of conditions in the Gold
Coast. Besides the land being owned by the dead and the widespread distrust of outsiders, there is the jungle in which a man can
snatch a living straight from nature herself. If you drive an Akan
at a pace that he thinks is too hard, he'll drop his work and head
for the "bush" where he can live, maybe not as well as he could on
a monthly wage, but he'll be living just the same!

In the south, in the Colony area which holds the Ga and the Fanti
tribes, one finds many Western attitudes, a high rate of literacy, etc.
These people have been in contact with Europe for centuries. The
Northern Territories, mostly Mohammedan, contain the most backward elements of the population, though they number more than a
million. To the north is grim poverty, nakedness. . . .

The most important native industry is cocoa farming, which
accounts for the bulk of the nation's income. Cocoa was introduced
into the country in 1879 by a Gold Coast African returning from the
islands of Fernando Po and San Thomé. Beginning with an export
of eighty pounds of cocoa in 1891, the Gold Coast today supplies a
third of the world's demand. In 1935 there were 950,000 acres under
cultivation; cocoa farming gives employment in all to some 195,000
people, including labor communally derived from African family
groups. If the cocoa industry should fail, the nation's attempt to rise
out of its tribalism would be strangled. Farmers, therefore, are today
battling desperately to save the industry from a blight called swollen
shoot, a disease which reduces the yield of trees and finally kills
them. In 1944 the disease had spread over such a large area of the
country that it was feared that the industry would be wiped out.

The government called in scientists who discovered that swollen shoot was caused by a virus which was being spread by mealybugs traveling from tree to tree, drinking the sap.

The only method found so far to check the growth of this disease is to cut out the infected trees, a method which aroused the opposition of the semi-literate farmers and caused a nationwide political uproar. But it was found that by controlled methods of cutting out infected trees over an eleven-year period, only a loss of about 7 per cent of the trees was sustained.

The government is now seeking a method of registering workingmen, providing them with identity cards, taking their fingerprints, etc. At first the tribal-minded suspected a white man's trick in this attempt to introduce standards of efficiency and classification of trades; they felt that the government was about to conscript them into a new war and they would not co-operate. But, as time elapsed, they saw the advantage of being identified; from tribal nonidentity, the working masses are now moving slowly toward personal identity, individuality, and responsibility.

An amusing tribal habit came to light in the mines of Takoradi, Kumasi, and adjacent regions. The clan spirit prevailing among the workers made them share and share alike in all details of life. Thus, if a boy felt that he didn't want to go to work one morning, he asked his tribal brother to work in his stead, telling his pal to use his name. The European bosses didn't know one African from another; all blacks looked alike to them. This widespread system of masquerading was not employed to cheat; its aim was simply to rest and while away the hours. And the boy substituting for his loafing comrade would not know how to do the work properly. . . .

One of the most serious employment problems in the country concerns the illegal recruitment of labor, a practice which constitutes a hangover from the slavery that was once widely (and to some extent, still is) exemplified in the institutions of the Akan. A loose sort of trade in human beings still goes on; it's not as blatant as in the old days, but it's serious enough to make trouble. This illegal recruitment is so skilfully organized along clannish lines that it's well-nigh impossible, so far, for the government to stamp it out.

At most of the northern borders, beginning with autumn, are unofficial labor agents with trucks, waiting to intercept the half-famished migrant who longs for food and work. These labor agents "buy" these hapless tribesmen by promising them food and lodging for as long as they remain under the tutelage of their "buyers." The agents finally "sell" the migrant to a cocoa farmer, for, say eight pounds. If the migrant does not like the work, he runs off, though the farmers watch these migrants most carefully. If a migrant succeeds in escaping, the farmer has to "buy" another migrant. In some remote districts there are migrants who have been with cocoa farmers so long that they do not know where to go; in a land of tight clannishness where everybody is related to somebody, these migrants feel that they do not belong to anybody; they become resigned and quite willing to work indefinitely for their keep.

There is an obscure but potent psychological element abetting slavery; the Akan has a terror of his family line becoming extinct, which means, in terms of his religion, that an ancestor's desire to return to the world through a reincarnation of the family blood stream would be impossible. . . . Hence, slaves occupy a strange and privileged relationship with African families. The offspring of masters and slaves are considered as a legitimate part of the family. If the family line is threatened with extinction, a slave can and has been elevated to the head of the family, enjoined to keep the property intact, to pass on the heritage to succeeding generations.

There are factors in the attitudes and habits of African workers that make them rather inefficient from a Western point of view. Conditioning, stemming not from a racial, but from a cultural background makes them feel that it is not necessary to measure up sharply to certain standards of performance. This does not mean that the African is lazy; he can work, can extend himself as much as any man when he wants to, but his grasp of the world is as yet too poetic and he is reluctant to pant and sweat to earn a living, especially if the work involves digging gold out of the soil of his own earth for Europeans!

African capitalism is practically nonexistent; it seems that the African possesses little or no desire to launch ambitious financial schemes. He distrusts long-range plans; he is the most materialistic of men, wanting his share now, cash on the line. He is a close and practical dealer in small and petty trading for a quick turnover. Many Africans do not trust banks; life insurance is rare among them. But when they feel that they are working or fighting for themselves, there is no limit to their exertions. . . .

XL . . .

I must plead guilty to a cynical though cautious attraction to these preposterous chiefs, their outlandish regalia, their formal manners, the godlike positions that they have usurped, their pretensions to infallibility, their generosity, their engaging and suspicious attitudes, their courtliness, and their thirst for blood and alcohol and women and food. . . . Their huge umbrellas are foolishly gaudy, their never-ending retinue of human slaves is ridiculous, their claims about their ability to appease the dead is a fraud, their many wives are a seduc-tive farce, the vast lands that they hold in the name of the dead are a waste of property, their justice is barbaric, their interpretations of life are contrary to common sense; yet, withal, they are a human lot, intensely human. . . . Let no one suppose that the knowledge that they possess about human life was lightly gained. Insights of that order are bought dearly, with streams of blood. As rulers of men, they know something that many twentieth-century rulers do not know, or are afraid to acknowledge.

I'd like to feel that, in the hoary days before the coming of the white man, they were superbly conscious of what they were doing in that fetid jungle. But, really, I cannot. . . . These chiefs dote too obviously on rituals involving babies, adolescent girls, women, mys-tery, magic, witchcraft, and war. I'd like to feel that they laughed to themselves when they were alone at how they duped their illiterate followers—or did they? Really, I doubt it. They were as illiterate as their simple-minded victims, so how could they have had that degree of reflective knowledge that would have given them the freedom to laugh? The odds are that they believed in it all.

But that guy (He intrigues me no end!) called Okomfo-Anotchi, that joker who evoked the Golden Stool from the sky on golden chains, that guy who drove that sword into the earth and nobody can pull it out, that chap who climbed that tree and left footprints that can be seen even now—he could not have been completely serious all the way! His deceptions are of so high an order that they imply a cosmic sense of humor. I'd like to regard him as being knowing, humanly cynical, compassionate, and deeply mindful of his people's future; I'd like to feel that when the time came for him to die, he turned his head discreetly to the wall and tried as hard as he could to repress a sad smile. But I'm afraid that that's hoping for too much. Most likely, when dying, he picked out ten or twelve people to serve him, to keep him company in the beyond. . . .

These chiefs are and were, one and all, scoundrels, some consciously, some unconsciously, some charmingly, and some with ill-humor. Yet, in a world where cause and effect rested upon a basis of magic, they were needed as mediators between the visible and the invisible. It must not be thought, though, that this propensity toward magic originated solely with the chiefs; it was there before they came; in fact, they were thrown up as functionaries as the result of the widespread belief in magic among the common people.

It is striking that all the cases of attempts at magic or witchcraft I heard about in the Gold Coast dealt with someone's trying to make something *concrete* happen. By that token, it would seem to me that the best possible demonstration against this thirst for magic would be, at all costs, an overt and highly publicized *increase in material production!* The African mind works logically, but, in the confines of tribal life, it works with the wrong material: spirits, bones, blood, funny little dolls and sticks. . . . The will to accomplish is there without doubt, and what makes verbal admonition so futile against belief in magic is that, on the emotional and psychological plane, magic does work, really accomplishes something in terms of suggestion and hypnosis. Omnipotence of thought makes it possible for the native mind to believe that it is transferring these subjective manipulations to the objective realm. . . .

Kobina Kessie, a young African lawyer, a member of the royal family of Kumasi, has lived long in England and views his country's culture with an admirable measure of objectivity; yet he assures me that the spell of the Stool House, its dread, gloom, awe, dampness, and silence are really impressive and moving things, that while in the Stool House something actually comes over you so deeply and penetratingly that you feel that you are in the presence of the departed. I do not doubt this. Confront me suddenly with a moldering pile of skulls and bones in a dank and narrow room and I would, too, for moments, feel the same. The tribal African thinks that when he confronts you dramatically with a detached human head, and you fall down in a faint, he has demonstrated some awful spiritual power. He divines that it is the spirit in that decapitated head and not the sheer horror that it evokes in you that makes you back up with a look of revulsion.

My last day in Kumasi dawned sultry and sunless. With Kojo behind the wheel, I set out for one of the big gold mines in Bibiani. Again green jungle loomed to left and right as the car lurched, dipped, slanted, curved, and mounted red laterite roads. Swish hut villages swung by, lost in the green uproar of vegetation. Occasionally we crossed a shaking wooden bridge spanning a small, stagnant river. The journey alternated between miles of cascading rain and miles of dazzling sunshine. Flanking the road were those streams of filing Africans, stripped to the waist, plodding along with gigantic and unbelievable loads floating atop their skulls.

Lying amidst dramatically plunging hills, Bibiani is a large-sized village divided into four main parts: the gold mine, the European community, the African community attached to the gold mine, and a native community rotting away in an unhealthy depression beside a huge, muddy, scummy lagoon. One can see the native section, called Old Town, a veritable city of mud, before arriving; it stretches out, dark brown and yellowish, fading toward the towering jungle. Its one main street is gouged with gullies and lined with stores selling cheaply made European goods. Lifting one's eyes, one sees the European community nestling high up in the cool hills: white bungalows gleaming among the dark green trees. Before the gold mine came, there was no village here; the natives who huddle here now work for the Europeans in their white homes high up in the hills or in their black mines deep down in the hot earth. Bibiani is a company town. . . .

In this gold mine some hundred Britishers direct a labor force of some four thousand Africans. Each year about half of the workers leave and a new batch take their places. Underground as well as above, so many different tribal dialects are spoken that sometimes as many as three interpreters are needed to know what one native is saying. When a mine sucks in natives from British and French West Africa, a Tower of Babel is truly created. The task of organizing, for political or industrial purposes, such a variety of tribes is stupendous. Floating fragments are these tribal men when they are compared with the tight, corporate unity of the Europeans above them.

I wandered down the narrow, winding lanes between the mud huts in Old Town and saw the bleakness, poverty, and dirt. Indeed, sanitation, just simple animal cleanliness, is the crying need here. The gullies, cut into the red earth by eroding water, were filled with excrement. Flies buzzed lazily in the still, hot air. Physical disorder was rampant; nothing repeated itself; the only time I saw anything in series was when I came across a batch of flashlights for sale.

I glanced up the hill at the gold mine; I could hear the faint, regular, rhythmic clang of the machinery even down here. In the mud huts life was being lived by the imperious rule of instinct; up there, instinct had been rejected, repressed, and sublimated. I passed a tall, naked black boy; he stared at me, at my camera, my sun helmet; then, seemingly unaware of what he was doing, he squatted and evacuated his bowels upon the porch of his hut, still staring at me. . . . It was clear that the industrial activity upon that hill, owned or operated by no matter what race, could not exist without the curbing and disciplining of instincts, the ordering of emotion, the control of the reflexes of the body. Again I felt that pathos of distance!

I was told that *juju* interferes with the working day of the men in the mines to a surprising degree. If a boy has a curse put on him by another boy, the cursed boy becomes terrified and must forthwith

leave for his tribe to become purified. No persuasion of his more
learned brothers or Europeans is of any avail. When ill, though the
company maintains a hospital, many African workers prefer their
own native witch doctors, believing their illnesses to be the results
of spells cast by someone. They do not trust the "white man's"
medicine. And, often, it is only when they are so ill that they cannot
resist that many of the miners in this area will accept modern
medical treatment.

That afternoon I watched the elaborate mechanical and chemical
processes by which gold was extracted from rock. Endless tons of
crushed ore ran over conveyer belts and poured into huge revolving
bins which emptied into vast steel drums that whirred and groaned,
pulverizing the ore for twenty-four hours a day. From crusher to
crusher I followed the ore until finally I saw vats in which the ore
had been reduced to the consistency of talcum powder. At last I
came to that section where, from a shaking table covered with cor-
duroy, water washed down a trickling stream of golden flakes into
a metal pail over which stood, stripped to the waist and barefooted,
a black boy keeping track of the wet gold dust. Behind him stood an
armed Britisher.

"You chaps must have a time keeping track of this gold, hunh?" I
asked my guide.

"How did you guess that?" he asked me.

"Because if I were that boy, I'd swallow that gold if I had a
chance," I told him.

The guide laughed uneasily.

"The anxiety we have keeping track of this gold!" he exclaimed.
"As soon as we discover one method they use in taking the gold out
of here, they've got another. Talking about eating gold: now and
then we *do* have to have a man assayed. If the armed man at that
table simply sneezed, that boy would swallow a handful of that gold
dust. . . . By swallowing a bit each day and recovering it, he'd make
a lot of money. It's smelly but highly profitable. . . ."

The white and black men lived in separate worlds; the blacks felt
that the white men were powerful interlopers from whom to steal
was regarded as "getting even." Though practically all the African

workers were illiterate, they had devised many shrewd schemes of getting the gold out of the mine. Those working at the tables from which gold dust trickled had to present themselves for duty completely nude; the company gave them something to cover their bodies. Despite that, they found ways of taking "their share" of the gold.

One ingenious method the Africans used in getting the gold out of the mine involved the utilization of rats. The boys would catch rats —the mine was full of them!—and kill them and disembowel them and secrete their corpses in nooks and crannies. While working, they would come across bits of gold, or sometimes they'd dig gold out of the quartz with their penknives—I saw veins of gold as thick as pencils!—and hide it until they had a pile worth getting out. They'd take the dead rat, fill his rotting carcass with gold dust, and toss his reeking body atop a heap of debris to be carted upward and thrown away. Bound by clannish ties, they could work like this with little risk of detection by the British.

One day a British guard saw such a moldering rat arrive at the surface atop a pile of rubbish. He saw a black boy pick up the dead rat with the tips of his fingers, wrinkle his nose in disgust against the foul odor, and fling the rat away. But this time there was something just a little odd about how the rat fell upon the ground. It landed with a thud and lay completely still. . . . Despite the repelling scent, the guard went to it and kicked it with his foot. The dead rat did not budge; it was too heavy! Examining the rat, the guard found it stuffed with gold. . . . It was never known which boys had been involved.

The most typical story of gold stealing related to a tribal boy working in a department where the gold was cast into bars. One day, after a bar of gold had been cast, the African boy—a model worker who had been employed for many years—walked slowly and boldly up to the counter upon which the golden bar rested, lifted it, and started unhurriedly, confidently toward the door. . . . For a moment the African guards and the European officials were too stupefied to move. When the boy, clutching the bar of gold, reached the door he was, of course, stopped by an armed guard. What puzzled everybody was that the boy exhibited utmost surprise at being interfered with and, gently, tried to disengage himself from the guard. His lips were observed moving soundlessly; he squinted his eyes; but, when he was shaken sternly, he relaxed and surrendered easily enough.

Questioned as to what he thought he had been doing, the boy told a pathetic story of a long and futile attempt to learn how to become invisible! For a hundred pounds a witch doctor had told him that, if he followed instructions faithfully, he could become invisible and be able to walk out of the mine with a bar of gold. . . . Having adhered to the witch doctor's routine, the boy reached that point where, he thought, by saying a certain combination of weird sounds, he could become unseeable to the naked eye. That was why he had so slowly and calmly lifted the bar of gold, why he had walked with such confidence with it to the door, why he had at first ever so gently tried to disengage himself from the guard, and why he had been seen moving his lips soundlessly—he'd been reciting the magic formula to make himself totally invisible!

The company has made itself completely self-sufficient, self-contained; it has its own water supply, its own powerhouse, its own schools, churches, movies, hospital—in fact, it is more than a company; it's a little city. Black life and white life flow daily around each other, not touching, yet generating charged currents of cooperation and hostility. There is no doubt but that the black boys who are working here are learning trades, slowly absorbing the techniques of the Western world. Though the government taxes the mines almost 50 per cent, the wages paid are fantastically low and the profits make it well worthwhile for these British to be here.

It is not the profits that this company makes that worries me; there is a profound wrong here creating a sense of tension and uneasiness. This black world is reflected in the minds of the white world in a strange and warped way, and the white world is reflected in the minds of the black world in a manner that is just as distorted. In the hearts of both races there rages a silent war of pride, of face-saving, of jealousy; attitudes on both sides tend to become total in their hate or distrust.

I don't say that this company ought to be made to leave the Gold

Coast; the elaborate methods of industrial chemistry, the vast machine shops that are maintained, the punctuality, the order, the cleanliness—all of these are qualities that the African must learn to master. But can he learn them under conditions whose objective configurations smack of intimidation? Of black against white? Of master against slave?

I observed orders being given an African; I saw him listen, nod his head to signify that he had understood. Five minutes later the African returned and asked for his instructions again! The first time the African had not been listening; he had been exhibiting what he felt was the necessary degree of servility; he had returned the second time for the actual instructions! The emotional and psychological factors involved in the mere confrontation of the African by his white master is enough to reduce his efficiency and intelligence immeasurably. Europeans will *never* be able to command the same degree of skill, loyalty, devotion, and intelligence of the Africans that the Africans can command of their own people. Centuries of invasion, war, plunder, indirect methods of exploitation have enthroned themselves in tradition, structuralized themselves in institutions, and kept alive the sense of the conquered and the conquerors.

Repeatedly Europeans of the Gold Coast told me how amazed they were at the manner in which the black politicians of the Convention People's Party drove themselves night and day. Naïve attitude! Those politicians were working for themselves and they knew no limit to their devotion save sheer exhaustion. It can be said that the presence of this company getting the gold out of the earth with its complicated machinery is helping the African to understand just what he most needs to learn. I've no doubt about it. In the compounds erected by the company for the African workers to live in, there is a visible improvement in local standards of living; but the same cannot be observed in the Africans' moral attitude. . . . They know that the company leased the land for a song from their illiterate chiefs. In their hearts they do not respect the British.

For several days now I've been observing, without quite knowing it, a living example of clannishness, its meaning, its merits, and limitations. Kojo, my driver, is a man of the Ga tribe. Whenever we

arrived in a village or city, Kojo would disappear at night to seek
lodging. But when we entered Bibiani's company town, a crisis
arose. Kojo approached me, frowning, and a little intimidated.

"Massa, small complaint," he said.

"What's the matter? You run out of money?"

"Nasa. Like to find my people, Massa. I need help."

"Your people?" I asked, bewildered.

"Yasa, Massa."

"You mean your family?"

"Yasa, Massa. My brothers and sisters."

"I didn't know you had relatives here."

"Nasa, Massa. Not proper, you know. But my tribe—"

"Oh! But how can I help you?"

"Massa ask big white man where Ga people live."

I got the point. I put the problem up to the officials of the gold
mine who quickly located a Ga settlement, and Kojo, smiling and
happy, was sent there. . . . The members of all tribes save that of the
Ga were strangers to him; he could not quite trust them and would
rather have slept in the car than to have stayed among them. Kojo
told me that his "family," when he appeared suddenly like that, fed
him, entertained him, took him around to meet and make friends.
If you are a tribal stranger, you seek out your tribe and you are
taken care of. If you are a European, you seek the shelter of the
European community. But an American Negro is an oddity; he has
one foot in both worlds and he pays through the nose for what he
gets from each.

The gold-mining officials informed me that the diet of mostly
starch that the African workers eat definitely lowers their productive
efficiency. After some astute figuring, the mining bosses felt that they
could safely open a cafeteria and sell solid food that made a balanced
diet at very cheap prices. They made no bones about the fact that
it was to increase their profits that they made this charitable gesture;
but, to their chagrin, the pumping of more vitamins into the African
did not obtain the sought-for aim. The mining officials had failed to
reckon with the temperament of the swarms of "mammies" who,
with calabashes and boxes atop their heads, waited at the gates of

the mine to sell the traditional *fufu* and *kenke* to the workers. When the miners began taking their meals in the company cafeteria, they naturally ceased patronizing the "mammies" who forthwith called a meeting and passed a resolution to demand that each wife exact a promise from her husband not to eat in the cafeteria! The cafeteria closed down and the mining officials are now trying to devise other means of eradicating *fufu* and *kenke* from the miners' diet, in short, some subtler means of getting more vitamins into the workers so that the production of gold bars can be increased!

XLI...

On a sunless, sultry morning I struck out for Samreboi, the world's largest plywood and timber mill, built by the United Africa Company in 1945. I was entering an area where rain had not fallen in two weeks and red dust coated the leaves of the trees and turned them a dull, brownish tint, making the jungle green seem even more dreamlike, unreal. It was around three o'clock in the afternoon when the jungle terminated abruptly and before me lay a vision of paved streets, electric-light poles, painted houses, stores. . . . I'd arrived in Samreboi.

"Kojo, drive around a bit. I want to see what it looks like," I said.

"Yasa, Massa."

It was a vast industrial plant; everything had a look of newness. The roads had been but recently cut through hills; steel structures reared toward the misty sky; paint gleamed on wooden doorways; European cars were parked row upon row; and even the Africans I saw walked with a quicker stride.

We came to a wooden bridge and Kojo slowed the car to a stop.

"Important river, Massa. Tano," Kojo said.

"Really?"

I leaped out of the car. The word "Tano" had evoked in my mind a sense of mystery, of ceremonies of purification, and rituals of sacrifice. This was the most sacred river of all Ashanti and I wanted to see it. But, being a stranger, it looked just like any other river to me.

It was about the size of the Seine or the Tiber; I walked to the bank and watched the swift, muddy current and tried to feel what others could have felt about this all too ordinary stream. I felt nothing.

I later learned that, because of this river, no goats could be kept in this area; they were taboo. Only sheep were allowed to graze and to be sacrificed. A person bringing in a goat would find himself in serious trouble.

I was the guest of an English couple, a Mr. and Mrs. Y, both of whom rushed themselves with almost frantic anxiety to show me this sprawling industrial town. Interspersed between questions of: "Have you had enough coffee?" or "Is there anything you want?" were questions touching upon politics. Mr. Y was delicate and knew that it was considered bad taste to press such matters, but Mrs. Y waded boldly in where even British officials felt it wise not to tread. . . . Her attempts to determine if I were a Communist or not almost made me laugh out loud at times.

"The poor company's losing so much money, you know," she told me.

"Oh, really? I didn't know that."

"Oh, yes. They haven't recovered their initial investment."

"I'm sure they will eventually," I assured her.

"People do not realize what it takes to build a big plant like this," she confided in me. "Now, there's the union talking about higher wages already. But they are being paid more money than they've ever had in their lives. . . . What would they have if we had not come here? Don't you think we're fair?"

"Really, I know nothing about local economic conditions," I lied.

"Managers of businesses are human beings, just like anybody else," she said stoutly.

"I'm sure of it," I agreed.

"I say," she asked me suddenly. "When you are riding from place to place here in the Gold Coast, do you sit up in the front seat with your chauffeur?"

"Oh, no. I sit in the *back*," I told her as if she had affronted me. "He's my driver."

She'd been trying to determine if I felt that Kojo was as "good" as I was! And in such a transparent manner! She had the queer notion that a Communist would have ridden up in the front seat with his chauffeur! And she felt that if I had been a Communist, I'd have told her that I did!

"Frankly, are you for or against colonies?" she asked me directly at last.

"When you put it that way, I don't know what to say," I told her. After all, I was her guest; she was feeding me three meals a day. . . . How could I tell the lady that I thought that she ought to be back in England . . . ?

Though the officials at Samreboi were fluently vocal about how much money they had invested in this gigantic undertaking, how efficient was their medical care, how fair their wage scales, etc., they were always silent about their secret methods of regulating the ceilings of wage rates. A shy, well-spoken black boy had whispered some information to me and I checked its accuracy; it was correct. . . . There existed an unwritten agreement between the mining industry and the timber industry that each would not *exceed* certain wage rates paid to workers. In short, wages had been fixed through inter-industrial agreements.

The company holds a ninety-nine-year lease and it employs some four thousand Africans and about sixty Europeans. In the beginning, in 1945, in trying to establish itself here, the biggest problem faced by the company had been the obtaining of food for the African workers, their kind of food; cocoa yam, cassava, groundnuts, palm oil, corn, and pepper had to be brought in each evening. If this diet was not available, the workers left.

The tribal workers had to be taught how to use complicated machinery. Formerly, I was told, only Europeans operated the huge saws that sliced the many-tonned mahogany trees and a theory prevailed that Africans could not possibly do such work with precision. But now, they were proud to tell me, the Africans were handling all the machines, though the Africans were not being paid what their European predecessors had been paid!

This timber concession spreads over an area of a thousand square miles; just what had been given the chiefs in return for this vast tract, I could not learn. The region was virgin forest and the jungle was so filled with elephants and leopards that it was not safe to go alone for more than two miles, unless one was prepared to defend one's life against sudden attack. The loggers, as they penetrated deeper into the jungle, came across scattered human bones, blackened and half buried in a carpet of rotting leaves. These bones were no doubt the remains of people devoured by jungle beasts.

En route to my British host's home a woman came yelling and running across a field. She was a European.

"Hold it a second, won't you?" Mr. Y asked me.

I called to Kojo to stop.

"What's the trouble?" my host asked the woman.

"Oh, God, I'm so scared," the woman whimpered.

"What happened?"

"They just killed a big snake in Mr. ——'s living room—"

"Really?"

"Oh, I'm so frightened, I'm weak," the woman sighed. "They say that snakes travel in pairs, husband and wife. Now, maybe the husband'll come back and bite somebody. . . . Do you think so? I'm scared to go home. . . ."

Overhearing this, I grew slightly suspicious. Maybe the public-relations department of Samreboi was putting over a "big one" for my benefit. Killing a snake in the living room seemed fantastic to me. I'd see. . . .

"I'd like to see that snake," I said.

"But it's dead," my host told me.

"That makes it perfect," I said. "Let me get a glimpse of this—"

"All right."

We drove about half a mile and came to a white bungalow. A scared steward came from behind the house.

"I'd like to see that snake that you killed," I told him.

"He dead, Massa."

"Well, where is he?"

"In a bucket, Massa."

"Well, bring me the bucket."

The stunned steward disappeared and a few seconds later he

came carrying a bucket that was obviously heavy. The top of the bucket was covered with a white towel. Why? I did not know and forgot to ask. The steward set the bucket gently upon the earth and backed off, as though he felt the snake still lived. . . .

"Uncover it and let me see the snake," I said.

Trembling, he yanked the towel off and leaped away. It was a monstrous reptile, bluish black, curled round and round, coil upon coil.

"What kind is it?"

"He black mamba, Massa."

"Dangerous?"

"Oh, he bad, Massa."

"Did *you* kill 'im?"

"Yasa, Massa."

"How did it happen?"

"Well, Massa—*my* Massa—he chop and he sleep in living room in chair. He sleep 'fore he go to work. Massa wake up 'cause he hear swish-swish-swish. . . . Massa, he open eyes and snake coming for Massa. Massa, he jump outta window. . . ."

"And what else?"

"Massa call me. He say, 'Kill snake!' I catch stick and I kill snake, sar."

From the jerky, nervous movements of the steward's body, he was still killing that snake. No; it was no put-up job; the jungle snake had come right into the living room of the European man. . . .

Establishing a town in a dense jungle was not easy; there were no roads; to send tractors to clear away the bush was not possible. The jungle roots were so tough that even steel would bend under the pressure of tearing them from the earth. Armies of workmen, carrying their tools on their heads, had to whack with cutlasses for each inch of space. Once an area was cleared by hand, fires were lit to the east, west, north, and south to keep snakes away. In the clearing a base would be set up so that they could send another army of workers ahead still farther into the jungle. The men were inexperienced and the accident rate was high.

When they finally reached the spot where they wanted to establish the town, they offered ten shillings to the natives for each bamboo hut that was erected. Place names originated in a most interesting fashion. When gangs of workmen were building a road, they would come to a spot on a hill where, say, many monkeys were perched high up in trees, whole colonies of them. . . . The workers would send word back to headquarters that they were located on Monkey Top Hill, and such names stuck.

As in Bibiani, so in Samreboi, all the needs of the European staff had to be anticipated; water, schools, movies, electricity, all of the appliances of modern life had to be brought here or the many European workers needed would not have come.

Then there was the task of getting the tribal people integrated into the project, or else they would have simply stood by and looked on with amused detachment. The chiefs had to be assembled, sheep had to be slaughtered and blood offered to the ancestors, libations of gin had to be poured, promises had to be made. . . . When the Europeans asked for African women to work as cooks, none was forthcoming. The tribal African male fondly believed in keeping his women out of sight. The educated Africans working for the company slowly persuaded the women to come forth, and I saw them cooking in public canteens. . . .

That night I attended a party at the home of the general manager; some fifteen company officials and their wives were present. With the exception of the white-clad, barefooted, slow-moving African stewards serving drinks and sandwiches, one could have thought that one was in New York, London, or Paris, so freely did the cognac, scotch, and sherry flow. The party got under way with a blanket introduction of me to the group; the general manager intoned:

"I know that we are all glad to have Dr. Williams from the States here with us tonight!"

I was of a mind to protest my being identified as Dr. Williams, but I thought, what the hell . . . ?

Amid wild hilarity, they began telling jokes about the natives. A man began:

"You know, one of those savages working at a saw this morning had an accident. . . . He was there cutting a slab of timber and the damned fool looked up and off went a finger. I heard a commotion and went running to see what had happened, and there stood the fool staring down at his hand, blood spurting out. . . . I was so angry that I could have spat lizards. I said:

" 'How in hell did you do that?'

"He rolled his eyes up at me and said:

" 'Like this, Massa. . . .'

"He stuck his hand near the whirring saw and another finger came off, flying up in the air over the machines. . . ."

The heads of men and women tilted back and laughter gushed up in the room.

"I was about to ask him how he had managed to lose that second finger, but I didn't want him to lose a third one; so I just took the monkey gently by the shoulder and led him to the doctor."

A relaxed silence ensued, then another man cocked his head, smiled, and began:

"That reminds me of the time when I was general manager of UAC. . . . The cocoa crop had come in and the place was swimming in money; those 'ink spots' had so many pounds they didn't know what to do with them. . . . One bugger came in one morning and wanted a sack of cement to make a floor for his bathroom, and he wanted a sack of fertilizer for his yam patch. . . . He laid down cash for the two sacks and hoisted them atop his head and off he went. . . . Well, the damn fool couldn't read. He plowed the sack of cement into his yam patch and mixed the fertilizer with water and smeared it over the ground of his bathroom. . . ."

Happy laughter went around the room. . . .

"So the next year he came to see me, looking all sad and bewildered. He said:

" 'Massa, there musta been something wrong with that cement and fertilizer you sold me. 'Cause when I take a bath, my feet get muddy and I'm standing in weeds. And that fertilizer was no good; my yam patch didn't grow a single yam this season.' "

Laughter and the serving of more drinks. I sat with a tight smile. I was wondering if Kwame Nkrumah knew the kind of British friends he had. . . .

Another man launched forth:

"Say, did I tell you about the half-educated guy who organized a reception for Winston Churchill? Well, Churchill came to this particular colony to make a major address. This African monkey worked day and night to organize the thing, and he was perfect. . . . Everything was just right. . . . Churchill rose to speak and, as he started, a naked African woman ran into the crowd, holding one of her breasts. . . . Churchill paused and the woman ran away. Churchill resumed and the naked woman came running again, holding her breast. . . . This time Churchill ignored the woman and continued speaking. . . . But, when his address was over, Churchill sent for the African who had arranged the meeting.

" 'My good man,' Churchill said, 'I know that you have a lot of customs here that we don't know about. But why did that woman run into the meeting hall holding one of her breasts, like that . . . ?'

"The African frowned, surprised. And he said:

" 'But don't you know, sir? That happens every time you make a speech in London, doesn't it?'

" 'Why, man, you're mad,' Churchill said, flabbergasted. 'Never at any meeting in London at which I spoke did a naked woman run into the hall holding onto one of her breasts—'

" 'I beg your pardon, sir,' the African scholar protested, his eyes bright and knowing. 'I recall reading, sir, that at your last public meeting in London, at which, sir, you spoke, that, as you spoke, a *titter ran through the crowd . . . !'* "

That one brought the house down and they laughed loud and long. The guffaws would die down for a moment, then swell forth again as each person present visualized the foolish joke. They sat sniffing, sipping their drinks, well satisfied with themselves; finally silence prevailed, one of those silences which, for no reason, settles upon a group of people.

At that moment the newly installed plumbing was heard throughout the house; a coughing, sucking sound went through the pipes. One of the young men lifted his eyes cynically toward the ceiling and announced in stern tones, struggling against the laughter that tried to break through his lips:

"SOMEBODY IS BEING DESTOOLED!"

The room actually exploded with laughter. The men stood up, holding onto their drinks, and yelled. The women bent over, clutching their stomachs. It was fully five minutes before the thigh slapping and the yells died down.

"That's a hot one, eh, Dr. Williams?"

"That's a hot one, all right," I said. "God, I never thought I'd hear one as hot as that!"

I forced a smile, sitting tensely, holding my drink. Why were they acting like that? Did they think that they'd win me over to their point of view? Or were they trying to see if I'd object? Or did they take it for granted that I was on their side? (In talking over this incident with Africans in Accra, I was informed that the Britishers felt that they had been acting quite normally, that they were used to black Sirs and black Orders of the British Empire sharing such jokes and attitudes.) Well, this was Africa too; the conquerors were godlike, aloof; they could derive their entertainment from the lives and gropings of the people whom they had conquered. . . . These were cold, astute businessmen and I knew that self-government for the Gold Coast was something hateful to their hearts. On and on the storytelling continued until the small hours of the morning. At last we all stood in the humid darkness on the veranda, saying good-bye. The general manager shook my hand warmly and said:

"It was a pleasure, Sir Williams, to have you with us."

"It was an *unforgettable* evening," I said.

We shook hands again. An hour later I was in my mosquito-proofed room in a modern bungalow. My emotions and my body felt bleak. I got ready for bed, then stood at the window and looked out into the blackness. . . . Jungle lay out there. Then I started, my skin prickling. A sound came to my ears out of the jungle night; something—it was a tree bear, I was told afterwards—began a dreadful kind of moaning that stabbed the heart. It began like a baby crying, then it ascended to a sort of haunting scream, followed by a weird kind of hooting that was the essence of despair. The sound kept on and on, sobbing, seemingly out of breath, as if the heart was so choked with sorrow that another breath could not be drawn. Finally, a moan came at long intervals, as though issuing from a body in the last extremities of physical suffering. And when I could no longer hear it, I still felt that it was sounding in my mind. . . .

XLII...

It's said that the Tano, the sacred river, requires one human victim each year, and if it does not get it, there is trouble. About six weeks ago, it seems, there was an unusually heavy rain and the river rose to the level of the only bridge spanning it in this area. It was across this bridge that the native workers had to come from their compounds each morning. The officials of the company became alarmed because, if the bridge was swept away, the vast mill would have to close down until another bridge was built. In that event the loss of man hours would be stupendous.

Both Africans and Europeans gathered on the bank of the swollen river and anxiously watched the progress of the rising water. It was disclosed through gossip among the natives that the chief, a new one, had forgotten to sacrifice a sheep to the river that year, and that, they said, was why the river was behaving so angrily. Tano would claim a victim in revenge for its neglect; then, as the crowds stood watching, the current uprooted a huge tree which fell athwart the stream and inched its way slowly toward the bridge. . . .

The European engineers got busy at once; that tree had to be anchored or the bridge would be lost. After much desperate work, they succeeded in tying a rope about one end of the tree; but would the tree, so big and heavy, hold with just *one* rope? No! It was decided that another rope was needed, and it had to be tied onto the tree at its middle. The Europeans called for volunteers from among the Africans and none was forthcoming. The raging torrent frightened them. Finally an African from another tribe, to whom the god Tano meant nothing, said that he would try. The Europeans fitted him with a lifebelt; the man was an excellent swimmer; and, to make sure that he would assume no risks, the Europeans secured the man with an extra rope tied about his waist.

Cautiously, I was told, the man waded out toward the tree, then swam. He actually made it, tied the rope about the middle of the tree. The tree budged and the rope grew taut, like a violin string. His work done, the man reached up and caught hold of the taut rope; then a strange thing happened. Just as the man was ready to launch himself into the water, he let the weight of his body suspend from the rope; he was seen bobbing, then the taut rope shot the African into the river, like an arrow from a bow. . . . Frantically, the workmen began hauling on the rope that was tied to the man's body; they pulled it out of the river, but the man's body was not tied to it. He was lost. . . . The man's body was never recovered.

That was proof! A lamentation set up at the riverside. Tano had had its victim! You see, you can't ignore that river! These Europeans, they don't know what they're talking about, the Africans said. They think that they are so smart, but look at what they did. . . .

I went out into the jungle to see how those huge trees, weighing many tons, were cut down. The ground was sodden with decayed leaves. In the jungle proper it was so cool that a faint vapor came from my mouth as I breathed. Solid walls of leaves and branches and creepers and plants whose names I did not know rose from sixty to a hundred feet all round me. It was so quiet that the voices of the workmen seemed muted. All kinds of insects swarmed; it was there that I saw my first soldier ant, that black, almost inch-long creature which, when sufficiently mobilized, could wipe out human life on this earth, could devour man and animal. I did not see them at their worst; there were simply long black lines of them, busy tunneling, making bridges of themselves for their brothers to pass over, frantically rushing about on their mysterious errands.

Trees, some of them forty feet in diameter, towered skyward. I was told the names of some of them: the African Walnut, Mahogany, Cistanthera, Gedu Nodor, Guarea, Cedrata, Idigbo, Opepe, Sapelewood, Iroko, Abrua, Omu, Colawood, Piptadenia, Akomu, Antiaris, Canarium, Celtis, Limba, Mimusops, Apa, Ekki, Ochrocarpus, Okan, Avodire, etc.

An eagle swooped through the skies; there came a sound like someone pounding an anvil with a hammer; it was a bird cry and it kept up for a moment, then stopped. There is a jungle denizen called the golden spider who spins a vast golden web, the strands of which are thick, wet, sticky, and glisten brightly.

That evening I had an interview with the leaders of the African Plywood Timber Employees' Union. The organization had a membership of about a thousand; it was two and one-half years old; the illiteracy rate was established at 75 per cent. The wage rates ran from four to six shillings a day; the workers got free rent, medical care, etc.

I could detect no special problems about the workers' being able to relate themselves to industrial conditions. The management informed me that they were punctual, diligent. There was but one terror: the manner in which the African drivers handled the trucks carrying logs weighing fifteen tons or more along the dirt highways. The accident rate was appalling. The logs were chained to the trucks and a sudden putting on of brakes would send the fifteen-ton logs plunging forward against the driver's cab, crushing the driver to death. Also there were hundreds of Africans, bedeviled by the problem of transportation, who would sneak rides atop the logs. I was shown a blotch of blood on the roadside where one such rider had been caught beneath a twenty-ton mahogany log. . . .

"But doesn't this awful accident rate make them want to be more careful?" I asked one of the more intelligent union leaders.

"With a Westerner, yes," he told me. "But the African believes that when an accident occurs to him, it's because of *juju*. . . . So he goes right on speeding, not caring, with death loaded behind him in the form of a tree weighing twenty tons. . . ."

The union members were athirst for technical education; the hammering of this point by Nkrumah had sunk home in their minds. Yet, almost every question they asked me about education was couched in terms of somebody somewhere beyond the Gold Coast giving them something. Does this curious attitude of dependence stem from tribal life?

"Self-reliance is the only sure way to freedom," I told them over and over again. But I doubt if they grasped what I meant.

Politics was the one topic about which they were most vocal. In a colony, trade unions are not and cannot be simply economic organizations; they must, of necessity, if they are to hold their membership, enter politics in a vitally active way. The drive toward self-government was more urgent to them than wage rates. Most of their meetings, I was told, were taken up with questions of nationalism and political strategy. Their standard of living could not be thought of as being separate from their colonial status, and nobody could ever fool them on that fundamental point.

Adhering, according to my instructions, to my itinerary, I had to leave Samreboi and head for Takoradi, that most industrialized of all Gold Coast cities. The opportunities for employment had caused this port to become clogged with migrants for whom living space had not been found. Indeed, migration was so great that there was some unemployment. The process of urbanization was reflected in the attitude of the people, their speech and walk.

Economic activity dominates life here: the building and repairing of locomotives, fishing, furniture making, house construction, leatherwork, and the fashioning of gold into ornaments, transportation, etc. Almost one-tenth of the population of forty-odd thousand work for the government or public services. Poverty is acute and stares at you from the overcrowded compounds. Detribalization has proceeded further here than at any other spot in the Gold Coast.

The inflation of prices that took place during the war has not been adjusted and the laboring masses find it almost impossible to make their scanty wages cover the bare cost of existence. Dr. Busia's *Social Survey Sekondi-Takoradi* indicates that many of the young people cannot marry in terms of their tribal customs; their wages simply do not permit it. In some instances laborers earn barely enough to feed themselves and must take on extra work after the work day is over in order to pay rent. A great part of the food that is eaten in this city comes from either the interior of the country or from Europe, a condition which augments the prices of staples.

The impulse to organize for economic betterment has thrown up a multitude of occupational organizations whose membership is composed of fish sellers, carpenters, shoemakers, chauffeurs, seamen, sugar sellers, cooks, stewards, gold- and silversmiths. . . . (Busia's *Social Survey Sekondi-Takoradi*). It seems that these organizational efforts are really an attempt to fill the emotional void in their lives left by their former tribal identification. The African, even when he comes to the city, hangs onto his feeling about death for a while; hence, large funerals are a much desired end to one's life. Dr. Busia reports that two recent funerals in the city cost £85 14s. 10d., and £87 12s., respectively. Items for these funeral celebrations included: whiskey, beer, mineral water, palm wine, gin, food, a silk shroud for the corpse, etc.

Upon my arrival I ordered Kojo to drive me around so that I could get the "feel" of the city. Riding through what seemed a respectable quarter, I heard the yelling of men, women, and children.

"Find the place where that noise is, Kojo," I said.

"Where they act wild, Massa?"

"Yes."

The car turned and drove into a crowded compound. I got out and stood stockstill, unable to believe my eyes. Though the streets were paved and the houses were made of cement, I was witnessing the wildest funeral I'd yet seen. . . . There was an unpainted coffin in the background, near a veranda, resting on the bare red earth. Around this coffin about twenty men were running and sweating and panting and jabbering furiously. Their eyes were smeared with some black substance and their mouths were dabbed with red. Crisscrossing their foreheads were white strings of cowrie shells, cutting deep into the flesh. In each right fist was a long, evil-looking knife. They were naked to the waist and a grass skirt covered their buttocks. Around and around in a circle they went, chanting; but, at some signal, they would all halt, crowd about the coffin, pointing to it, stamping their feet; they puffed their cheeks and swung their heads from side to side with intense passion. Then they would resume their running in a circle. . . .

A woman, presumably the dead man's wife, went to the coffin and pointed to each nail. Strangely, the nails had not been driven home; it was as though they were expecting the dead man to push aside the lid, rise, and live again. Then the woman knelt and placed a small bottle of clear liquid at the head of the coffin.

To one side was a row of men beating drums, blowing horns, and brandishing sticks. Some people were prancing, others dancing, while the onlookers made wild and meaningless grimaces with their faces. I jumped; several muskets had gone off in back of me. I took out my camera and focused. A painted man came running to me.

"You take no picture!" he said, turning hurriedly away.

But another man yelled:

"No; no. . . . Stay here! We want you take picture!"

I stopped. I explained that I was an American, that I wanted somebody to explain the meaning of the funeral rite to me. I waited while they consulted among themselves. Finally they said that I could take two pictures. But, as I tried to focus my camera, the first wild man who had objected rushed forward, waving that awful knife. . . .

"Take no picture! I kill you!" he screamed.

The others caught him and held him. I stood, undecided.

"You work for British!" the wild man yelled.

"I'm an American!" I yelled back.

"You lie! You work for British!"

"I'm an *American!*" I screamed, hoping that the crowd would sympathize with me.

But the crowd looked on with detached curiosity and I knew that they would not have moved a finger if that crazy man had got ever so close to me with that knife. I started backing discreetly off.

"Naw; don't go— Stay and take pictures!" another man said.

I thought hard. People who carry on in this manner over a dead man's body might just as well get the idea into their poetic heads that I was some kind of a ghost, or a prospective sacrificial victim. One flick of one of those monstrous knives would yank me straight into the other world. I managed two more shots with the camera, but my sweaty hands were trembling. The wild man was struggling to get free from his pals.

"He be drunk, Massa," Kojo warningly whispered to me.

"Let's go," I said.

I turned and started toward the car, almost colliding with a tall, handsome woman.

"Take me," she said.

"Hunh?"

"Take me," she said again, putting her hands on her hips.

I got out my camera; I'd take a shot of her just to show this wild and mean-tempered crowd that I was a sport, a well-meaning sort of fellow. . . .

"No, no," the woman said, blocking my lens with her hand. "Take me, *me*," she repeated.

I blinked. Then I understood. She was selling and she thought that I would buy.

"Nuts," I said, whirling and making for the car.

The crowd guffawed. The painted men were still rushing in circles about the coffin. I got into the car, slammed the door and locked it. The "take me" woman was smiling invitingly.

"Let's get away from here, Kojo," I said.

A fairly well-dressed man came to the door of the car and tapped on the window glass. Cautiously, I lowered the window an inch.

"You'd better go," he said.

"I'm going," I said. "But what in God's name are they doing?"

"They're trying to frighten away the dead man's spirit," he said.

"Thanks," I said, rolling the window up again, tight.

The motor roared; the car pulled off and I felt better. I lay back and closed my eyes and tried to relax. I don't know if those painted men with their long knives were successful in scaring away the dead man's spirit or not; all I know is that they sure scared the hell out of me. . . . Next day at noon I told Kojo to drive nonstop to Accra.

XLIII...

I cast my accounts and found that I was near the end of my pounds. Since the 4th of June I'd been reacting to the reality of Gold Coast life every waking hour.

Through a travel agency I booked passage for Liverpool for the 2nd of September, which gave a few days' breathing spell and allowed me time to visit the forts and castles on the way back to the port of Takoradi.

In response to an advertisement I had inserted in a local newspaper asking to buy an out-of-print book, R. S. Rattray's *Ashanti*, I received a neatly written reply informing me that the book was to be had; and, at once, I set about locating the gentleman who held the book I so urgently wanted. His address was in care of an educational institution; but, when I applied there, I was told that:

"This gentleman comes here for his mail sometimes, but we don't know him."

"You receive his mail and don't know him?"

"We do that for many people, sir," a mild black man told me. "You see, many people have no fixed place of abode."

"But I thought that that only applied to juvenile delinquents—"

"Oh, no, sir. Many respectable people have no work and, consequently, no home."

"How can I locate a man with no fixed place of abode?"

"You can't, sir. You'll have to wait. He'll show up."

"But I need him urgently."

"Why do you need him urgently?"

"He has a rare book for sale. I want to buy that book."

"Oh, just a *book*, sir?" he asked, surprised.

"Yes."

"Well, I can't help you, sir," he said.

I left my address, which was a post-office box number, with the official and told him to tell the man possessing the book that I wanted to see him at once. A few days later I got a note asking me to telephone a certain number; I did. It was my man with the rare book. I instructed him to meet me in a bar.

He came wearing a dirty native cloth, holding an oblong, flat package wrapped in frayed newspaper under his arm. It was the rare book. I'd thought that maybe a thin, hungry-looking professor would have come; I hadn't expected this rather rough-looking fellow. . . . I bought the book, then asked him:

"Haven't you got an address?"

"No, sar."

"Where do you sleep at night?"

"I got a big family, sar."

"Where does your family live?"

"All along the coast, sar."

"Your family, your clan, or your tribe?"

"My family, sar. I've many brothers—"

"Blood brothers?"

"Yes, sar."

"Are these brothers sons of your mother?"

"Not quite, sar, you see. . . . But men are brothers to me, sar, blood brothers."

"What's your tribe?"

"Ashanti, sar."

"And your blood brothers are Ashanti men?"

"Yes, sar. We know and help each other, sar."

"But, why?"

"Because we are brothers, sar."

"But how did you *get* to be brothers?"

"We grew up together, sar."

The men with whom he had shared life were his brothers; men of the same generation were brothers. They knew a look and feel of the world that other men of other generations did not know. I watched him stuff the money somewhere under his dirty cloth, pull on his battered hat, and walk out. A man with no address? A nomad. . . . I regretted that I had not had time to talk with him. . . . And he hadn't seemed worried. He had brothers, not the sons of his mother, but men to whom he felt a blood relationship, brothers who fed him when he was hungry, let him sleep when he was tired, consoled him when he was sad. . . . He had a large "family" that stretched for miles and miles. . . . I tried to visualize it and I could not. . . .

XLIV...

To think about Africa is to think about man's naïve attempt to understand and manipulate the universe of life in terms of magical religion. Africa, until now, was religious. Africans hold their lives as being sacred. And it is ironical that the men of Europe who plundered this continent for four hundred years did it in the name of religion! It was religion against religion. That is the only manner in which the insane thirst for gold and slaves could possibly have felt itself justified. The white masters of Africa were and are remarkably akin, emotionally and spiritually, to their black slaves.

The African conception of life is neither evil nor criminal; it is simply pitiably human. His conception of the state is symbolically derived from his love and reverence for the family. The state as well as the universe are symbolically conceived of in a way that is but a sweeping projection of his concept of and feeling for the family. To understand the Akan idea (and it's a pretentious, inordinately vain one!) of the state, one has to unite two distinctly different ideas: the family and the universe.

The African does not distinguish absolutely between good and evil. No matter how malignant he thought some of the "spirits" of the universe were, he never succumbed to feeling that the world as a whole was evil. Maybe he has more than paid for that mistake, a mistake that was squarely on the side of the angels.

It was only when adversity drove him to feel evil that he felt it, and the white men of Europe contributed more than their fair share to that psychological process by their wars and oppression. One would have thought that Christian Europe, discovering people serving God in an Old Testament style, would have been deeply mindful of the fact that only a nuance separated their religious beliefs from those of the African. Compassion could have served here better than scorn or bungling uplift. . . .

The state is owned by a female king, just as a child is regarded as being owned by its mother; the state is ruled by a male king, just as a family is headed and its affairs managed by a father. Hence, female kings are founders of states, the "mother" of everybody in the state; the female companion of the king is called queen mother, though she is not actually the mother of the king at all; she is either his sister or some other worthy female.

The symbolic nature of these relationships have been rather well worked out in a book entitled *The Sacred State of the Akan*, by Eva L. R. Meyerowitz (London: Faber and Faber, 1951). Though some Ashanti intellectuals sneer at what this book has to say, it does fill a void when one tries to explain what meets the eye in the Gold Coast. Thus, to the queen mother the emblem of the spiral, the sign of birth and motherhood, has been assigned. The female king is also considered as the daughter of the moon, for the moon is regarded as having given birth to the sun. The sun is then the king and the moon the queen. . . . Now, I don't believe any of this, but I see nothing barbarous in it.

The moon (that is, the sense of woman) created the universe and in that universe are seven aerial bodies—the Moon, the Sun, Mars, Mercury, Jupiter, Venus, and Saturn. Consequently, any state or universe that wants to rule must have seven parts. . . . The universe is regarded as being a mother and the basic origin of all things, families as well as solar systems. A woman's giving birth, her menstrual period, her moodiness and irrationality—all of this tended to envelop women in an atmosphere of general awe, justifying the Akan mind in projecting out upon her a contradictory and dubious mixture of honor, fear, worship, and loathing.

The moon, being the color of silver at times, made them feel that the mother must be symbolized by silver; and the sun, being yellow, made them think that the man was symbolized by gold. When a queen died in the old days, silver dust was stuffed into all the opening of her corpse: eyes, ears, nostrils, mouth, anus, vagina. And when a king died, gold dust was packed into his eye-sockets, etc.

These primal symbols, derived from the reality of mother and father, female kings and male kings, created many of the Akan details of life. The female kings introduced lamps, codes for women and girls, laws governing sexual offenses, etc., and the male kings and his advisors, in the name of their ancestors, elaborated laws and rules for the state, war, trade, etc.

The Akan people *believed* these poetic conceptions, the only conceptions available to them. Blood relations were replaced by mystical ones which were believed to be based upon "blood." In this manner came about the matrilineal conception of descent and inheritance. It was an intuitive grasp of life dictated by endemic wisdom, tracing relations between objects that really had no relations, but establishing such relations by similarity, proximity, succession, etc. I still do not believe a single word of all of this, yet I do not endorse the killing of a single flea if that flea happened to believe it. I cannot say that imperialism is right because it blasted the lives of people holding such notions. . . .

The king is the son of the sun, and is, thus, sacred. The king's greatest dangers are death and unclean women in their menses; hence, the king's food must always be cooked by men; if a menstruating woman touches a king, rites of purification and sacrifices must be made. The king wears sandals to keep his feet out of touch with the earth which contains the countless bodies of the dead.

Since he partakes of the divine, the king never really dies; his soul becomes a part of that in which it resided before it was born, that is, the sun; and that "blood" part of him becomes an ancestral spirit which can, with proper ritual, words, and sacrifices, be evoked to enter those things which were once the intimate possessions of the king. Indeed, these spirits are conceived of as being capable of eating and drinking. All of which explains libation pouring, etc.

The corpse of the king in the old days was allowed to decompose under ritualized conditions. It was placed in a coffin which had holes in its bottom and then the coffin was set over a pit; when the body fluids had all dripped out, the remainder—the sodden bones—was taken from the coffin and scraped, dried, oiled, and the skeleton was strung together, bone by bone, with thread spun of gold. These skeletons were then wrapped in costly cloths and taken to Bantama where they were jealously guarded. A stranger intruding into such a place would be instantly slain. . . .

All of this seems bizarre to me; I can't conceive of myself ever believing any of it; but, still, I don't agree that people who do believe in such ought to be declared biologically inferior!

It is thought that forty days after the death of a king, his soul reaches heaven or the African counterpart of such a place; and a great deal of joy is evinced at that period by the general populace.

The Akan, acting upon the division of the sexes, erected two corresponding attitudes to denote them: *ntoro* implies the male principle of life, and *abusua* the female principle. *Ntoro* is the semen of the male and it is believed to possess the power of bestowing spiritual qualities of a male sort. *Abusua* is the blood of the woman and it is transmitted to the offspring, and, it is believed, it is *only* the woman, in conception and birth, who transmits blood and all of its magical qualities to the child. This is the erroneous conception that buttresses the matrilineal descent and inheritance, and the practice of exogamy to some degree in some clans of the Gold Coast.

The *ntoro* outlook actuated the impulse to create armies, to wage war, etc.; the *abusua* outlook prompted the religous role of woman. Both outlooks, hedged about with numberless taboos, account for the sexual segregation that cleaves African society in twain. Out of *ntoro* and *abusua* have come a multitude of gods and rituals and ceremonies, the dreaded apex of which is human sacrifice. For example, from *ntoro*, meaning semen, comes a deep and mystical regard for water, lakes, lagoons, rivers, etc. From *abusua* springs the conviction that blood, menstrual and otherwise, possesses powers allied to the hidden energies of the universe. With the fiery sun and silver moon as an eternal background, gold and silver assumed powerful meanings. Throughout Akan society emotional values are attached to these colors and projected onto objects, natural or fabricated, having those colors or some shades of them. Kola nuts, being red (like blood or gold), occupy a higher place of esteem than just ordinary nuts; brass, resembling gold, is used to decorate state chairs if gold itself is not obtainable. This is why Africans regarded the worthless trinkets of the Europeans with such delight. It wasn't simple-mindedness that made them feel that the beads were something for which one exchanged gold. It was religion. . . .

The moods born of this apprehension of existence gave birth to a

high order of simple poetry. Thus, the Earth Goddess *Assaase Afua*
is addressed as follows on the Talking Drums:

> *Spirit of Earth, sorrow is yours,*
> *Spirit of Earth, woe is yours.*
> *Earth, with its dust,*
> *Earth, while I am yet alive,*
> *It is upon you that I put my trust,*
> *Earth, who receives my body.*

A funeral song goes:

I am an orphan, and when I recall the death of my father, water falls
from my eyes upon me.
When I recall the death of my mother, water from my eyes falls upon me.
We walk, we walk, O Mother Tano,
Until now we walk and it will soon be night.
It is because of the sorrow of death that we walk.

Before the coming of the white man, matrilineal institutions conferred upon the African woman a special and mystical position. The
queen mothers had the right to veto much of the men's actions.
In the event of the death of the chief or king, she, in consultation with
advisors, selected the new head of the clan or state. . . . With the
establishment of the religously patrilineal English power, the chiefs
were recognized and the women ignored. Institutions were smashed
and no new ones were devised to perform their functions. The coming of the white man spelled the doom of the African woman; as
Christianity gained a foothold, she became "free" but with far less
real power than she had before. It is not without its meaning that the
last military effort of the Ashanti was led by a black woman! And
this same fact might well account for the great popularity of the
Convention People's Party among the women of the Gold Coast.

X L V . . .

I visited Christianborg Castle which was built by the Swedes in 1657
and taken by the Danes in 1659. In 1679 it changed hands again,
being bought by the Portuguese from the Danes, and in 1682 was

bought from the Portuguese by the Danes. This swift change of
ownership reflected the desperate struggles that went on between
European powers in the early days of the Gold Coast. The castle
was captured by Gold Coast native tribes in 1693 and resold by
them to the Danes a year later. In 1850 it was bought by the
British. . . .

It is at present the official residence of the Governor of the Colony,
Sir Charles Arden-Clarke. White, vast, standing at the edge of the
Atlantic, it dominates the tropic, sandy, palm-treed landscape. As I
entered the castle grounds, the armed Northern Territory guards
came to attention. I explained that I wanted to look over the castle.
Six of them spoke at once:

"Me, Massa."

They were eager because they wanted that inevitable "dash" at
the end of the tour. I mounted the broad, white, spick-and-span
steps and stood looking out over the rolling sea. . . .

"The ships that took the slaves to America and the West Indies
. . . Where did they anchor?"

The guide pointed to the sandy seashore. "Right out there, Massa."

"And where were the slaves kept?"

"Follow me, Massa."

I was led down winding steps until I came into a narrow and dank
passageway, then into small dark rooms whose only light came
through barred windows.

"Are these the same windows that the slaves looked out of?"

"The same, Massa."

The walls were incredibly thick.

"Just how thick is that wall?"

"Fifteen feet, Massa."

I was told that the same iron bolts which secured the doors to
keep the slaves imprisoned were the ones that my fingers now
touched.

"How did they take the slaves to the ships? Is there a passageway?"

"Yasa, Massa. Come."

He pointed out the route the slaves had taken when they had been
led in chains to the waiting ships.

"It was that simple?" I asked.

The guard showed his white teeth in a sad grin.

"Yasa, Massa. Very simple. But it gone now," he told me.

"And maybe you'll be free, really free soon?"

"We hope, Massa."

I looked at the chapel—it was quiet, dim, ready to cast its spell of awe and wonder. . . .

"Did you ever worship in there?" I asked the guard.

"No, Massa."

"Are you Christian?"

"I'se Moslem," he said.

"And what about the Christian's God?"

"He all right, Massa," the guard said, laughing.

I "dashed" him a few shillings and left. Outside, I gazed at the grim stone walls. The dramas that once took place in that castle were forever lost. The slaves sickened and despaired and the white men died of yellow fever and malaria. . . . I tried to picture in my mind a chief, decked out in cowrie shells, leopard skin, golden bracelets, leading a string of black prisoners of war to the castle to be sold. . . . My mind refused to function.

A few days later, with Kojo behind the wheel, I set out to see Cape Coast Castle which was built by the Swedes in 1657, captured by the Danes in 1659. Stormed by the local Fetus tribe, it was taken in 1660; in 1662 the English captured it, lost it to the Dutch, and recaptured it from them in 1664. Less impressive than the castle at Christianborg, it nevertheless shows by its moldering gun emplacements what went on in those days. It is now occupied by state officials, the post office, etc. Slaves had been kept here in dungeons, and then marched to the great slave headquarters of the Gold Coast, the Elmina Castle, and thence shipped to the New World.

I reached Elmina just as the sun was setting and its long red rays lit the awe-inspiring battlements of the castle with a somber but resplendent majesty. It is by far the most impressive castle or fort on the Atlantic shore of the Gold Coast. Built originally by the Portuguese in 1482 with stones prepared in Portugal, it is approached by a drawbridge which, when lifted, foiled any attack from either natives or Europeans in the old days.

I crossed the vast courtyard and entered the auction room in which countless slaves had been sold. One had to know how to pick a good slave in those days, for slave traders were tricky men. They shaved all the hair off the Africans, oiled their bodies, making the ill look as good as the healthy. I stood in a tiny enclosure which had slits in the wall; it was here that African chiefs would hide themselves while their captives were being bid for by Europeans. The chiefs didn't want their victims to know who was selling them. . . . I saw the dungeons where the slaves had been kept—huge, bare rooms with stone floors.

No one will ever know the number or identity of the black men, women, and children who passed through these walls, but there is no doubt but that the men who dealt in this human flesh waxed rich. Even today the castle bears marks of crumbling luxury; there are marble sills at many of the doorways; there are lofty, spacious rooms which you know at a glance no slaves had ever entered. The mighty guns that still point toward the horizon and the misty landscape must have cost heaps of gold dust; and the mere upkeep of such an establishment must have necessitated a staggering turnover in human flesh each year. . . .

Some of the walls are thirty feet thick. Towers rise two hundred feet in the air. What spacious dreams! What august faith! How elegantly laid-out the castle is! What bold and plunging lines! What, yes, taste. . . . King Prempeh I was kept in a large bare room in one of the towers by the British. I stood gazing into that room and wondered what could have passed through his mind. . . . How he must have prayed to his ancestors for help!

Rumor among the natives has it that there is a vast treasure trove buried somewhere in the depths of the castle fortress. I don't think there is; but the native, remembering the horrible tales of what went on within these walls, likes to think that there is gold dust here, thousands of tons of it. If there is any treasure hidden in these vast walls, I'm sure that it has a sheen that outshines gold—a tiny, pear-shaped tear that formed on the cheek of some black woman torn

away from her children, a tear that gleams here still, caught in the
feeble rays of the dungeon's light—a shy tear that vanishes at the
sound of approaching footsteps, but reappears when all is quiet,
hanging there on that black cheek, unredeemed, unappeased—
a tear that was hastily brushed off when her arm was grabbed and
she was led toward those narrow, dank steps that guided her to the
tunnel that directed her feet to the waiting ship that would bear her
across the heaving, mist-shrouded Atlantic. . . .

Dear Kwame Nkrumah:
      My journey's done. My labors in your vineyard are over. The ship
that bears me from Africa's receding shore holds a heart that fights
against those soft, sentimental feelings for the sufferings of our
people. The kind of thinking that must be done cannot be done by
men whose hearts are swamped with emotion.
      While roaming at random through the compounds, market places,
villages, and cities of your country, I felt an odd kind of at-homeness,
a solidarity that stemmed not from ties of blood or race, or from
my being of African descent, but from the quality of deep hope and
suffering embedded in the lives of your people, from the hard facts
of oppression that cut across time, space, and culture. I must confess
that I, an American Negro, was filled with consternation at what
Europe had done to this Africa. . . .
      Yet, as grim as the picture is, its grimness is somewhat relieved
by the fact that African conditions are not wholly unique. The suffering that your people bear has been borne triumphantly before,
and your fellow countrymen have shared that burdensome experience
of having had their destinies dictated by alien powers, from above,
an experience that has knit together so many of the world's millions
in a common consciousness, a common cause.
      Kwame, let me put it bluntly: Western lay and academic circles
utter many a hard saying against Africa. In defending their subjuga-
tion of Africa, they contend that Africa has no culture, no history,
no background, etc. I'm not impressed by these gentlemen, lay or

academic. In matters of history they have been more often wrong than right, and even when they have been right, it has been more by accident than design, or they have been right only after facts have already been so clearly established that not even a fool could go wrong.

I found only one intangible but vitally important element in the heritage of tribal culture that militated against cohesiveness of action: African culture has not developed the personalities of the people to a degree that their egos are stout, hard, sharply defined; there is too much cloudiness in the African's mentality, a kind of sodden vagueness that makes for lack of confidence, an absence of focus that renders that mentality incapable of grasping the workaday world. And until confidence is established at the center of African personality, until there is an inner reorganization of that personality, there can be no question of marching from the tribal order to the twentieth century. . . . At the moment, this subjective task is more important than economics!

Manifestly, as in all such situations, the commencement of the injection of this confidence must come from without, but it *cannot* and *will* not come from the West. (Let's hope I'm wrong about that!)

Have no illusions regarding Western attitudes. Westerners, high and low, feel that their codes, ideals, and conceptions of humanity do not apply to black men. If until today Africa was static, it was because Europeans deliberately wanted to keep her that way. They do not even treat the question of Africa's redemption seriously; to them it is a source of amusement; and those few Europeans who do manage to become serious about Africa are more often prompted by psychological reasons than anything else. The greatest millstone about the neck of Africa for the past three hundred years has been the psychologically crippled white seeking his own perverse personal salvation. . . .

Against this background one refrain echoes again and again in my mind: *You must be hard!* While in Africa one question kept hammering at me: Do the Africans possess the necessary hardness for the task ahead?

If the path that you and your people had to tread were an old and tried one, one worn somewhat smooth by the past trampings of many people; had Europe, during the past centuries, dealt with Africans differently, had they laid the foundations of the West so securely that the Africans could now hold Western values as basic assumptions—had all this happened, the question of "hardness" would not have presented itself to me. (I know that some Europeans are going to say: "Ah, look, a black man advocates stern measures for Africa! Didn't we tell you that they needed such as that?") But Kwame, the truth is that nothing could have been more brutally horrible than the "slow and sound" educational development that turned into a kind of teasing torture, which Europe has imposed so profitably upon Africa since the fifteenth century. . . .

The accomplishment of this change in the African attitude would be difficult under the best of circumstances; but to attain that goal in an Africa beset with a gummy tribalism presents a formidable problem: the psychological legacy of imperialism that lingers on represents the antithesis of the desired end; unlike the situations attending the eruptions of the masses in Russia, China, and India, you do not have the Western-educated Africans with you; in terms of mechanization, you must start from scratch; you have a populace ridden with a 90 per cent illiteracy; communication and transportation are poor. . . .

Balancing these drawbacks are some favorable features: West Africa, thanks to climate, is predominantly *black!* You can pour a libation to the nameless powers that there are no white settlers to be driven out, no knotty land problem to be solved by knocking together the heads of a landed black bourgeoisie. And, though the cultural traditions of the people have been shattered by European business and religous interests, they were so negatively shattered that the hunger to create a *Weltanschauung* is still there, virginal and unimpaired.

If, amidst such conditions, you elect, at this late date in world's history, to follow the paths of social and political evolution such as characterize the history of the institutions of the Western powers,

your progress will go at a snail's pace and both of your flanks will
be constantly exposed and threatened.

On the one hand, just as you organized against the British, so
will other Nkrumahs organize against you. What Nkrumah has done,
other Nkrumahs can do. You have made promises to the masses;
in your heart of hearts I know that you wish hotly to keep those
promises, for you are sincere. . . . But suppose the Communists out-
bid you? Suppose a sullen mood sets in? Would not that give the
Communists *their* opportunity?

On the other hand, I cannot, as a man of African descent brought
up in the West, recommend with good faith the agitated doctrines
and promises of the hard-faced men of the West. Kwame, until they
have set their own houses in order with their own restless popula-
tions, until they have solved their racial and economic problems,
they can never—no matter *what* they may say to you at any *given*
moment!—deal honestly with you. Given the opportunity, they'll
pounce at any time upon Africa to solve their own hard-pressing
social and political problems, just as you well know that they have
pounced in the past. And, also, I'm convinced that the cultural
conditioning of the Africans will make it difficult for them to adjust
quickly to values that are solely Western, values that have mocked
and shamed them so much in the past, values that go against the
grain of so much in the African heart. . . . After all, you have already
been down that road.

Your safety, your security lie in plunging full speed ahead!

But, how? What methods? Means? What instrumentalities? Ay,
there's the rub. . . . The neurotically fluttering attempts of missionaries, the money lust of businessmen, the cool contempt of
European soldiers and politicians, the bungling cynicism of states-
men splitting up families and cultures and indigenous national
groupings at their pleasure—all of these have left the task of the
redemption of Africa to you and yours, to us. . . . And what a task!
What a challenge! What an opportunity for creation . . . !

One simple conviction stands straight up in me: Our people must
be made to walk, forced draft, into the twentieth century! The direction of their lives, the duties that they must perform to overcome

the stagnancy of tribalism, the sacrifices that must yet be made—all of this must be placed under firm social discipline!

I say to you publicly and frankly: The burden of suffering that must be borne, impose it upon *one* generation! Do not, with the false kindness of the missionaries and businessmen, drag out this agony for another five hundred years while your villages rot and your people's minds sink into the morass of a subjective darkness. . . . Be merciful by being stern! If I lived under your regime, I'd ask for this hardness, this coldness. . . .

Make no mistake, Kwame, they are going to come at you with words about democracy; you are going to be pinned to the wall and warned about decency; plump-faced men will mumble academic phrases about "sound" development; gentlemen of the cloth will speak unctuously of values and standards; in short, a barrage of concentrated arguments will be hurled at you to persuade you to temper the pace and drive of your movement. . . .

But you know as well as I that the logic of your actions is being determined by the conditions of the lives of your people. If, for one moment, you take your eyes off that fact, you'll soon be just another African in a cloth on the streets of Accra! You've got to find your *own* paths, your *own* values. . . . Above all, feel free to *improvise!* The political cat can be skinned in many fashions; the building of that bridge between tribal man and the twentieth century can be done in a score of ways. . . .

You might offer ideology as an instrument of organization; but, evidently, you have no basis for that in Africa at this time. You might, by borrowing money from the West, industrialize your people in a cash-and-carry system, but, in doing so, you will be but lifting them from tribal to industrial slavery, for tied to Western money is Western control, Western ideas. . . . Kwame, there is nothing on earth more afraid than a million dollars; and, if a million dollars means fear, a billion dollars is the quintessence of panic. . . .

Russia will not help you, unless you accept becoming an appendage of Moscow; and why should you change one set of white masters for another . . . ?

There is but one honorable course that assumes and answers the ideological, traditional, organizational, emotional, political, and productive needs of Africa at this time:

AFRICAN LIFE MUST BE MILITARIZED!

. . . not for war, but for peace; not for destruction, but for service; not for aggression, but for production; not for despotism, but to free minds from mumbo-jumbo.

I'm not speaking of a military dictatorship. You know that. I need not even have to say that to you, but I say it for the sake of others who will try to be naïve enough to misconstrue my words. I'm speaking simply of a militarization of the daily, social lives of the people; I'm speaking of giving form, organization, direction, meaning, and a sense of justification to those lives. . . . I'm speaking of a temporary discipline that will unite the nation, sweep out the tribal cobwebs, and place the feet of the masses upon a basis of reality. I'm not speaking of guns or secret police; I'm speaking of a method of taking people from one order of life and making them face what men, all men everywhere, must face. What the Europeans failed to do, didn't want to do because they feared disrupting their own profits and global real estate, you must do.

Above all, Africans must be regimentalized for the "long pull," for what will happen in Africa will spread itself out over decades of time and a continent of space. . . . You know as well as I that what has happened in the Gold Coast is just the beginning; and there will be much marching to and fro; there will be many sunderings and amalgamations of people; there will be many shiftings and changes of aims, perspectives, and ideologies—there will be much confusion before the final redemption of Africa is accomplished.

Do I sound gratuitously hard, cruel? How I wished I did not have to think of such measures! Yet, what could make such measures unnecessary? Only a West that could come forth and admit that it didn't do the job, that the job has to be done, and that it was willing to help you to do it. . . . Yet, I cannot conceive of the West acting in that manner, even though all the common sense of history, moral and material, is in favor of it. In its fight against Communism, Europe could bind Africa to her by such an act of help and understanding. . . . Of course, when this is pointed out to Westerners, they shrug their shoulders and say that they have timed African development according to their conceptions of what Africans can do; but, in saying this, they forget that they are not free to indulge in such fantasies. Western time today is being timed by another time: *Communist* time! It would seem that the issue of self-preservation alone would jolt Europeans out of their infantile dreams about Africa. . . .

And in exchange for aiding honest Africans to shake their people loose from their tribal moorings, the West could have all the raw materials it wanted, a larger market for its products. . . . And an Africa deliberately shaken loose from its traditional past would, for a time, be a more dependent Africa than the angry, aimless Africa of the present day. Such an Africa could menace nobody.

Why do I bring up the question of "menace"? Because the mere thought of a free Africa frightens many Europeans. Europeans do not and cannot look upon Africa objectively. Back of their fear of African freedom lies an ocean of *guilt!* In their hearts they know that they have long tried to murder Africa. . . . And this powerful Europe, with atom bombs in its hands, is haunted by visions of an eventual black revenge that has no basis in reality. It is this subjective factor, among others, that makes the West brutally determined to keep Africa on a short chain. . . .

Will the West come forward and head up these nationalist revolutions in Africa? No; it's a dream. If it comes true, I'd be the first to hail it. But since we cannot wait for dreams, let us turn to reality. . . . That is, the militarization of African life.

The basis, concrete and traditional, for the militarization of African life is there already in the truncated tribal structure. The ideological justification for such measures is simple survival; the military is but another name for fraternalization, for cohesiveness. And a military structure of African society can be used eventually for defense. Most important of all, a military form of African society will atomize the fetish-ridden past, abolish the mystical and nonsensical family relations that freeze the African in his static degradation; it will render impossible the continued existence of those parasitic chiefs who have too long bled and misled a naïve people; it is the one and only stroke that can project the African immediately into the twentieth century!

Over and above being a means of production, a militarized social structure can replace, for a time, the political; and it contains its own form of idealistic and emotional sustenance. A military form of life, of social relations, used as a deliberate bridge to span the tribal and the industrial ways of life, will free you, to a large extent, from begging for money from the West, and the degrading conditions attached to such money. A military form of life will enable you to use *people* instead of money for many things and on many occasions! And if your people knew that this military regime was for their freedom, for their safety, for the sake of their children escaping the domination of foreigners, they will make all the sacrifices called for.

Again I say: Would that Western understanding and generosity make these recommendations futile. . . . But if the choice is between traditional Western domination and this hard path, take the hard path!

Beware of a Volta Project built by foreign money. Build your own Volta, and build it out of the sheer lives and bodies of your people! With but limited outside aid, your people can rebuild your society with their bare hands. . . . Africa needs this hardness, *but only from Africans.*

You know as well as I know that politics alone is not enough for Africa. Keep the fires of passion burning in your movement; don't let Westerners turn you away from the only force that can, at this time, knit your people together. It's a secular religion that you must slowly create; it's that, or your edifice falls apart.

There will be those who will try to frighten you by telling you that the organization you are forging looks like Communism, Fascism, Nazism; but, Kwame, the form of organization that you need will be dictated by the needs, emotional and material, of your people. The content determines the form. Never again must the outside world decide what is good for you.

Regarding corruption: use fire and acid and cauterize the ranks of your party of all opportunists! *Now!* Corruption is the one single fact that strikes dismay in the hearts of the friends of African freedom. . . .

In your hands lies the first bid for African freedom and independence. Thus far you have followed an *African* path. I say: *So be it!* Whatever the West or East offers, take it, but don't let them take you. You have taken Marxism, that intellectual instrument that makes meaningful the class and commodity relations in the modern state; but the moment that that instrument ceases to shed meaning, drop it. Be on top of theory; don't let theory be on top of you. In short, be *free*, be a living embodiment of what you want to give your people. . . .

You and your people need no faraway "fatherland" in either England or Russia to guide and spur you on; let your own destiny claim your deepest loyalty. You have escaped one form of slavery; be chary of other slaveries no matter in what guise they present themselves, whether as glittering ideas, promises of security, or rich mortgages upon your future.

There will be no way to avoid a degree of suffering, of trial, of tribulation; suffering comes to all people, but you have within your power the means to make the suffering of your people meaningful, to redeem whatever stresses and strains may come. None but Africans can perform this for Africa. And, as you launch your bold programs, as you call on your people for sacrifices, you can be confident that there are free men beyond the continent of Africa who see deeply enough into life to know and understand what you *must* do, what you *must* impose. . . .

You have demonstrated that tribes can be organized; you must now show that tribes can march socially! And remember that what you build will become a haven for other black leaders of the continent who, from time to time, long for rest from their tormentors. Gather quickly about you the leaders of Africa; you need them and they need you. Europe knows clearly that what you have achieved so far is not confined to the boundaries of the Gold Coast alone; already it has radiated outward and as long as the influence of your bid for freedom continues to inspire your brothers over the teeming forests of West Africa, you can know that the ball of freedom that you threw still rolls. . . .

With words as our weapons, there are some few of us who will stand on the ramparts to fend off the evildoers, the slanderers, the greedy, the self-righteous! You are not alone. . . .

Your fight has been fought before. I am an American and my country too was once a colony of England . . . It was old Walt Whitman who felt what you and your brother fighters are now feeling when he said:

Suddenly, out of its stale and drowsy lair, the lair of slaves,
Like lightning it le'pt forth, half startled at itself,
Its feet upon the ashes and rags—its hands tight to the throats of kings.

O hope and faith!
O aching close of exiled patriots' lives!
O many a sicken'd heart!
Turn back unto this day, and make yourself afresh.
And you, paid to defile the People! you liars, mark!
Not for numberless agonies, murders, lusts,
For court thieving in its manifold mean forms, worming from his sim-
    plicity the poor man's wages,
For many a promise sworn by royal lips, and broken and laugh'd at in
    the breaking.
Then in their power, not for all these, did the blows strike revenge, or the
    heads of nobles fall;
The People scorn'd the ferocity of kings.

INDEX

United Trading Company, 273
University of Paris, 3

Volta Project, 188, 189, 249, 288
Volta River, 188

Ward, W. E. F., 118
Washington Park, 233
Watson, Aiken, 93
Watson Commission, 93
Weekend in Havana, dance arena,
    107

Wesleyan Collegiate School, 156
West Africa, 13, 26, 166; beggars in,
    50-51; Dutch in, 45, 46; English in,
    45; Portuguese in, 37, 42, 43, 44
West Africa Graphic Company, 186
West Indies, 11, 14
Westend Arena, 74
"When Malindy Sings," 134
Whitman, Walt, 351
Williams, Eric, 1, 7, 10, 12
Women's Division of the Convention
    People's Party, 101